"For all those seeking healing, and those who bring healing to others, this is an immensely powerful book filled with wisdom, understanding, and experience—and above all filled with hope. I highly recommend it!"

—**John Eldredge**, author of *Wild at Heart* and *Beautiful Outlaw*

"Through Dan's skillful and tender writing, I've been given a vision for how to love and walk well with the members of my community whose stories have been marked by sexual abuse. I'm so very thankful for his gentle, prophetic voice, and for the many ways his words have been healing and life-giving for generations."

—**Shauna Niequist**, author of *Savor* and *Bread & Wine*

"Brilliant and accessible, Allender has given us this incredible gift: a book that not only helps us understand the potent impacts and effects of sexual abuse but offers hope and a roadmap to healing. Thank you! I am thrilled this book exists."

—**Wm. Paul Young**, author of *The Shack*, *Cross Roads*, and *EVE*

"This book is like Dan—compelling, liberating, and a gentle salve that will transform wounds into holy scars. *Healing the Wounded Heart* will dust your mind and soul with itching powder, and even better, it will provide help, hope, and healing at the most intimate levels of your life. This book will become a classic for generations."

—**Dr. Dennis Rainey**, president of FamilyLife

"*The Wounded Heart* was a revolutionary book; over the past twenty-five years untold numbers of lives have been transformed through its reading. People who previously had no words for the unspeakable terror of sexual abuse finally had a language—and

permission—to express their suffering and move toward integration and wholeness. God was at work through this book, redeeming—saving—lives. Now, through thousands of stories in dozens of different cultural contexts and undergirded by recent, revealing research on the brain and the body, *Healing the Wounded Heart* travels more deeply into the dark caverns of sexual abuse. Knowledge, infused with the power of the gospel, illumines our precarious path, and we are able to psychologically and theologically understand our sexual brokenness and harm as never before. Thank you, Dan, for courageously and vulnerably leading us into this dangerous territory so that we can breech the walls of our shame and deception and clearly hear God's voice calling us into the glorious light of truth as 'beloved daughters and sons'."

—**Rev. Lauran Bethell**, global consultant for ministries with victims of human trafficking/prostitution, international ministries, and American Baptist Churches/USA; coordinator/founder of International Christian Alliance on Prostitution (ICAP)

"*Healing the Wounded Heart* is informed by Dan Allender's own story and his life on the frontlines with survivors of relational, sexual, and spiritual trauma. The stories are real and therefore the help is real. We benefit greatly from his lifelong investment in people and his humble, fierce honesty about the battle for our freedom and against the systems that harm us. Dan's holistic emphasis on the mind/body/neurological interplay in response to the trauma of abuse and his clarification of the role of evil (the dark intentionality behind all perpetration) is especially helpful and grounding. Likewise, the profound chapter on male victims is long overdue and welcome as is the chapter on caring for another's story. Many of us who counsel know that the sexual arena is one where the fighting is brutal, the casualties legion, and the cover-ups shocking, so it is relieving to hear Dan's familiar voice offering direction, seasoned insight, and renewed vigor. The call is not only to 'know or do the right things' with people but to engage relationally with wisdom and kindness. Thank you, Dan, for taking us to new depths that honor God and survivors alike."

—**William W. Clark, PhD**, clinical psychologist; co-founder and president of the Lay Counselor Institute; adjunct professor, Cairn University; visiting professor, Reformed Theological Seminary, Washington, DC

"With all of the information and wisdom we believe we have gleaned in the past twenty-five years about the topic of sexual abuse, one would think the world would be different than it is. But the ruthless danger of abuse is no less present. In *Healing the Wounded Heart*, Dan Allender does not settle for offering us a reprise of his earlier landmark work. Rather, our guide unflinchingly walks us through the necessary passages of the disintegrating nature of abuse to bring us to the light and the healing—with no apology for the rigorous work required—of redemption. This book is a triumph not only for the author but also for all of us who have been the grateful recipients of his lifetime of work—and who need it now more than ever."

—**Curt Thompson, MD**, author of *Anatomy of the Soul* and *The Soul of Shame*

"Dan Allender has, for decades, stood as a bright light shining into the dark and hidden world of sexual abuse. His work is the best guide I know toward a healing path for any victim of sexual harm. Beyond that, Allender's approach encourages readers toward a deeper theological understanding of God and the redemptive work of Jesus Christ amid experiences of trauma and evil. Anyone who has been sexually abused—or knows someone who has—should read this book."

—**Andrew M. McCoy**, assistant professor of ministry studies, Hope College

"*Healing the Wounded Heart* is classic Allender! In this long-awaited sequel to his earlier book on sexual abuse, Dan Allender skillfully unpacks the neurobiology of abuse, the role of spiritual warfare, and the profound impact of living in a sex-saturated culture. In my work as both a professional counselor and a counselor educator, I need this book. My clients need this book. My graduate students training to be counselors need this book. Therapists and pastors and family members need this book. Artfully weaving a theology of healing and recovery throughout the text, Allender offers hope and redemption to those who have been harmed."

—**Pamela S. Davis, PhD**, assistant professor of counseling, Wheaton College Graduate School

"This is a fiercely compassionate and hopeful book that is deeply rooted in real life experience. There is an earned and practical wisdom resonating throughout that can only come from a practitioner who has worked faithfully with those harmed and affected by childhood sexual abuse. If you have ever questioned or wondered whether God's love can remain even in the darkest and most dank places of human experience and suffering, you need to read this book."

—**Chelle Stearns**, author of *Handling Dissonance*

Healing
the
Wounded
Heart

The Heartache of Sexual Abuse
and the Hope of Transformation

Dan B. Allender

BakerBooks
a division of Baker Publishing Group
Grand Rapids, Michigan

© 2016 by Dan B. Allender

Published by Baker Books
a division of Baker Publishing Group
P.O. Box 6287, Grand Rapids, MI 49516-6287
www.bakerbooks.com

Printed in the United States of America

Library of Congress Cataloging-in-Publication Data
Allender, Dan B.
   Healing the wounded heart : the heartache of sexual abuse and the hope of
   transformation / Dan B. Allender.
      pages cm
   Includes biographical references.
   ISBN 978-0-8010-1568-7 (pbk.)
   1. Sexual abuse victimes—Religious life. 2. Sex crimes—Religious aspects—
Christianity. 3. Sex crimes. 4. Sexual abuse victims. I. Allender, Dan B. Wounded heart.
II. Title.
BV4596.A25A45 2016
261.8'3272—dc23   2015033037

Unless otherwise indicated, Scripture quotations are from the Holy Bible, New International Version®. NIV®. Copyright © 1973, 1978, 1984, 2011 by Biblica, Inc.™ Used by permission of Zondervan. All rights reserved worldwide. www.zondervan.com

Scripture quotations labeled NLT are from the *Holy Bible*, New Living Translation, copyright © 1996, 2004, 2007 by Tyndale House Foundation. Used by permission of Tyndale House Publishers, Inc., Carol Stream, Illinois 60188. All rights reserved.

In order to protect the confidentiality of those who have shared their stories, sufficient details have been changed to alter their identities. The stories are most often an amalgamation of a number of people; no story describes a single person unless otherwise noted.

This publication is intended to provide helpful and informative material on the subjects addressed. Readers should consult their personal health professionals before adopting any of the suggestions in this book or drawing inferences from it. The author and publisher expressly disclaim responsibility for any adverse effects arising from the use or application of the information contained in this book.

The author is represented by Yates & Yates, www.yates2.com.

21   22   7

To my holy, unpredictable, wild-hearted,
ferociously kind wife, Becky.
Nothing of this labor or life would have
been possible without you.

Contents

Contents

Acknowledgments

The past twenty-five years since the publication of *The Wounded Heart* have passed like a sun-drenched cloud. But as I begin to write a list of all whom I wish to thank for the gains of these decades, I am flooded with thousands of faces, stories, and names from Recovery Weeks, story workshops, therapy, lunches, airplane conversations, and long walks. These are the heroes of this book whom I am not free to name.

However, I am profoundly indebted to the woman who asked in our fourth session twenty-seven years ago, "What do you know about sexual abuse?" I am grateful I told the truth, and she took me into a mysterious land that I had never wanted to visit. As well, I feel that way about each person I have been privileged to walk with into heartache and hope. It has been a holy and unexpected journey.

There are so many I wish to thank that I first want to apologize to those who know they played a role in this process but whom I fail to name. There are likely countless people I will eventually thank whom I will wish I had included here. Thank you. Thank you. It is not enough and it is but a beginning, but thank you.

To those who helped me create a lasting legacy, our Recovery Weeks for men and women: Shannon Rainey, Al Andrews, Karla Denlinger, and Nancy Lodwick.

To those who have helped facilitate Recovery Weeks and taught me the power of radical care and the pursuit of truth: Lynn Todd Wynn, Allyson Baker, Sue Cunningham, Linda Busse, Amy Anderson, Jan Meyers Proet, Shannon Rainey, Nathan Eckland, Andy McCoy, Wendell Moss, Andy Ide, Linda Royster, Susan Kim, Abby Wong, Amanda Webb, Cathy Loerzel, MaryJane Apple, Sharon Hersh, Stan and Marcia Smartt, Gina Waggoner, and Jennifer Walker.

To those who were part of the original (exciting and exhausting) start-up of the Allender Center for Trauma and Abuse: Keith Anderson, Cathy Loerzel, Jeanette White, Abby Wong, Susan Kim, Rachael Clinton, Andy Ide, Wendell Moss, and Trapper Lukaart.

And to those who have joined us through the years in the Allender Center: Sam Lee, Debi Franz, Lisa Fann, Andrew Bauman, Jon DeWaal, Jay Stringer, Matt Tiemeyer, Melanie Lindell, Cameron Cary, and Ella Chang.

To my dear friends who have helped me maintain sanity, follow Jesus, and laugh and weep often: Tremper and Alice Longman, John and Stasi Eldredge, Mike and Myra McCoy, Dave and Meg Dupee, Jane Barry, Russ Teubner, Lauran Bethell, Bill and Janet Lenz, Barbara and Lou Giuliano, Chris and Julie Rothrock, Len and Sherry Bundy, Dave and LaJean Rohland, Mark and Debi Warrender, Steve and Lisa Call, Pam Davis, Laurie and Dave Proctor, Allyson and Brent Baker, Michelle and Steve Ruetschle, Scotty and Darlene Smith, JoeCarol and John Thorp, Frank Tomlinson, Elizabeth and Kip Tournage, and David and Shannon Rainey.

To those who at some point bore the burden of organizing and shepherding my life: Linda Pfeiffer, Patty Warwick, Susan Rice Berthiaume, Laura Wackman, Linda Busse, Jill Stenerson, Lisa Philabaum, Kate (and Jon—hilarious, isn't it, Jon?) Weinstein, Hope VanDyk, Jeanette White, and Cameron Cary.

To those who have sung the glory of the Father, Son, and Holy Spirit into my writing: Laura Hackett, Audrey Assad, Lowland

Hum, and the ever glorious and endlessly passionate Ashley Cleveland.

To my most favorite people at the Seattle School of Theology and Psychology—the intrepid, incomprehensibly gifted librarians: Cheryl Goodwin, Mary Rainwater, Erin Quarterman, and Molly Kenzler (you can leave us but you will never be forgotten).

To those whose direct assistance in helping form this book was crucial and kind . . .

John Eldredge: thank you for helping me to pray, reorganize the book, and write with joy.

Susan Kim: thank you for your careful and wise way of guiding our research.

Heather Mirous: thank you for offering your rich understanding of the human mind and your deep sensibility in guiding those who have been abused.

Chad Allen and Rebecca Cooper: your love of language and the way truth is meant to sing made this labor much less painful.

Traci Mullins: it is hard to fathom my good fortune to have had you edit *The Wounded Heart* twenty-five years ago and then work your magic of thought and word to make this book as true as what we completed when we were both so young.

Sealy Yates: dear sir, you are a generous, wise, formidable presence who makes me laugh every time we talk. Thank you for letting me play in your stable.

Rebecca Anne Allender: oh, my love, each iteration, every word, passed through your thoughtful and kind review. The hours of tedium and the decades of passion that you have given for the sake of this calling are beyond comprehension. I can only hope that the full glory due your life is one day poured out like the sands in the ocean.

To my children: Annie, Amanda, and Andrew. First, I am so grateful for the immense wisdom and goodness in your lives, especially seen in those whom you chose to marry: Driscoll, Jeff, and Elizabeth.

I love you. I love your spouses. I especially love your children. I wrote this book for your children. I pray they never endure sexual harm, but their young lives can't help but be thrown into a sexually mad world. May we all know the wonder and grace of a love that never dies because the Son died and was raised to sit at the right hand of the Father for eternity. May it be!

Introduction

Why a New Book about Sexual Abuse?

My oldest daughter, Annie, was nine when I wrote *The Wounded Heart*. It was during that season of writing that I received an unmarked cassette tape from a musician who had asked me to review a song she had written about her sexual abuse. I sat at our kitchen table; Annie was sitting to my left and talking with me as I opened our mail and pulled out the letter and the tape.

She often sat with me and talked about her day or asked a wide variety of questions that I usually had no clue how to answer. As we sat and talked that day, she asked a question I had never even thought to consider. "Is that a tape about sexual abuse?" she asked. I had no time to think. "Yes," I said. "How did you know?" Instead of answering, she looked at me fiercely and asked, "How do I know that you will never sexually abuse me?" I assured her that while I would likely fail her in countless ways, she would never need to be worried about me harming her sexually. But instead of diminishing her concern, my answer prompted another disturbing question. With even more intensity, she asked, "Yes, but what if you lose control just like you sometimes do with your anger?"

13

As is the nature of all memory, what I have described feels bright, intense, and sharp, but what happened next is pure conjecture. It is likely I mumbled some meaningless words and broke off or redirected the conversation.

My daughter turned thirty-five this year, and I wish I'd had the courage then to ask her what she knew about sexual abuse and why it was a concern. I wonder to this day how my entry into this field affected her, my other children, my marriage, and the course of all our lives.

There have been scores of times in the past twenty-five years when I have felt like one of the most fortunate men on the planet. The privilege to be invited into the stories of thousands of women and men as we explore some of the darkest chapters of their lives is a gift that precious few on earth experience. This journey has taken me from the jungles of Thailand to the savannah of Ethiopia and into countless homes, churches, and conversations that all in some sense define my life and calling. I am a therapist, theoretician, speaker, writer, professor, administrator, husband, father, and grandfather. I am also a victim of sexual abuse. Sexual abuse has affected for good and ill everything I have done and likely will do on this earth. The harm from the past simply doesn't go away.

Decades ago we were in a car accident in Anchorage, Alaska. An intoxicated woman ran a red light and crashed into the driver's side of our car, just a few inches from crushing my upper body. I sustained a neck injury that over twenty-three years has cost me thousands of dollars of chiropractic care, and it still aches as I write this. I can't imagine what my condition would be without the immense care I have received, but even more so I can't allow myself to consider what my life would be like if that accident had never occurred. The same is true with sexual abuse in that I can never fully eradicate the consequences of the harm I have endured—yet unlike the car accident, it has given me the opportunity to be transformed with each tear I have shed.

Would I trade these benefits for not being harmed? Of course, without a doubt; I'd do so in an instant. But that is not an option, and until God's final victory over darkness fully removes the harm of living in this world, it is best to embrace heartache and determine to use it for larger purposes. It is to that end that I write this book.

When I began writing and teaching about sexual abuse in the late eighties there was little material available from which to glean those first putative steps on the journey. At that time it was assumed that informing people about the diabolical damage of abuse would decrease the likelihood that it would continue to occur at the same rate, and I wanted that outcome with a passion.

I have learned a lot in the past twenty-five years. Mostly I have learned from my clients. I have also gleaned an immense amount of understanding from fellow professional and lay therapists who continue to lean into darkness that most fear to name, let alone enter. While I am encouraged by the advances that have been made in bringing the reality of sexual abuse into the light, I have seen the culture flip from massive denial to indifferent minimization. In spite of the growing body of research that underscores how one abusive moment can shadow a human life for decades, date rape, sexting, pornography, unwanted sexual advances, sex when intoxicated or stoned, groping, and other behavior that is sexually suggestive, demeaning, or harassing have become so common that in many people's minds they hardly warrant being called sexual abuse.

In reality, our day is vastly more adversarial, opportunistic, shallow, and violent than ever before.[1] Abuse often creates a twenty-eight-car pileup with massive debris, bent metal, and wounded victims. It spirals into generations. It sinks into the depths of the heart. I believe there is value in writing a twenty-five-year retrospective because so much new data and research have enhanced our understanding of the nature of the harm of abuse and trauma.

For example, we understand the human brain better; it's as though we have landed in the new world and discovered the first few miles of a vastly unexplored continent. We are clearer about the need to involve the body in the process of addressing the by-products of abuse, especially dissociation and triggers that prompt addictive behavior, sabotage, and self-harm. The role of the internet, pornography, and post-traumatic injury to the body and soul are understood today in ways they were not twenty-five years ago. Most important for me, I am clearer about the work of evil—both human and in the unseen realm of spirits—in the design and devastating consequences of sexual abuse. As disconcerting as it may be to some to be asked to consider the realm of foul and dark spirits, it would be cowardly for me to ignore that dimension.

If there is a central, driving factor as to why I am writing a new volume about sexual abuse, it is because I am a grandfather of four wonderful, wild, beautiful grandchildren. Each of them will grow up facing the dark prospects of an earth heating up from global warming, oceans that may see a radical deficit of fish, shorelines being swallowed by encroaching water, and nations rising and falling due to calamities that go far deeper but involve no less than the weather.

As the winds blow foul, there will be upheaval in this century that will directly and indirectly turn the strong against the weak, resulting in what has occurred for millennia: more women and children and men will be sexually victimized. It is in this world that my grandchildren will become men and women. While I have no guarantee they will ever read my work or know or follow my life trajectory, I can't stand idly by and not fight a little harder and longer for their sexual future.

I am blessed to be working with a small cadre of therapists in the Allender Center for Abuse and Trauma whom I trust will carry on our labor far after I am residing in another world or am unable to speak and write as I wish. There is good reason to hope that we will continue to make progress in addressing the harm of sexual abuse. However, the war will not ever be finished until the Lord Jesus Christ returns to set his kingdom right in the midst of this broken and scarred world. Until then, this labor of inviting those who know sexual brokenness and scars to wholeness and beauty is an endeavor worthy of all the suffering, struggle, and sweat.

When I reread *The Wounded Heart* in preparation for writing *Healing the Wounded Heart*, I found myself grateful beyond words that I would not recant or change any of the major categories I addressed when I was a young theorist and therapist. You may wonder if you need to first read *The Wounded Heart* to understand what I am saying in this book. Every author hopes his or her work is read in a somewhat progressive fashion; however, I am realistic enough to know that few will read all of my work, let alone in sequence. If you read *The Wounded Heart* years, if not decades, ago, a review of what you underlined will be immensely helpful, but it is not required before reading this book. However, if I have my druthers, I would want you to read both *The Wounded Heart* and *Healing the Wounded Heart*.

I also view the workbook that accompanies this book as an indispensable part of processing and applying the thoughts I offer in the pages ahead. It is one thing to consider the concepts as they relate to your life; it is an entirely other experience to welcome the process of healing into your life. The workbook invites you to reflect and write your way to greater freedom. It is best to join with others in reflecting on the questions that are provoked and ally yourself with a group that is working out the implications of past sexual abuse. The material in this book is also given further clarity through podcasts and videos found at theallendercenter.org.

It is my dream that my readers will see the massive war clouds and not turn back due to fear or hopelessness. I long for a few more brave, foolish, and wild-hearted men and women to embrace the calling to engage this scourge with the hope that what God has begun he is faithful to bring to completion. He will bring about passionate, holy delight in sexuality, and in his design for sex he will draw our hearts into the depths of wonder and gratitude and, ultimately, to the worship of the Father, Son, and Holy Spirit. It is to this end that we proceed.

Part One

The Wounded Heart

1

The New Face of Sexual Abuse

The period in which we now live may well go down in history as the Erotic Age. Sexual love has been elevated into a cult. Eros has more worshipers among civilized men today than any other god. For millions the erotic has completely displaced the spiritual.

A. W. Tozer, 1959

Hookup sex is fast, uncaring, unthinking and perfunctory. Hookup culture promotes bad sex, boring sex, drunken sex you don't remember, sex you could care less about, sex where desire is absent, sex that you have "just because everyone else is, too," or that "just happens."

Donna Freitas, 2008

The majority of people believe sex is just sex. It is good, not so good, and most of the time just average. It titillates and serves as the currency for lots of conversations, prompts the purchase of products, and sustains the superficial connection with a stranger. Sex just *is*, and as one person said, "If you think about it too much, it exposes the middle-aged bald guy behind the curtain. I want my fantasy to be uncontaminated by reality."

But sex is more than sex, and sexual harm is more than a mere violation. It reverberates to the deepest parts of our humanity and returns with an echo that doesn't stop even decades later. It is imperative that the noise of abuse—even if it has been turned down to an imperceptible level—be turned up so that we don't allow it to settle into the background of our stories.

For many, this means giving up the presumption that we have not suffered sexual harm. We all have. Each and every individual on the earth has known some assault against their gender and/or their genitalia. Some of the harm is obvious and severe. Other harm is so subtle and normalized that it seems ridiculous to call it abuse. But sexual abuse is often far subtler and extensive than most of us have considered.

Monica, a young woman whom I counseled, told me that while she was in college sex for her was like eating at a sketchy diner. Most of the time sex was not great, but it was also not a big deal. There were a few times when she "got food poisoning" and it took a long time to recover. When I asked what she meant, she shrugged and said, "I didn't say yes or no. I didn't want him to do what he did, but I was high and it went further than I wanted, but it was my fault, so why cry over spilled milk?"

The goal of a hookup is sex that in no way obligates either partner to any level of a relationship even a minute after it is finished, let alone in the future. My client expressed a sentiment I have heard countless times: "Sex just happens—whatever." But as Monica began to explore her indifference regarding her sexuality, she began to acknowledge how seldom she had a voice or registered her displeasure. It took far longer for her to own that several of the "food poisoning" interactions were demeaning and cruel. And even after doing the work to name the exploitation and violation, she could not call the experience rape.

She balked to call what happened rape because, she said, "I didn't stop it. I shouldn't have had three beers, and I should know better than to hook up with a guy who treated me so poorly from the beginning." She was violated and she took responsibility for the harm—then, like many, she chalked it up to a bad night and was grateful it didn't happen more often.

Monica was not on this earth when I wrote *The Wounded Heart*, and her experience is one of the new faces of sexual abuse. She is sexually sophisticated and cynical. Sex has been woven into her childhood through music videos, sexting, hallway gossip, and sexual violations that are dismissed as no big deal.

The reality of sexual abuse is dark and torturous terrain that many choose not to walk because too much is at stake; it is far easier to shrug it off, take the blame, and be more wary the next time. Why is this deep harm against the human heart, soul, and body so difficult to address? The answer is compelling and simple: God loves sex. But Satan, God's enemy, despises sexual joy and is perversely committed to marring it.

Sex is God's idea, and he delights in the sensual pleasure and soul intimacy that grow when one gives fully from the heart to pleasure and be pleasured by one's covenant lover. God thrills when his creation enters the complex interplay of making love within a covenant relationship. Sex is meant to be both a sacramental gift and a riproaring sensual feast. God made sex for our pleasure and to offer us a glimpse of what it means to be known by him. It is that simple. Sex is earthy and sacred—a blessing of body and soul that glories in the earth of creation and the breath of God's kiss to animate our dust. The sensuality of being a body is woven into the wonder of being more than a body. We are far more than a set of physiological processes and biochemicals lighting up through movement and touch; we are people engaged with others in a process that calls us to be more than we are in the moment. The moments of sexual engagement are potentially the most intense, alive, intimate, and holy moments one can know on this earth.

Monica's story at first glance might be called a tragic story of promiscuity and poor choices. Further, it is not hard to imagine someone saying, "Sadly, she is reaping the consequences of sin and needs to get right with God." This sentiment is not merely cavalier, irrespective of how biblical it sounds; it is cruel and blind to the legion of influences that shape how a young man or woman becomes sexual in our culture.

Many months into our work, Monica told me about how her older brother had taken a video of her when she was showering as a twelve-year-old. She covered herself, but her developing body was clearly seen. He threatened to post it anonymously if she didn't grant his friends sexual pleasures. The encounters were, in her terms, "some groping and slobbery make-out sessions with boys who didn't have a clue how to kiss."

When I asked her what she would call this whole narrative, she said, "Gross and weird, but no big deal. Even my mom told me to chalk it up to boys being boys." I asked her if her mother knew of the video and the "make-out sessions." She stammered, "Sort of, I guess, maybe not the groping part, but she found out about the video and kissing."

Monica's brother was her mother's favorite. He could do no wrong, and he got away with little more than a slap on the wrist. Monica, on the other hand, took the brunt of her mother's anger. Monica never did exceptionally well in school and didn't play sports like her brother did. Perhaps most problematic, she was the apple of her father's eye. He had divorced Monica's mother when she was eight and overtly gave her more time and gifts than any of her siblings. Her brother and his friends had sexually abused her, but she not only didn't have the language to name it but she was also determined not to call it abuse. She could not say that her mother failed to protect her from the abuse and gave implicit permission to

24

her brother to do whatever he wanted to her without consequences. Her sexual and family story felt like no big deal to her; in fact, compared to her friends who had "really been sexually abused," her story felt almost innocuous.

Without a doubt, Monica had made some deeply harmful choices, but they simply can't be summarized and swept away under the rubric of "immorality." She is far more than merely sexually immoral; she is living out significant sexual harm against herself and others without much of a clue as to what throws her into those sexual scenarios. The cost for Monica to understand what she actually experienced was to step deeper into all that had led her to cross the border into sexual nonchalance. Once the category of sexual abuse became a smidge wider than her original understanding, she began to tell me of countless experiences of being groped in the cafeteria line, shown pornography on the school bus by girlfriends and male acquaintances, and flirted with by older men who dated her mother. The story of sexual marring seemed endless. But Monica refused to see the harm in her story, nor could she name it in her culture.

Sexual Harm Is on the Rise

Just as a fish is unaware of the water that sets the parameters of its world, so we often fail to take in the milieu in which we live. In the past twenty-five years girls have become far more sexualized. Examples of the pressure to grow up sexually are legion. Britney Spears, in her 1998 music video "Baby One More Time," depicted herself as a Catholic schoolgirl who breaks out of the humdrum of school boredom through a pornified exhibition of erotic desire. More than fifteen years later the ante was upped when the infamous Miley Cyrus twerked to the fascination and denigration of the teddy-bear-wearing dancers surrounding her. Beyond the glorification of sexual acts, far more disturbing to me was her choice to wear a teddy bear outfit and act out her "liberated" sexual power through debasing innocence. Whether her goal was to mock innocence or not, it accomplished what she desired: she furthered her brand.

The sexualization of young girls has been addressed as a growing trend. The American Psychological Association developed a task force that released its findings in April 2007.[1] One of the members of this task force, Sharon Lamb, wrote a compelling analysis (with her coauthor, Lyn Mikel Brown), *Packaging Girlhood: Rescuing Our Daughters from Marketers' Schemes*, in which she detailed the ways in which Bratz dolls, youth thongs, and "sexy dressing" are sold to preteens. Another researcher, Donna Freitas, writes:

> There is an emerging cultural trend where many young women learn to trade sex and its allures—sexual favors and/or sexy dressing—for popularity, long before they step onto a college campus. Young girls and women as early as middle school and certainly by high school barter their sexed-up bodies for status.[2]

In many ways the trend is not just the sexualization of our children but the normalization of pornography as not merely a rite of passage but a mark of sexual liberation. Innocence is considered a burden, a constraint; it appears that breaking its bonds offers status and benefits.

Perhaps the greatest social change regarding sexuality in the past twenty-five years and the structure that has increased the sexualization—if not the pornification—of our children have come from the ubiquity and godlike status of the internet. Monica's story included sitting on the bus in fifth grade and having her friend show her pictures on her cell phone of two women having sex. She was both fascinated and disgusted. Her friend was an intense, powerful force in her class who could turn classmates against someone in an instant. Monica knew not to withdraw or show revulsion; instead, she regularly watched whatever her friend wanted to show her.

Young adolescents turn to their peer group far more than to any other group of people or institution to normalize their social interactions and define their identity. As pornography becomes more ubiquitous and acceptable, it is becoming entrenched in children's daily interactions with their peers.

Research indicates that internet porn is first encountered between the ages of ten and fourteen.[3] It is likely that this age is dropping as digital devices become more common and pornography is normalized in our culture. Pornographers often utilize the technique called "typosquatting," in which frequently accessed children's internet sites that might be misspelled by a child are used as portals to funnel children to pornographic sites.

It was estimated in 2006 that 13 percent of website visits in America were to sex-related sites.[4] There is, of course, a significant and unresolved debate as to the level of addiction, relational impact, and identity formation issues related to the use of pornography; the direct and immediate result of watching pornography is difficult to assess. But what is impossible to ignore is the vulgarization and degradation that seem to arise in a sexually pervasive and exploitative culture. It is impossible to deny that ever more egregious sexual harm, including bestiality, child pornography, and sadomasochistic harm, is depicted and being accessed by a wide range of men, women, and children.

Whatever the factors are that promote degradation, it is unquestionable that there is a rise in sexually violating harassment and intimate partner violence. The extent of sexual harassment in our schools between elementary school and high school is staggering. In 2001 the American Association of University Women study on harassment indicated that 89 percent of girls and 60–79 percent of boys were sexually harassed.[5] The onset of the harassment was in sixth grade. In this group 59 percent experienced harassment occasionally and 27 percent often. And the incidence of sexual harassment increased through high school.

Harassment has often been viewed as a form of bullying, but the problem with the term *bullying* is that it is seen as relatively innocuous and not against the law, whereas sexual harassment has a specific, legal definition: it must be "sufficiently severe, persistent or pervasive to deny or limit a student's ability to participate in or to receive benefits, services or opportunities."[6] It is all too easy to dismiss "teasing." Kids will be kids and boys especially will be boys. However, what is being addressed in these studies is far more insidious and abusive than being teased about being overweight or remarks made about not developing quickly enough. A significant percentage of children and young women and men are being marked by verbal sexual violence, touch, and gossip. Simply put, sexual bullying mars many children's ability to go to school and learn on a daily basis.

As well, research indicates that 40–60 percent of teenagers experience intimate partner violence, including psychological, physical, and sexual abuse.[7] Over 13 percent of girls in the study had been raped by a boyfriend. It is not an exaggeration to say that growing up as a girl occurs in a sexually hostile environment. One young woman, when asked if she had experienced sexual harm, turned her eyes away and said, "Being touched in places I don't want, by people I don't want, is another way of saying being at a dance party."

And both boys and girls are the victims of sexual harm. One high school senior told me that where one stands on the pecking order of sexual cruelty is a constant issue. If you are high up the ladder it means you must either participate or at least ignore the harm done to others who are not part of your group. To stand against degradation and mockery is to lose one's social standing. If you are on the bottom rung, you likely undergo a weekly, if not daily, experience of being made into the scapegoat for others' cruelty.

If there is a darkening of this era through pornography and harassment, there is an even darker shadow over what has been called the hookup culture. Hookup sex is not primarily about the sexual experience but far more about maintaining social status and avoiding being viewed as a social outcast. Hookup sex is defined as having three core elements: (1) casualness: the design is to keep relational entanglements, expectations, or desire out of sex; (2) brevity: the faster the better because the brief time spent in sex keeps expectations and desire at a minimum; (3) sex: a hookup might be simply making out or include sexual intercourse, or anything in between. (For many high school and college age men and women, oral sex is viewed as little more than a form of kissing.)

Hookup sex often occurs when one or both parties are significantly affected by alcohol, which is readily available, especially to college students. Binge drinking on college campuses is so common that between 25–40 percent of college students have recently consumed so much alcohol that they could not remember their activity.[8] Alcohol—either as a social lubricant, a justification, or a defense—is a perceived and/or real basis for entry into hookup sex.

It should not be surprising that a relationship exists between alcohol and sexual assault. An article in the *Journal of Interpersonal Violence* found that 62 percent of unwanted sex occurred because of alcohol impairment.[9] In a follow-up study,

> approximately 44 percent of the women participating in the study reported at least one unwanted sexual encounter while in college, and 90 percent of this unwanted sex took place during a hookup. Of all the reported incidents of unwanted sex, 76.2 percent involved alcohol, which played a significant role in blurring the lines of consent. The researchers found that often, the victim was too drunk to properly give consent. Often, the victim did not really remember what had happened after waking up the next day.[10]

Bottom line: sexual harm has been normalized in a sexually indulgent and demeaning age. We live in a vastly more sexually indulgent, indifferent, impersonal, and hostile world where it is harder to name the abuse that has been normalized and ignored. Like Monica, we find it easier to shrug it off than to step into what feels overwhelming to engage. But sexual harm, like all brokenness, doesn't fade away because we minimize it or try to forget. Rather, it lingers in the crevices of our heart, slowly but surely dividing us from ourselves, others, and God.[11]

Sexual Harm Can Be Healed

Monica told me in no uncertain terms that she loved sex in her young adult life. It made her feel powerful, free, and desirable. She continued to deny the impact of her childhood sexual abuse, and she was proud to say that, unlike in her college years, she now made better choices in her relationships with men and didn't drink as much as she used to. She was "not as stupid, needy, or usable as I was when I was younger."

Her desire to see me professionally had nothing to do with her sexual history; rather, she was troubled by persistent patterns of frustration and failure in relationships with friends. It is never my task to get a person to engage what they are not ready to explore. Monica continued, episodically, to let me see even more of her sexual heartache, but once it came to light, she would yank it back under layers of denial and indifference.

That remained true until she took a job as a nanny for a family with an eleven-year-old girl whom she came to love. The preteen was starting to experiment with dressing sexy and flirting online with boys she didn't know (who could easily have been thirty-five-year-old predators). Monica freaked out. The lioness in her roared, and she took active measures to protect the girl and help her make better choices about exploring her sexuality in a crass, sexually absorbed, boundary-free world. Her new awareness and passion awakened Monica sufficiently to say that if this girl were to be harmed the way she had been violated, she would call it sexual abuse and respond accordingly.

No one, including Monica herself, had given her room to ponder her life. This is not done in an afternoon, and seldom is it done even in the closest of relationships. However, while the price to name our abuse may be high, it is far higher if we refuse to do so. Working with Monica was like putting together a jigsaw puzzle that had many pieces missing; it was painstakingly slow as we returned to moments of great harm with greater insight and care each time we traversed the terrain. There were countless sessions in which I was tested, accused, ignored, flirted with, and engaged. I loved the privilege of walking with Monica through the topography of her life, and in time she began to address the young, broken parts of her heart. Slowly, as she found the courage to explore the deep questions of life through the lens of her story, she began to heal.

Sex has the power to touch the deepest dimension of what it means to be human and alive to God; therefore, it stands to reason that it is hated more than any other dimension of humanity by a kingdom that opposes the glory of God. There is a power that uses sexual violation as its choice means to turn the human heart away from the Creator. This opposition to beauty and innocence is at the core of all sexual harm.

2

The Role of Evil

I don't care if I sound mental to you, but I hear voices. They mock and threaten me. I'm not psychotic. I sometimes wonder if they are just an extension of myself, but there are times when the voices seem crueler than anything I have ever felt or done to someone else or myself. The only way to silence them is to do a little bit of what they ask, and then I feel quiet inside for a while. Then it all starts over again.

participant in a recovery group

Our sexuality is so deeply intertwined with and expressive of our gender, our heart, our yearning for pleasure and for love—it is core to our being. When harm is done here, it is done in the depths of our existence, and our enemy seizes the opportunity to access dark strongholds within us. Those places of oppression tend to be among the deepest forms of oppression people experience, because evil has accessed wounding done to core parts of our souls. Our hope is that as those holds are broken, we can experience a healing and freedom otherwise impossible apart from God banishing the darkness and reclaiming his own.

John Eldredge

I have come to believe that the most significant portions of a story of abuse are guarded not only by our self but also by foul spirits that threaten, mock, confuse, and shut down our internal world whenever we get too close to shame and heartache. Are they in us, outside of us, around us? Are they demons? Fallen angels? Speculation is not my goal—only discernment and engagement are.

The moment the topics of evil and spiritual warfare are brought into the conversation about sexual abuse, conflict or chaos seems to reign. I have talked with fellow Christian therapists about spiritual warfare and observed their amused incredulity and academic contempt that an educated professional psychologist in the twenty-first century would resort to such a "primitive" worldview to understand human suffering and psychological symptoms.

There is a second response, and I find it more troubling. It is from people who acknowledge that there is evil—in fact, personal or intentional evil, not merely a force or the consequence of human cruelty—but that this evil is so limited by the work of Jesus that it is like a distant thunder. It can be sensed but doesn't have to be addressed beyond praying the Lord's Prayer. Bright and educated people have told me they can't fathom why there is a need for therapy; if I would simply help abuse victims get free from their demonic warfare and get back to the Bible, they would be completely healed.

A participant in a sexual abuse recovery group told me, "Look, I know there is something working against me. I don't need to be convinced there is a dark presence in the world. But I was in a church that demonized every problem or mishap. I finally shared with an elder's wife that I had a history of past sexual abuse, and she told me she thought so. She said she felt a spirit of fear and seduction and that I needed to pray against these spirits. She gathered a few of her friends and prayed over me. I thought it was weird. I know they are sincere, but one woman started waving her hands over me and said, 'You are haunted by a spirit of perversion.' I got angry. She might be right, but I felt like I had to agree and do what she was demanding or I'd be told I had a spirit of defiance or something. I either agreed or was written off. Frankly, it didn't feel that different from how one of my abusers set me up. It was all or nothing. In this case, I walked out of the 'deliverance' and I have not been back. I feel sick because I liked them and the church until I became their project to rid me of demons."

When I wrote *The Wounded Heart*, I believed evil existed but it was not my calling to directly address its presence or consequences. If asked then what my therapeutic approach was, I'd say I simply didn't want to consider the presence of evil other than in systemic and impersonal terms. Then I changed. How? By listening to my clients. Through their stories I have come to the conclusion that evil is very much at work in the world, in our mind, and in our body.

Theories about the nature of evil, let alone how to address it in life, have little consensus even among those who acknowledge that it exists and is deeply engaged in all aspects of human affairs. This lack of common ground leads me to offer my thoughts and experiences with pause and caution. We have much to consider and learn, and I don't write from a position that is dogmatic. It is important for me to put forth a number of core convictions:

- Evil exists and is not infinite but is a creature, a fallen angel (and his cohorts) in opposition to the glory of God and God's plan for his creation.

- Evil is limited by its existence as a creature. Evil is not omnipresent, omniscient, or omnipotent. Only God is God. Nevertheless, the kingdom of darkness is intentional, well informed, relentless, and perverse.

- Evil's primary way of operating is in darkness and secrecy, subtly using its cunning to reach its ultimate goal: ruining the glory of God. It will expend no more energy against a person, marriage, family, institution, or community than it needs to achieve its goal. If a person can be seduced by hours of television, sabotaged through a depression, or lulled into self-sufficiency through money, a degree, or a set of convictions that limit curiosity, then evil will likely focus more attention on those who are more dangerous to its kingdom.

- Evil hates what God reveals in and through the creation of humanity, especially with regard to gender and sexuality. Nothing brings evil greater delight or power than to foul our joy in being a man or a woman through sexual harm or gender confusion on the one hand or dogmatism on the other.

- Evil is involved in all human suffering indirectly, but it is dangerous to equate any specific event directly with the work of evil. Illness, relational conflict, or psychological struggles can never be approached with a univocal, singular understanding; instead, the effects of evil, direct or indirect, must be approached from many perspectives that include the body, heart, mind (brain), and self, as well as cultural systems that involve family, race, ethnicity, and culture.

- Evil gains access and power to ruin a part of our life by seducing us with lies that tempt us to form an alliance or covenant with the kingdom of darkness. No human being is immune to this seduction, and therefore every person, whether aware of it or not, struggles in a war that eventually affects every dimension of life. (Let this not be read to say that evil cannot be directly and profoundly thwarted and disempowered through prayer.)

- Evil delights in sexual abuse because the return on investment is maximized. It takes but seconds to abuse, but the consequences can ruin the glory of a person for a lifetime.

- Finally, he who is in us, Jesus, is greater than he who is in the world, the prince of darkness. And through the Spirit of God we are empowered to do direct harm to the kingdom of evil through the skillful use of faith, hope, and love.

Evil's Plan for Sexual Abuse

I view Satan as a thief, murderer, and destroyer who seduces us into making a covenant that thwarts God's plan and ruins God's creation.

When we covenant with another it is binding and irrevocable unless a greater authority supersedes to free us. The plan of evil is to get us, through lies, deceit, accusations, and threats, to make a vow of loyalty to it. The endgame of evil is to destroy our trust in God and then offer us any alternative that further distances us from the healing God longs for us to experience.

Evil Is a Thief

Evil steals innocence and joy. It hates our potential intimacy with God, therefore it uses the desire he created in us for beauty and sensuality, and our hunger for wisdom, to seduce us away from him. Its tactic is simple: use desire to tempt us away from our deepest desires and then turn us against desire as the enemy that got us into trouble. It is like a sting operation.

Evil particularly enlists the abuser's "grooming" of his or her victim to do its bidding. The abuser woos the child or adolescent through reading the desires of his or her heart. He reads the child's absence of care and attachment through his or her insecurity and begins offering what the child's caregivers have failed to offer. The child is given delight and told secrets. Relational intimacy is then deepened with touch that feels life-giving. Over minutes or months the abuser begins to use the child's desire to annul his or her sense of danger or wrong. The tentacles of the grooming reach deeper until the will of the child is broken. The abuser crosses the line of honor, and sexual abuse occurs. Usually it is covered over and hidden, and more secrets and threats are used to ensure silence. It is through this insidious seduction that more sexual abuse is likely to occur at even more egregious levels.

And all to what end? It is inevitable that most victims of abuse will unwittingly join the abuser in blaming themselves for what occurred. The well-meaning therapist, parent, or friend stands with the victim and nearly shouts, "It is not your fault. How can you blame a ten-year-old child for what happened?" But as intense as the desire to help is, those words fall like plastic pellets against the metal hull of a ship. What is usually not addressed is the way evil has bound the victim's heart to a hatred of the desire for intimacy, a hatred of the body's arousal, and a hatred of the sweetness of trust. It all happens so quickly that the victim is unable to see the con game of the abuser.

The calling of a good therapist is to follow the story of abuse and its aftermath closely enough to see the tracks of evil. There will always be a unique configuration of debris, a pattern of evil's intent that gives an indication of the covenants the victim has made, consciously or unconsciously, with the realm of darkness.

Sometimes the covenants or agreements are as simple as, *Your body is evil, and desire will always get you in trouble.* Other times evil weaves accusations and threats with promises. *You will never be loved because you are ugly, but at least your body can be used to get the closest thing to love—attention.* Evil is brilliant at then setting up experiences that bring us "evidence" of its deceitful accusations. The more we believe and bind our heart to evil's "truth," the more pathways it can develop to other lies.

A client told me about the moment she decided never to love again. She was abused by her father often and had been sold to various people for money, power, and drugs. He had a girlfriend who was the first woman ever to be kind to her. This woman was the first person who held her when she cried and even gave her counsel on how to escape some of the abuse. The day came when the girlfriend left the girl's father and she came to the girl's bedroom to say good-bye. After she left, my client said audibly: "I will never love anyone again and feel this alone."

My client is a good woman, strong in faith and faithful. She is resolute and passionate about helping others; she is stubborn and unwilling to ask for or receive help from anyone else. She made a vow soon after her one source of care and protection abandoned her to never trust or need anyone again. The vow she made unwittingly gave a portion of her heart to darkness, and this foothold allowed evil to pound away at her every time she let herself "need" a friend. She would hear a voice in her head that mocked her for being so needy and then threatened that her friends would talk about her and make fun of her.

Is my client's struggle psychological or spiritual? The question is tedious. The fact is there is nothing about our spirituality that doesn't intersect with our personality; there is nothing about our personality that isn't a reflection of our spirituality. Therefore, my client's paranoia is as much a spiritual issue as it is an issue of the body and soul.

There is nothing that will open our eyes to our bondage to the kingdom of darkness other than the kindness of God. It is the love of God that called Jesus to become the one to bear the full weight of all the accusations and debts claimed against us. The apostle Paul tells us:

> You were dead because of your sins and because your sinful nature was not yet cut away. Then God made you alive with Christ, for he forgave all our sins. He canceled the record of the charges against us and took it away by nailing it to the cross. In this way, he disarmed the spiritual rulers and authorities. He shamed them publicly by his victory over them on the cross. (Col. 2:13–15 NLT)

Jesus intends to stand against every accusation and claim made against us. When we are assaulted by a half-truth contemptuously hurled at us, he intends to take the blow first. His death is a covering against every assault of contempt and every claim of debt owed. The more freedom we gain from evil's brutal lies, the clearer we will see how past events have been used to capture and kill parts of our heart.

Evil Is a Murderer

Evil is a killer that delights in taking life and destroying hope. It does so through mocking our sense of powerlessness to escape the harm that evil has inflicted.

The news is a prime example. It is nearly impossible to hear of the suffering of the day without some sense of exhaustion, futility, and despair. It is beyond our capability to bring about change in any dimension in the "big" crises of the day. And, in fact, we feel we can't substantially change the problems at work or even alter our tendency to procrastinate. What seems true is that we don't really have any power or capacity to change anything. It is a lie, of course, but it feels true deep in our bones.

Evil knows that to the degree we are discouraged and defeated, we will not fight for survival. To not fight is to capitulate, to surrender. Evil doesn't primarily want to kill us; instead, it wants us to spend our lives in worry or regret. Its design is to take life from life, or in other words, to kill hope. It loves for us to sour ourselves through ruminating on failure and obsessing over the disasters we anticipate in the future. Both regret and worry sap creativity and plunge the heart into the slough of despair.

There are two primary consequences of despair: dissociation and indulgence. Dissociation is a deep inner disconnection from reality that turns the heart to a world of indulgence that for a brief moment satisfies. Dissociation is inevitable for a child or adolescent caught in the web of abuse. In fact, it is the gift of a boundary to separate us from the immensity of the horror.

Dissociation is not a choice; it is a survival mechanism.[1] And as much of a gift as it can be, evil ruins it by telling us that the only way we will ever be able to handle the struggles of reality is to escape. We often add to this impulse other things that increase our ability to numb out, such as food, drink, sex, work, television, video games, or pornography. These means of escape then become a context for evil to condemn, threaten, and mock us. To escape the shame, we numb ourselves even more.

The goal of evil is to kill desire, creativity, and the passion to war against its kingdom. It should be clear that we must stand against this impulse to surrender to a life that is a mere repetition of the past.

We are not powerless nor do we go into this fight without weapons. Scripture tells us to resist the devil and he will flee (see James 4:7). We have been given weapons and gifts to fight against evil because Jesus has ascended on high to sit at the right hand of his Father and has been given all power and authority over all that is seen and unseen. But how do we enter this fight?

We must love life and embrace the courage God has given us through the gift of the resurrection. G. K. Chesterton writes:

> Courage is almost a contradiction in terms. It means a strong desire to live taking the form of a readiness to die. "He that will lose his life, the same shall save it" (see Matt. 10:39; 16:25; Mark 8:35; Luke 9:24) is not a piece of mysticism for saints and heroes. It is a piece of everyday advice for sailors and mountaineers. It might be printed in an Alpine guide or a drill book. This paradox is the whole principle of courage, even of quite earthly or quite brutal courage. A man cut off by the sea may save his life if he will risk it on the precipice. He can only get away from death by continually stepping within an inch of it. A soldier surrounded by enemies, if he is to cut his way out, needs to combine a strong desire for living with a strange carelessness about dying. He must not merely cling to life, for then he will be a coward, and will not escape. He must not merely wait for death, for then he will be a suicide, and will not escape. He must seek his life in a spirit of furious indifference to it; he must desire life like water and yet drink death like wine.[2]

Furious indifference. How do we hold the paradox of giving up our life in order to find it? I believe Chesterton is saying that the more we open our heart to both heartache and hope, the more we can look death in the face and say, "Where is your sting?" (1 Cor. 15:55). We must love all that bears the mark of life: the sound of an owl finch and its call that sounds like the meowing of a kitten. We must love Bach, Ethiopian berbere, and the smell of freshly baked bread. Life is teeming with goodness. We must also experience death and powerlessness, but darkness will not win. Life and love will have the final word.

To love life is to defend against the one who would take it. It means taking up the weapons of God, the full armor, to live a life of love. It requires defiance that calls forth a deep rumbling in the soul to say, "Hell, no" and "Heaven, yes." This enables the heart to move with ferocity and kindness, openness and confidence, strength and humility. It refuses to say that the damage of abuse is irrevocable and all we can do is learn to live with it.

To love life is also to acknowledge that all we wish to see changed will certainly one day occur even if we do not see it in our lifetime. The resurrection promises that restoration, full and complete, beyond our wildest imagination, will dawn even if the night seems to last for eternity. The blood spilled by the murderer will not be forgotten and will not be in vain, and justice will bloom as surely as flowers do after a long winter.

Evil Is a Destroyer

Evil destroys. I don't believe its primary commitment is to utterly and completely blow up God's glory or wipe it off the face of the earth. In reality, it is far more sinister than that. If evil has the choice to incinerate a work of art or put a mark across its canvas, it should be clear that it prefers to mar. To destroy is to foul, to soil what is still before us but has lost its glory because of that mark. With regard to sexual abuse, evil's plan is to foul our beauty through shame.

There is shame in betrayal—*Why did I trust him?* There is shame in powerlessness—*Why didn't I stop it?* But our greatest shame is in responding to the touch of our body with arousal and pleasure. It is the darkest work of evil to mar our sexuality through the experience of touch. *My body felt arousal through all my senses, and therefore sensuality is dangerous and dark.* If there is a shadowing of all our senses, then that is especially true for our genitalia. *My sexual being and body are dark and dangerous.*

What is felt sexually, even for a child who doesn't know the word or its meaning, will inevitably leak into other intimate relationships. A client told me that even as a young girl, every time her father hugged her and walked with her hand in hand to the playground, she could feel the presence and touch of her uncle who abused her. She knew the two men were different, but she didn't know what to do with her genital arousal when her father hugged her. He was a good man. She felt aroused, therefore she had to be a very, very bad girl. Over time, the evil one drew her to renounce her goodness and accept the accusation that she was bad. It offered her the resolve to work extremely hard in school and never do anything wrong in order to gain the love that she might earn from her father. Then she vowed to hide all that was happening inside of her mind and body lest someone discover and expose her ignominy.

Let's be utterly clear about this next point: she was never a mere passive victim of evil's seduction and harm. Her own bent to find life apart from God, like that within us all, delivered her naturally to the lies of evil. But, that said, it is also crucial to understand that she was totally, 100 percent, a victim of her uncle.

She was also a child of Adam and Eve, who naturally fled and fought against the goodness of God. This is true of every human being from birth to death, unless our heart is disrupted through repentance. Her proclivity to turn against the invitation of God to trust in a legion of lies and false gods is also our natural bent. But this in no way lessens the full and utter responsibility of her abuser for using her fear, desire, and shame for his purposes. The mixture of her natural bent with the insidious assault of evil created havoc in her life, as it does in the life of every human being.

This havoc shows itself in countless ways, but centrally it disposes us to doubt, flee from, and try to control love. We are inveterately made for love, and at the same time we are terrified and defiant against receiving and giving love for the sake of God's glory. We want love on our terms—which, of course, is never love. We want love but not the deep humility, openness, curiosity, and vulnerability that it requires. It is evil's intent to stain our joy of receiving by shaming us for the arousal we felt with our abuser. Evil works to mar the joy of giving through blaming us for the arousal our abuser experienced through our touch. Evil wants us to suffocate in shame and to drown in the self-contempt we use ineffectively to resolve our shame. Shame and contempt spin the web designed to keep us from living boldly from our heart.

How Then Are We to Live?

I can't offer a method, a formula, or a series of steps. But I can point to where the journey of restoration will take us. If we are to heal, we must do the following things, which are rooted in the rich soil of faith, hope, and love.

We Must Become More Awake, Articulate, and Story Sensitive

Faith is a network of beliefs, convictions, and presuppositions that allow us to locate ourselves in the world as a distinct person and yet connected in relationships. Faith grounds us and helps us establish our identity. It serves as a compass to help us navigate who we are and how we relate to others. The Bible calls faith an anchor for our soul (see Heb. 6:19).

Faith begins through the attachment process of bonding to our primary caregiver(s). It grows through hundreds of thousands, if not millions, of experiences that enable us to test the world and our growing assumptions. A child learns who and what to trust, including the self; he or she learns what failure means and what is required to restore a bond with others and the world if trust is broken. Abuse severs the natural attachment bond of trust. We become leery of being fooled again by an abuser. This agreement—*I will never trust again*—lessens the inevitable heartache of betrayal. The vow is like a bubble that insulates and protects while simultaneously suffocating and killing. What protects us begins to ruin our core relationships in the long run.

The majority of people I see for therapy come because their relational realm is broken. Something has penetrated the bubble, and though it has been resealed, the ache can't be denied. Most want the fractured relationship restored without having to give up their insulation. It is simply not possible. But seldom are the roots of the core issue addressed; to do so means to reenter memories of betrayal that are full of pain and bitterness. It is better to wall off the memory, insulate themselves, and carry on. That works until the bubble gets pierced and the ache demands attention that harshness or denial will not resolve.

Reentering terrain we have fenced off as forbidden is an act of profound courage. It requires learning to read our story with eyes that see as God sees. We grow in faith to the degree we do what seems counterintuitive: open our heart to remember, grieve, and ask God to engage our heartache with tenderness.

Start with a simple assumption: every human life bears the marks of evil's hatred of human glory. Evil in its hatred has stolen, killed, and destroyed. It is not hyperbole to say that every life must be explored as wisely and methodically as a CSI agent inspects a crime scene. We can reclaim only what we name. If we refuse to enter our past with honesty, sensitivity, and wisdom, the harm of the past will continue to war against us in the present.

Most of us tell stories regarding the heartache of the past in a manner that allows us to tell the truth without being transformed by it. We tell without telling. We allow details to be generalized and painful parts to be suppressed. And no one seems to notice or enter the forbidden terrain with a call to clarity or an invitation to grieve. The result is that our memories don't call us to God in the present.

People seldom remember in a way that causes them to be desperate for God to be God.

Later in this book we will address the dynamics of memory and how to tell stories of harm to allow our past to increase our need for kindness and care. Telling the stories of past harm is meant to open our heart to mourn and to receive the comfort of God. It is comfort that enables our heart to imagine a day and a world transformed by hope.

We Must Become Angrier and Bolder in Our Refusal to Participate in the Repetitive Reenactment of Despair

Hope refuses to believe that the inevitable is so. What has always been and can't change is an illusion; if anything is true, it is that change is inevitable, not that the inevitable will not change. But evil caustically replies, *Nonsense. It is what it is. You will only be more discouraged and frustrated until you accept reality.*

We all live in the tension between the already and the not yet. What is isn't that bad, so why risk what is unknown and may be worse than what already is? *Be careful what you wish for; you may get it.* The known is a safer enemy than the unknown. Yet we were made for the unknown and to risk danger. In our day we crave danger that bears no consequences. We want to feel the rush of speed but in a context where we know the rules of engagement allow us to sue. This is equally true of how we hope—we want to dream and create but without risk of harm. And so we settle for addictive patterns that we repeat with the wish that finally we will get what we want.

Repetition of destructive or empty behaviors drains us of hope. As we reenact patterns that lead to the same heartache as in the past, hopelessness increases. Reenactment is being bound to a loop, a repetitive pattern of living out the unaddressed and unresolved harm of the past. Hope demands that we challenge our habitual reenactment with boldness, honesty, and kindness. This is counterintuitive. But we will not regain the ground of hope by force or mere self-control. No addict has changed merely because of the pain.

What changes us, then, if it is not pain? A passionate desire for goodness. Pain may alert us to the reality that something is wrong, but only when desire is freed to imagine the goodness and kindness of God does our heart turn toward joy. In a later chapter we will consider how engaging repetitive patterns of reenactment with a heart open to receive kindness begins to grow hope for transformation.

We Must Not Hide from Shame but Engage the Accusations with Courage and Embrace the Delight of God with Humility

The experience of shame sends a shudder so deep through the soul that most human beings would rather disappear, lie, or give up all that feels dear to escape the cataclysm. It is no small matter that the first story after the rebellion of Adam and Eve is about their frenzy to do whatever was necessary to escape exposure. Adam and Eve had to know that hiding from an infinite, all-knowing God was impossible. Shame makes a person mad, if not insane, and is the impetus for some of the most harmful acts against other human beings. Adam and Eve were willing to turn against one another in a heartbeat to blame each other and God in order to diminish the horror of exposure. Loyalty freezes in the ice of shame.

If we are to discard the heavy mantle of shame we must allow others to enter what feels like a festering wound and risk reengagement with evil, the destroyer. And in turn we must open our heart to what seems impossible and inconceivable: the delight of God. We must bless what God blesses and curse what he curses. Healing requires entering our stolen story to grow faith by remembering the past and learning to grieve. In turn we regain hope by receiving kindness that disrupts the reenactments that kill our dreams. Finally, we must bless what our body experienced in the suffering of arousal and curse only what God curses: the shame and contempt of evil.

3

The Body's Response to Abuse

I wasn't sure about all this health related to abuse stuff. If you start digging around, of course you'll find something, but I remember in a class I took in psychology that correlation is not causation. So how do I know that the illnesses I have are related to the abuse or are just genetic? Plus, I'm afraid to put things together sometimes . . . to blame it on him. . . . There are many things that happened in my life, not just my sexual abuse.

participant in a recovery group

I don't know if there is a relationship between the autoimmune disease and the abuse, but I'm willing to explore it. But can something from way back then be affecting me now? I guess I don't want to believe that the abuser is still messing with my body. Seriously? Is there any part of me that isn't screwed up? Is there any hope?

participant in a recovery group

Mountains of evidence now demonstrate with unshakeable certainty that the body suffers from abuse and trauma well after it has ended. The destruction of childhood

This chapter is cowritten with Dr. Heather Mirous, PhD in cognitive psychology, Northwestern University.

sexual abuse manifests itself long-term in our physiology, moving us away from God's original plan of perfect health and toward accelerated death through evil's physical, mental, emotional, and spiritual sabotage.

Physically, evil's sabotage may manifest itself in the form of chronic emotional upheaval (such as stress), frequent illness, and even grave disease. Mentally, evil would love to confuse and distract us from ever connecting the dots of our past abuse to our body's current suffering. Emotionally, evil would be delighted if we would feel powerless and hopeless about finding anything we can do to restore our health. Spiritually, evil would love to bar us from reclaiming our body, literally God's holy territory, in order to move toward restoration here and now on this earth.

In preparation for writing this chapter, I asked the members of one Wounded Heart recovery group to begin the process of investigating any potential connections between their past abuse and their current physical health. The questions I asked them to consider for several weeks included *What is your attitude toward your body and illnesses?* and *What cost may be incurred if it is true that your body is profoundly affected by past abuse?* Their response was stunning: "We have been engaging the material in *The Wounded Heart* for more than three years, and we have never once spoken about the effects of the abuse on our health. I don't think we have consciously avoided it, but it has not come up. We have never thought to make it a matter of discussion. Once we did, it was as if the walls came tumbling down. There were a lot of questions and discussion, as well as a great deal of skepticism, fear, and despair."

Scripture tells us that we are created in the image of God (see Gen. 1:27); therefore, we can conclude that our mind and body are intimately connected. God is not divided even though he reveals himself in the three persons of Father, Son, and Holy Spirit. We are likewise created whole and one, yet with the complexity of many parts meant to work in a harmony that can be called *shalom*. Shalom is the Hebrew word for peace. It is not the absence of tension or conflict; instead, it is the holy interplay of the parts into a compelling whole. Just as it would be a mistake to segment God into three parts, so would it be to see our body, heart, mind, and soul as merely compartmentalized units that are not integrally connected. While we may find comfort in thinking that what happens in one compartment does not spill over or contaminate another, this would be foolish and allow evil to further divide us.

When the heart and mind and soul are injured by sexual abuse, we must recognize that the body was not on a protected island but was also injured and is likely still suffering. Like the mental, emotional, and spiritual scars, the physical injury does not simply go away with time. In fact, if not tended to, like any injury it will likely fester, breed infection, and manifest itself in nastier ways.

Instead of tuning out the pain, we must listen to it as a gift that contains an important message worthy of being heard and honored. This listening is a compassionate and powerful leap toward restored health. The enemy would love for us to believe that what we are suffering in our body is just another unfortunate thing that has befallen us, something we are powerless to do much about. Or, better yet, the enemy would have us believe that what we feel in our body is simply "all in our head," that we are being hypochondriacs, an even more dismissive and dishonoring stance. Sadly, abusers and naive or negligent caretakers may have uttered these harmful and wrong sentiments, and even our most trusted doctors have probably suggested these ideas with some condescending authority. We also may have shamed ourselves with these thoughts, once again thinking that we are making too much out of nothing. This lie has the dark power to shut down our search for meaning and remedy, even when we *know* that something is wrong in our body.[1]

The truth is that what we are experiencing in our physical frame is also in our head; in fact, it's in our mind, our heart, our soul, and our body—our entire being. Modern science is finally beginning to catch up with how intimately the mind and body are connected. On one hand, this seems like a silly revelation—of course the mind and body are connected! After all, the brain is not only part of the body but the body's control center. Nevertheless, really honoring the connection between mind and body is a paradigm shift, especially in Western medicine, in which the mind and body have historically been kept separate. As one renowned doctor and scientist says, "Not only does the doctor or clinician suffer from the lack of an integrated viewpoint of a patient's disease, the patient suffers even more. He or she is left ricocheting from one specialist to another, none of whom can really address the patient's needs in their entirety."[2] Not that these specialists do not offer expertise in a focused area, but in some ways they represent the insanity of fractured modern medicine.

Today, we are fortunate that more and more doctors and scientists are bringing the body, mind, heart, and soul together. Doctors are being trained to practice integrative medicine, considering the holistic picture of mental, emotional, and spiritual precursors of physical ailment in each patient. There are now whole branches of psychology devoted to studying the impact of thoughts and feelings on our physical health and, even more specifically, the physiological implications of stress in the body and brain.[3]

In this chapter we will briefly highlight current research findings in order to help you examine your own body and mind, to pray over these truths, and to bring to light any form of physical harm that evil has worked to keep in the dark.

Healthy Physiology

Before we begin to explore the ways in which trauma disrupts our physiology, it is helpful to briefly explore God's design for healthy physiological functioning, especially within intimate relationships. God has wired us—body, heart, mind, and soul—for connection with one another and for truly intimate connection with a select few (including him). He has also wired us to move, to take hold of our world and explore, create, and shape it into new configurations of glory.

> God blessed them and said to them, "Be fruitful and increase in number; fill the earth and subdue it. Rule over the fish in the sea and the birds in the sky and over every living creature that moves on the ground." (Gen. 1:28)

We are created to be in relationship and to generate goodness in the world. To be fruitful and fill the earth requires a body that is wired for care and empathy and sexual desire and pleasure. To reign and rule requires a body that is wired for movement, curiosity, adaptability, caution, and management of risk and danger. All of this wiring begins in the womb and is evident at every level, from single cells to brain structures to whole body systems throughout the entire course of our human development.

Before we even take our first breath, for example, God has equipped our body with an amazingly intricate cocktail of biochemicals that send messages to receptive brain areas and drive us toward connection with one another—and signal fear when that connection is not safe. For example, oxytocin,[4] sometimes called the "love hormone," is released in the infant and in the mother as she nurses her baby (or even thinks about nursing her baby, often stimulating milk letdown) or nurtures her baby through loving touch,[5] bringing about feelings of mutual pleasure and connection, bonding, security, and attachment. With this sensation of love comes dopamine, which fills the receptors of multiple brain areas, including the nucleus accumbens ("reward center"), bringing about feelings of satisfaction, reward, and anticipation for more—not too different from the way addicts feel euphorically high after their fix of choice. Truly, we are addicted to love.[6]

To make us able to send and receive such chemicals, God has equipped us with specialized cells and structures throughout the brain and body, all designed to work in concert and provide unity within the body and mind within the context of relationship. One interesting set of such cells was accidentally discovered in the 1990s in primates (we now know that humans possess even more): mirror neurons.[7] These neurons are motor neurons in the brain that activate the motor cortex when we observe the intentional action of another person, as if to mimic them, even without our body making a move (or perhaps only a subtle one). This mirroring also enables us to instantaneously read and identify the other's emotion through even the faintest movement of his or her muscles and to subtly feel what that other is feeling. This facilitates empathy and attunement between one another and promotes deep connection, relational intimacy, and secure attachment.[8]

When connection happens well and in the context of safety and trust from our early days, these biochemicals, cells, brain structures, and so forth prompt us to approach our world instead of withdrawing from it, to explore it with an unbridled sense of freedom and awe, play and connection, all to the glory of God.[9] System-wide, the sympathetic part of our autonomic nervous system gears our body up for these approach behaviors by increasing heart rate and respiration—literally getting our blood pumping, supplying us with energy to go, go, go and engage our world. Then more dopamine rushes in as we discover or create something fascinating, or humbly work hard and feel fulfilled in our accomplishment. Our serotonin level, linked to feelings of happiness and well-being, rises.[10] Our body smiles, and our face reflects the glory of God.

God has also created our sexuality to intersect with these chemicals, cells, and structural components of our brain and body. For example, as sexual desire increases, dopamine levels rise and serotonin levels decrease. An orgasm creates a whopping 400–500 percent rise in dopamine![11] God intended for sex to feel *really* good and to do really good things for us, physiologically and relationally.[12]

And then it's back to balance. After we spend energy engaging our world, God designed us to rest. The sympathetic nervous system takes a break and the parasympathetic nervous system takes over, slowing the body down, reengaging the more long-term maintenance processes such as digestion, repair, growth, and rest. God planned all of this for good, for healthy physiological function, for true intimacy and integration—oneness in our body, oneness with each other, oneness with him.

What happens, then, when intimacy has gone bad, been misused or abused? In short, we become divided, disintegrated—internally, between one another, and often with God. Before we look at this process of disintegration, we'll explore how God has programmed our body to react and recover from normal states of stress.

Our Body's Natural Stress Response System

Our body is well equipped to handle short bouts of stress. (Stress, by the way, can also include intense good feelings—unexpected joy, excitement, and so forth—anything that moves the body out of internal balance or *homeostasis*.) Homeostasis is the body's automatic, nonconscious, nonvolitional return to shalom, or optimal tension in balance.

God has programmed our body with an amazing cascade of biochemical, neural, and physiological responses to immediately swing into action and manage acute (sudden onset but short-lived) stressors, whether they are physical or psychological. Our human limitation in fully understanding God's amazing design compels us to look at the brain in small, manageable chunks, and therefore the following basic description is not perfectly accurate or complete but is merely a helpful heuristic in understanding the way God has equipped our brain and body to process stress.

One way our brain can be thought of is *triune*, comprised of three major systems that are evolutionarily and developmentally built from the bottom up: the reptilian brain (which contains the cerebellum and brain stem and regulates the body's vital functions such as breathing, eating, sleeping); the mammalian brain (which comprises the limbic system, including the hippocampus, hypothalamus, amygdala, and thalamus, and is responsible for memory, emotion, and multiple body functions); and the neocortex (the "newest" part of the triune brain, which contains the two hemispheres of the cerebrum and is responsible for the many types of executive function such as language, abstract thought, logic, and reason, which set humans apart from all other creatures).[13]

Part of the limbic system, the thalamus (nicknamed "the cook" by van der Kolk[14]) merges all the sensory input we receive from our surroundings—sights, smells, sounds, sensations—into coherent perceptions and sends these messages simultaneously to the amygdala and prefrontal cortex. If the amygdala (the "smoke detector"[15]) detects threat, it immediately signals the hypothalamus to activate the stress response. Our autonomic nervous system and endocrine system are then sent into action, resulting in an activated sympathetic system (gearing the body up by signaling for a quicker heart rate and blood flow to circulate oxygen and glucose to needed muscles), a suppressed parasympathetic system (immobilizing nonessential bodily maintenance and promotion functions such as digestion, growth, repair, reproduction, and immune function),[16] and a rush of adrenaline and cortisol (called the "stress hormone").[17] Because all of the above happens before we know it, literally, our body may be in motion before we are even consciously aware of it.

The prefrontal cortex receives the message just a bit slower (by milliseconds, via a different pathway[18]) than the amygdala. The medial portion of the prefrontal cortex ("the watchtower"[19]) evaluates the message and then signals the body to either restore homeostasis, if the threat is a false alarm, or bring the threat to conscious awareness, if it is indeed real, and devise an effective strategy to navigate through it or away from it. These physiological responses aim to keep our body safe by directing all energies to fleeing or fighting.

(If, however, the situation is too dire to flee from or fight off, we may instead freeze, or become immobilized.[20])

After the stressor is over, the system is meant to come back into balance. The elevation in cortisol subsides, heart rate and breathing come back down to normal, glucose clears from the bloodstream, and energy is again guided back to other long-term maintenance functions that were put on hold. If balance is not restored, trouble begins.[21]

When the stressor is sudden and disruptive, it is considered acute. When an acute stressor occurs and we cannot restore safety within a reasonable period of time, our brain and body become flooded with a continued cascade of these biochemical and physiological responses. This buildup leads to dysregulation in our body, often culminating in chronic illness and disease—right in line with the enemy's continued mission to steal, kill, and destroy our body, literally.

Acute Traumatic Stress

Some stressors are just too intense for our normal physiologic stress response to adequately process; even though they may be acute (sudden onset, short duration) they are also traumatic—not the type God equipped us to handle well. So, what do our brains and bodies do with these horrors?

Through recent advances in technologies like PET (positron emission topography) scans and FMRI (functional magnetic resonance imaging), neuroscientists have been able to see what happens in the brain, not during actual traumatic events themselves (as this would be impossible to catch, not to mention unethical to create) but during remembering of such times. Intuitively, it would seem that simply recalling a traumatic event in the past would not be as traumatic as living through it the first time. However, our brain and body say differently.

When participants are prompted to simply recollect a traumatic event, the part of the brain that processes what we see, the visual cortex, activates as if it were literally seeing the event unfold. At the same time, the physiological stress response springs into action—heart rate and blood pressure increase, adrenaline and cortisol spike, and breathing becomes quick and shallow.[22] While it's intriguing that these brain and body responses happen while simply recalling the traumatic event, even years later, they make sense in that these same responses would be expected to happen during the actual traumatic event.

What's more striking, though, is what else the brain does (or doesn't do) that is less expected. While the participants recalled the traumatic event, their brain scans showed that the area of the brain that processes language, Broca's area, located in the left inferior frontal gyrus, suddenly deactivated or significantly decreased in activity. Literally, during trauma, language goes offline. The loss of functionality in this area is similar to the way stroke patients lose their ability to form recognizable words and speak. It is no wonder that we struggle to put into words the atrocities that have happened to us. "Trauma by nature drives us to the edge of comprehension, cutting us off from language based on common experience or an imaginable past. . . . When words fail, haunting images capture the experience and return as nightmares and flashbacks."[23]

It is not just the language area in the left hemisphere that goes offline; much of the left hemisphere itself shows deactivation during a flashback. Among other things, this leads to the phenomenon wherein the event from the past loses its place in the context of time, making it seem as if it were happening in the present. While the executive function areas of the left hemisphere are deactivated, the limbic system of the right hemisphere, specifically the amygdala ("smoke detector"), is acutely activated, warning the participant that something very dangerous is happening, seemingly in real time.[24]

For participants who froze during the traumatic event (versus responding with fight or flight), during a flashback even more than the left hemisphere deactivates—it is nearly the whole brain. This ominous lack of activity accompanies the utter lack of feeling that these participants experience when reminded of the traumatic event, similar to the way their bodies and minds completely went numb, shut down, blanked out, or severely dissociated during the traumatic event. This behavior is medically described as "depersonalization" from the actual event (most likely evoked when in a position of powerlessness during the traumatic event, such as being physically immobilized by a perpetrator).[25] In these cases, the physiological stress response does not kick in when the person is being reminded of the event—no increased heart rate, breathing, and so forth. Do not be fooled, however. The body is still experiencing extreme amounts of stress, and in any form this is debilitating over time.

Chronic Stress

Our body is beautifully designed to immediately and effectively gear up for short bouts of stress, but we are not designed to continue operating at that crazy accelerated pace. The body is meant to come back into our natural state of internal balance, homeostasis—shalom.

If this does not happen, over time this dysregulation becomes our body's new normal through a process known as *allostasis*[26]— our body's attempt to adapt in order to maintain homeostasis by changing our normal physiological responses (such as increased stress hormone secretions and all of the accompanying physiological reactions throughout the body's systems) in order to process the continued stress signals from the brain. Whether that stress is actual or perceived doesn't matter—the brain and body are still ramping up to a new normal to handle the continuous stress.

With continued allostasis, our body begins to suffer wear and tear, or "allostatic load." This represents the cumulative burden on the body from compensating for the continued stress, and its effects are individual to each person, given his or her genetics, lifestyle, history, and so forth.[27] By some counts, this load can be quantified. A higher allostatic load means more dysregulation and deterioration in the body and the brain, and more fertile ground for susceptibility to stress-related ailments and diseases.[28] Literally thousands of empirical research articles, review articles, meta-analyses, and books have been written on the fallout of carrying chronic stress, or a high allostatic load, in our body. It is rather scary to begin to open our eyes to the masses of research about the ways in which the body "keeps the score"[29]—from the lowest level of analysis, the cell or neuron, up to organs, all the way up to interrelated systems within the body.

In the brain, for example, it has now been well established that the architecture of multiple areas is changed through trauma and chronic stress. While the amygdala grows and becomes hypersensitive, the hippocampus and prefrontal cortex shrink[30] (especially in females, as estrogen plays a role[31]), making the interconnections and functions of these brain areas less efficient and less effective, thus distorting our everyday experiences. What is even more shocking is that it's not just experiences as extreme as trauma, chronic stress, depression, or PTSD that change the brain; even circumstances as "benign" as jet lag or lack of physical activity have been shown to shrink the hippocampus.[32]

In terms of a system, as the brain continues to signal the stress response, it may not be surprising that the stress-response system (in particular, the hypothalamic-pituitary-adrenal [HPA] axis, which helps regulate emotion) develops atypically in children who have been abused.[33] There is a disruption in cortisol output—either too high or too low. Dysregulation throughout development[34] increases susceptibility to physical, mental, and emotional illness.

In fact, there is now evidence that *many*, if not all, bodily systems suffer dysregulation and susceptibility to disease as a result of prolonged imbalance (even those we may not readily relate to stress[35]): respiratory,[36] digestive,[37] metabolic,[38] endocrine,[39] cardiovascular,[40] immune,[41] reproductive,[42] and more.[43] The biologically protective process of inflammation, by which our body fights off foreign invaders

60

or pathogens, turns against us when stress continues the process of inflammation and overactivates our immune system—the root of autoimmune disease.[44] Basically, any condition ending in "itis" can be traced back to inflammation—arthritis, thyroiditis, ulcerative colitis, vasculitis, and so on (and there are plenty of other inflammatory disorders that do not end in "itis").

Bottom line: prolonged stress moves our body away from God's plan for health and toward accelerated aging and death. (Literally, our body's "molecular clock for cellular aging," our telomeres—the protective end caps on our chromosomes—show us how our time here on earth is shortened when our body and mind are not well cared for by shrinking in size and ability to protect our DNA.[45]) The ravaged body of a survivor is left vulnerable, susceptible, and fragile long after the abuse has ended. Whether we have experienced acute stress or chronic stress, our body has suffered; it has been overstressed in multifaceted, interrelated ways that are more complex than we even know. The delicate balance of shalom in the body has been disrupted, the dance between systems that regulate activity and rest (sympathetic and parasympathetic) has been altered, and you are likely carrying an allostatic load heavier than you were ever meant to bear.

What's even more evil is that the emotions of shame and powerlessness that accompany abuse significantly intensify this physiological discord[46]—each on their own, but even more so in combination. In a meta-analysis of over two hundred laboratory stress studies, the conditions that elicit feelings of powerlessness and shame together triggered the largest cortisol response in research participants, and that was just during relatively simple and ethical laboratory tasks such as public speaking.[47] Just imagine the larger impact of sexual abuse on our system. It is no wonder that with this inconceivable level of unrest, our mind and body often drive us to desperately seek external ways to calm our overstressed system—the least of these, perhaps, is reaching for an alcoholic drink or scavenging for bits of chocolate just to feel at ease, even if for a moment.

Redemption and Resurrection of the Body

Evil not only intends physical harm but also intends to destroy through the usual suspects of confusion, doubt, self-blame, self-contempt, hopelessness, and powerlessness. The good news is that we have an amazing amount of control and power in regaining our physical health because God, in his sovereign creation and provision, offers us ways to restore shalom. Modern science has provided countless data to support and expand upon the principles he originally provided. So we are well armed with ammunition against the evil one to take back our rightful territory and restore our health, first through identifying our body's suffering from abuse and then by taking hold of our power to heal.

Identifying the Damage

The body remembers. It is chronically calling out to us that our allostatic load is too heavy. Often, rather than listening to our body, we sabotage or mute it through activities such as excessive drinking or eating (or not eating enough), exercise, busyness, or shopping.[48] The enemy works hard to keep us in the dark, to the point that we are not even aware of the relationship between our health issues and past sexual abuse.

There is immense power in just naming the consequences of our past abuse on our current physical functioning. Bringing these physical connections to light dismantles the dark hold on our mind, and therefore our body. The quantity and quality of the connections between past abuse and current physical ailments are probably about as vast as the number of cells in our body. Some connections are obvious; others are not. Here are some survivors' insights:

> Fever blisters, cold sores—*"I find it interesting that only those of us abused by Daddy got them, but not the two siblings who were not."*

Arthritis—*"It started on the drive home from the abusive uncle's place."*

COPD and asthma—*"What can I say . . . it's horrible. Horrible. Horrible. When you get that short of breath, and your mind is instantly back in the closet."* (Her place of abuse.)

Vertigo—*"I've only felt that way once before, and I believe God was reminding me that I was completely incapacitated during the rape."* (A body memory relieving the shame of why she didn't fight her perpetrator off and take some action.)

Hair loss—*"My adrenals and thyroid finally crapped out, just too much stress for far too long. My doctors never asked about my emotional history or current stress. Instead, I was sent to separate specialists, and each tried to treat my physical symptoms—acne, irregular periods, and then the worst—hair loss, a lot of it and all of a sudden. Finally a holistic doctor helped me realize it's all been stress-related. It's devastating, and I am so angry at what else was taken from me."*

Bed-wetting and sleepwalking—*"Both started shortly after the abuse, and ended years later when my grandfather (the abuser) died. I never connected these until we were working on our health stories."*

There were many others mentioned: migraines, heart palpitations, more cold sores, TMJ (temporomandibular joint disorder), eating disorders of various kinds, stomach and digestive problems, overactive bladder, chronic urinary tract and yeast infections, anal retention, intense pain during sex, fibromyalgia, other autoimmune diseases such as vasculitis and Hashimoto's thyroiditis, and the list goes on. This collection of symptoms came from only thirteen members of one Wounded Heart group! Several symptoms seemed to appear in relation to the onset of abuse and/or the physical presence of the abuser, and some symptoms disappeared after the death of the abuser or after beginning the process of naming past abuse.

How readily do we connect these dots? Recognizing the correlation between current physical symptoms and past sexual abuse is often met with skepticism and denial: *I don't have a health story.*[49] This recognition can be especially muddy for victims who have strong reasons not to listen to their body. There are few "streets" that connect our cortical mind with our limbic system. One street that links thinking to feeling runs through the medial prefrontal cortex, a part of the brain that supports self-awareness. In fact, self-awareness is better described as sensory awareness, which is the ability to feel and register how our body is engaging the here and now—a process called interoception.[50] This "looking inside" is not a skillset that a Western approach to medicine or education has valued, and when abuse brings up feelings of shame, fear, disgust, arousal, or self-hatred, we are even less inclined toward self-awareness. Even if we do look inside, we may be silenced by evil's message of shame. Somehow the harm inflicted on our body is now either our own fault or a blemish too embarrassing to admit.

Beyond identifying what it has attempted to steal, kill, and destroy in our body, the last thing evil would want is for us to believe there is any shred of hope that we can do anything about the trauma our body is still holding. Hope moves us away from destruction and toward wholeness. Hope begs for vision and motivates action toward a better state—in this case, restored health in body, mind, heart, and soul.

Hope for Healing

Can we recognize the common weapons of the enemy to keep our hope from surfacing? There is deceit: any distortion from God's truth, such as self-doubt, hopelessness, illusion of control, or erroneous thinking that *God does not care about* _____. There is accusation:

any version of self-blame, shame, self-contempt, or thinking, *It's my fault.* There is also threat: the message that we will always fail and that we are powerless.

Can you hear the messages of evil in these survivors' words?

> *"I have the blood work data, which I can't do anything about."* (powerlessness) *"Then I have the pain that I can't deny, but is it really that bad? Am I giving it too much credence?"* (self-doubt)
>
> *"I used to blame myself. You're ugly, you're fat. You deserve whatever."* (self-blame, self-contempt)
>
> *"I attributed my arthritis to my sin, my relationship with the abuser . . . that God was punishing me."* (a different source of self-blame)
>
> *"It's hereditary, in my genes . . . so it's out of my control, nothing I or any doctors can do."* (powerlessness) *"Plus, God does not care about my face breaking out or my hair falling out; that's just vanity."* (deceit, hopelessness) *"I don't want to talk about it."* (shame)
>
> *"I need to be in control of everything concerning my body—food, drink, sex, emotion—and I never let myself rest. I've worked very hard to remain in a numb state. I'd prefer to be a robot."* (self-contempt, distortion, and false responsibility)

What does God say?

> Do you not know that your bodies are temples of the Holy Spirit, who is in you, whom you have received from God? You are not your own; you were bought at a price. Therefore honor God with your bodies. (1 Cor. 6:19–20)

The issue of our physical resilience is actually a fundamental biblical construct. Our body is called a temple, literally the place where the Spirit of God dwells. Not taking the utmost care of our body neglects and destroys the home of the Holy Spirit. Our body is deeply honored by God and so we are to honor our body, which in turn honors God.

What does it mean to honor God with our body? This survivor describes it well:

> I wasn't making myself a priority before, and now I am. . . . I used to blame myself. *You're ugly, you're fat. You deserve whatever.* And now I say, *Well, God made you. God loves you.* And it's time to honor that. And what can I do today to honor my body? I'm not going to worry about tomorrow, or what I did or didn't do yesterday. Today, I'm going to open the blinds and let the light in. I'm going to take care of myself today.

Honoring our body entails bringing it back into balance, restoring integration and shalom in the soul, mind, heart, and body by acknowledging the holy interconnectedness of God's design. Survivors have an even higher level of responsibility in honoring their body than those who were not abused, requiring a more informed, proactive, and protective mindset. Do not be surprised if you do not get help from your doctors and "specialists." Health care professionals and even therapists seldom recognize or honor the relationship between past abuse and current health. Pursue this internal investigation on your own or with trusted others (you might also consider finding some new doctors). Do not be swayed by our culture's denial of God's beautifully intricate design in each of us. As Socrates said, "Know thyself." This is good advice. "Know yourself, listen to the signals that your own body is sending you, and get to know the relationship between what is happening in your life and the mental states you are experiencing as well as the physical changes you are going through. Be ready to communicate these observations in an honest way to your clinician. Be a scientist; make notes in an impartial and logical way, even if it is painful and not flattering to yourself."[51]

Caring for the Body

Medical texts and research seem to center on a few common goals when it comes to caring for our body. There may be others, but some common health goals include:

- decrease stress activation
- decrease inflammation
- balance hormones
- increase serotonin (our body's stress buffer)[52]

When we move toward these goals, all kinds of good things happen. It is even possible for new neurons to grow and atrophied brain areas to rebuild![53] While the abuser took control of our body to inflict harm, there is much we have control over in our current body to restore health.

Keeping in mind the goals above, we should consider some of the healthy habits and bits of practical advice below as if we are window shopping: let each item on this list represent an entire store, rich in detail and context, multifaceted and requiring extensive time and experience to really get to know it. Each item is supported by much research (years or even decades in many cases) on the health benefits it provides our body. Resources are listed in the endnotes that offer a more complete picture of how stress affects our brain and body and how to care well for both.[54] The *Healing the Wounded Heart Workbook* also provides more time and space to help us think through the sabotage and repair of our body and mind.

Bear in mind that approaching this as a to-do list or a way to "fix it" will cause more harm than good; instead, we should approach it as a banquet of options to cultivate kindness toward our body, mind, heart, and soul. Just start somewhere, and enjoy the process.[55]

- Sleep[56]
- Eating well[57]
- Exercise (even a little helps a lot)[58]
- Sunlight[59]
- Prayer[60]
- Gratitude[61]
- Kindness/service[62]
- Laughter[63]
- Music[64]
- Social support[65]
- Mindfulness and body connection[66] (for example, yoga,[67] meditation,[68] EMDR,[69] breath work)
- Body work[70] (for example, massage, cranial sacral, acupuncture)
- Aromatherapy[71]
- Supplements [72]
- Medication[73]
- A holistic-minded doctor (now termed "integrative medicine")[74]
- Becoming your own body scientist[75]
- Stress journal[76]
- And, of course, sex[77]

May this list empower and inspire you; God has supplied us with much power in restoring what the enemy has attempted to steal, kill, and destroy.

Odds are you have been able to identify some links between your current health and past abuse. If, however, after reading all of this, you don't recognize yourself and you don't have an "itis" moment, then what? PRAISE GOD! Praise him for his protection over your body and mind. And ask him to help you be open to the messages your body may be sending you, or will send you in the future. Be vigilant. Listen to subtleties. Take your body seriously.

All victims of sexual abuse must learn to identify the devious schemes and voices of evil and then separate themselves from them. Evil directly harms our body through abuse and the physiological fall-out afterward. Evil continues to work overtime indirectly to sustain our body's harm by cunningly masking the source of its complaints. If we get wise to our body's ailments, evil then works in our mind and heart to keep us sedated, oppressed, and miserable. All of these devious schemes result in unbridled stress running rampant through our mind and body, leaving daily doses of literal destruction in its wake. As we embrace the path to healing, we must curse this evil but praise God for his truly *awesome* creation, resilient and ready for restoration.

4

Cursing the Body

But Christ has rescued us from the curse pronounced by the law. When he was hung on the cross, he took upon himself the curse for our wrongdoing. For it is written in the Scriptures, "Cursed is everyone who is hung on a tree."

Galatians 3:13 NLT

I have been at war with my body as long as I can remember being a body. I didn't like wearing dresses. I hated having my mother rip a brush through my hair. I hated having to wear shirts when the boys got to go shirtless. And then my grandfather's touch made me sick. Nauseated. My body had to be covered and then it could be opened up whenever he chose to pleasure himself. And after all of the battles, what was I supposed to do with what my body felt when he touched me? I hate what my body provokes in men and what it makes me feel.

participant in a recovery group

The abuser's tactic is always the same: groom, arouse, shame, and condemn. Once the heart joins evil in condemning pleasure and desire, the process repeats itself through an endless cycle of self-harm that leads to more condemnation and contempt.

The tactic is repeated as often as it takes to entrap. What changes is not the strategy but the particularities of each story.

One of the darkest I have heard over these twenty-five years involves a client whose abuser used cruelty and power to weave incomprehensible torture together with arousal and kindness. He bound her in handcuffs and used both whips and other devices of torture to wreak havoc on her body until she collapsed. After torturing her, he would anesthetize her and then gently nurse her, rubbing salve into her wounds.

She was kept in a coffin-like box at night, and by the time morning came she was desperate to escape, even if it meant another day of agony and humiliation. The sexual abuse was perpetrated in the fog of terror and dark dependence. Her abuser's craft and artistry, learned in a clandestine cult and perfected in a paramilitary context, enabled him to wage a war against her soul, each attack more devastating than the last. In her own words:

> I had survived the blows that had rained down upon me in various forms, my body battered but still mostly intact. My interior landscape has been forever altered by the conflict inside those terrible days. My body and soul felt burnt, barren, whole hills blackened and smoldering—still, little green shoots rose tremulously, defying the bloody siege. But he always returned. Again he smoothed down my arm, occasionally tapping when a possible vein emerged. I relaxed into the gentle rhythm. Even now I want to weep remembering. He smoothed away the hair that had fallen over my face. Oh, the agony of that kindness. An eternity later he wrapped a tourniquet around my arm. Rubber biting into my arm, I welcomed that sharp nip. The needle, a much desired distraction, found its home in my arm. Officious taping, an adhering tightness on the skin, wrapping, more taping, and the catheter was in. Then, "I must attend to your back now. This will hurt a little bit." He would begin rubbing some kind of ointment over the torn areas below my shoulders. In curious fashion, the stinging sensation grew less and less bothersome. I grew warm in

what seemed like extravagant care. Never before had I experienced a touch that soothed and comforted in this way. I cannot bear to go on.

The contours of this woman's torture and sexual abuse are beyond comprehension, but the pattern is the same: bring arousal through pain and fear, then replace with tenderness and pleasure, then elicit pain and fear through arousal, then soothe that pain and fear through tenderness and kindness. The ambivalence that results is tortuous and haunting. What is difficult to believe is that the tenderness and pleasure of care and gentle touch, especially genital arousal, are more tormenting than the original fear and pain.

Pain calls forth defiance and resilience. It impels the abused person to defend himself or herself by going far, far away into the dissociative regions of the soul to languish until the agony is over. But pleasure, especially tender, arousing genital pleasure, draws the soul back through the layers of damage to the surface to suffer again what is both humiliating and enjoyable.

This brilliant and dark torturer knew how to rip the flesh off my client's back and then care for her pain, brush her hair, and gently soothe her wounds as he groomed her for his eventual sexual violations. Listen again to her final words: "I cannot bear to go on." It is not the searing pain or terror that elicits those words but the soothing and comfort that aroused something in her heart that had never been touched before.

Another story involves a single friend who shared with me her struggle with a married man at church who offered her playful, seductive affection. He was flirtatious and near the border of inappropriate, but he never crossed the line to physical touch. She found herself thinking about him often and felt cheapened and silly for her growing interest in him.

I felt like I was able to be fairly stable at the end of the year and things seemed to fade away. In January I saw him at church a few times; he has asked to borrow some books, and I have chatted with him a few times in the parking lot. Seems quite harmless—yet I am aware that I still feel drawn to him, that he somehow has some kind of power over me. So, for example, when I lent him my book I really didn't want to, but I felt like I wasn't able to say no to him. I can see how this could quickly escalate into an addictive relationship. I feel broken and also determined that my beauty will not again be marred. I do feel terror too. I was so broken by the last destructive relationship I had in another church, my whole body is screaming—I never want to go through that again!!! Yet to live without some kind of fantasy also evokes terror; it was how I coped with trauma—to always have some kind of fantasy. It wants to linger.

My friend has a history of emotional entanglements with married men that began with a convoluted relationship with her father. The last friendship she'd had with a married man in another church did not escalate into a physical affair, but it did become a source of arousal, shame, condemnation, and obsession. She reenacted an abusive dynamic similar to the one she'd had with her father, and she'd handled her childhood trauma by escaping into fantasy because it was in that realm that she found comfort. Fantasy enabled her to flee from the blight or banality of reality and reconstruct life as she desired. It was easy to imagine a man who was paying attention to her as her platonic soul mate who would not ask her to be sexual but would shower her in delight. This time, even though she wasn't aware of what her new friend was arousing in her, she knew there was something wrong about his care. Still, it felt like a gravitational pull she could not escape. The arousal brought self-condemnation, which only seemed to intensify her obsession.

The closer one gets to one's shame-filled story, the harder it is to remain kind or desire kindness. This is especially true when a victim of sexual abuse gets near the story of grooming where the abuser offered care and delight.

In *The Wounded Heart* I wrote about how every act of abuse involves the development of trust (excepting the experience of random, jump-out-of-the-woods child sexual abuse). The abuser grooms the child by watching to see what the child needs that is so often missing in their primary caregiver's nurturance. The abuser reads the heart and life of the child and positions himself or herself as a trusting presence that offers what the others fail to provide.

This stage of grooming bears incalculable power. Whether the grooming period lasts a few minutes or months, trust is gained and access to the heart is assured. What is most diabolic is that the abuser sows seed that is often life-giving. God has created us to be studied, read, and interpreted, and the more accurate and deep the reading, the more life-giving is the experience. It doesn't take long to be won by a careful reader.

I was flying home from a trip and my flight was canceled. I rearranged my flight on the phone with the personnel who deal with the elite frequent flyers. But I had to get a new ticket, and to do so I stood in line for what felt like an eternity. Finally, my turn came and I gave the lady behind the counter my old ticket and told her I wanted a ticket for my new flight. She informed me the flight was already well past full. I was exhausted and irritated and told her in a condescending tone that I was already booked and only needed a ticket printed.

She looked at me and said, "Dr. Allender, you are clearly irritated and a man not to be trifled with." I looked at her directly for the first time. Her eyes indicated she was neither returning my condescension nor was she apologetic. She was direct and strong. I mumbled, "Oh, I am sorry, and yes, I am exhausted." I felt my body relax. Her warmth increased and she smiled. "No worries, it is my job to know how to deal with our most important customers who keep us in business and also feel entitled and extra-irritated when their lives don't work as they wish."

I laughed. In one sentence she lauded me and then told me that my self-absorbed, self-righteous entitlement was something she was a specialist in addressing. And her brilliance in dealing with me was worthy of my full respect. She read in me both exhaustion and entitlement—and I would have done virtually anything she asked. I was like a puppy that had been both scolded and then given a warm blanket.

If a stranger can alter my mood and circumstances that quickly, and I am a fairly self-aware and high-functioning (at times) adult, then what match is a child who is read well? We melt into people who offer us a taste of life. The brilliant reader of our heart wins access, and we become indebted and further open to their intentions.

It is one thing to be read well, but it is even more special to be *chosen*. It is the deepest hunger of our heart to be chosen above all others. We hunger not only to be known but far more to be the one who brings delight to the eyes of the beloved. The teacher who smiles at us brings us pleasure. The teacher who sees our joy and responds with delight increases our pleasure beyond words. It can all happen in a flash of a few seconds, but it literally changes the biochemistry of our brain.

When a perpetrator uses tenderness and care as part of the dynamic with his or her victim, the victim loses the ability to separate delight and beauty from harm and evil. The deeper we enter the realm of harm, the more we must see the diabolic intent of evil. This demands an understanding of the role of shame, the violence of contempt, and the resolve to curse what God blesses.

Arousal → Shame

Arousal comes through each stage of abuse. The first stage is the abuser's grooming through reading the needs and unique character of the victim. The grooming stage offers what has often been missed by one's primary attachment figures. It is a heartbreaking reversal. The abuser offers what is lacking in the relationship with one's caregivers to gain access to the heart.

76

I have had to say many times during therapy that the abuser was a better picture of God than one's parents or other primary caregivers. It is this radical statement that allows the abuse victim to see the dark reversal of what was meant to be. An inattentive parent fails. A parent who fails to see the inevitable marks of abuse fails. It is here the abuser wins.

The second stage of abuse—the touch of primary and secondary sexual parts—is bound to the rise of fear (cortisol), bonding (oxytocin), and pleasure (dopamine and opioids). It is this lethal combination of competing biochemical impulses that stream through the body of a young child or adolescent. How is a child to make sense of what feels like alien and contradictory impulses? A child will likely believe, *I am "bad" because I feel aroused; therefore, I will get in more trouble if anyone knows.* The isolating shame binds the young heart that much more deeply to the one whose touch is both intoxicating and shaming.

Expect the victim of sexual abuse to curse his or her body if he or she felt any arousal during the abuse. Living accursed is dark but familiar, and it requires little more from him or her than numbness. This can be true even when arousal is the result of fantasy rather than touch. The person's self-disgust and ambivalence toward tenderness from others result in a return to the quagmire of self-contempt, betrayal, and powerlessness he or she experienced during the original abuse.

Abuse becomes even darker and more confusing to the degree that fear and pain are part of the package. As cortisol rises even higher in the context of fear and pain, the body's excretion of opioids rises to numb the suffering. The body is doing nothing other than what God intended, and yet the victim of abuse experiences even more confusion and shame for being aroused in the context of violence.

In this regard, the body is "stupid." Having suffered back problems, I know that when the body perceives pain, it freezes that section to keep movement at a minimum. Long after the problem is resolved, the muscles remain tight and defensive. What the body meant for good is now doing harm. Care must be given to coax the body to relax and rest rather than to remain in a position of fight. Over time, if this tightness is unaddressed, other systems including posture, muscle alignment, and overcompensation will be affected.

The abuser's grooming increases the victim's brain's production of oxytocin (our bonding biochemical), and as primary and secondary sexual parts are touched the body secretes dopamine and opioids. As the body is physically aroused, the victim feels relationally entangled with the abuser while also experiencing fear, shame, and confusion. The mind simply doesn't know how to make sense of this contradictory and trauma-infused madness. This inability to understand and name the damage being inflicted usually leads the victim to turn on both self and others with violent contempt.

Shame → Contempt

Shame demands hiding and isolation. Exposure intensifies the volcanic meltdown of the self, fragmenting, sluicing, and congealing the exposed parts in a frozen mess. One client referred to shame as an avalanche that sweeps all life away and then merges it into a broken, unified field. The self is whole but in a bizarre configuration. It functions but not in the way it was meant to. The external face hides the internal fused debris field. As another client said, "No one knows what is happening in me or what I might be doing to their body or mine, because my face is put on and is as acceptable as the makeup I wear."

What keeps this veneer in place and the interior bound to remain hidden? Contempt is the shield that blocks the gaze of the other, diminishes desire, and warns or threatens the inner world to remain quiet. This inner violence also serves as a shield, whether it is self- or other-centered contempt.

Contempt is spiritual, relational, and intrapsychic violence. Self-contempt unleashes hatred against some aspect of the body or self that seems ripe for judgment. The focus of our cruel judgment becomes the scapegoat for causing shame. *I am stupid, fat, lazy, easily fooled, and have a big nose.* Almost any feature(s) can serve the purpose of explaining our shame and doubly serve as what we sacrifice to cover our shame.

It is no different with other-centered contempt. We turn against a person or group with the same violence that drains away our en-gorging shame. The technical process is called *projection*, and it involves turning against the "other" because of something that we fear or despise in ourselves. Our mockery of a gay man reflects some fear regarding our own sexuality. Our intolerance of the political right or left involves an unacknowledged fear of power. The level of justification for our contempt always feels eminently reasonable—reasonable enough to start wars, stone heretics, and refuse entry to our favorite clubs to those who are not like us.

We can even have contempt against our struggle with contempt. I have frequently been brought up short by how often the awareness that one is riddled with violence leads to more violence—contempt for contempt. I recall one man snarling at me: "Okay, I see how I hate myself, so how does that help me to do anything more than add more fuel to that hatred?"

Insight into our war is never sufficient to bring change. In fact, it may at first sharpen the clarity and intensify the depths of violence. Contempt over time becomes a judgment that moves us to align our heart with darkness through a curse.

Contempt → Vow

Shame and contempt set us up for the seductions of the evil one. "Did God really say not to eat from this tree?" The serpent mocked the law of God and then tempted Eve to disregard the one prohibition in the entire garden (see Gen. 3:1). Because the fruit was pleasing to her eyes, promised to fill her hunger, and gave her access to what she knew God didn't want her to know, she ate. Two things are to be noted: (1) evil knows how to use creation to seduce the heart, and (2) evil is brilliant at using words to seduce. Evil is pernicious, relentless, and cruel. It senses through reading the trajectory of our stories when our heart will be most vulnerable. It is in those moments it whispers or shouts alternatives to the will of God. It arouses—grooms, sets up harm, abuses—in order to mar the beauty of God in humanity.

Evil is envious of humanity. It can't bear that we are made in the image of God, nor can it bear the commitment of God to beings that evil must view as utterly lacking in glory and majesty. It lusts to break our covenant with God and craves to replace it with a covenant with the kingdom of darkness. It is working daily to subvert the loyal love of God with its flimsy counterfeit promises.

God has made a vow to bless and redeem humankind. A vow is a promise made to bind one heart to another. It is more than a commitment; it is an "I will die if I break this bond" agreement. A vow binds our heart to whomever we make it and to its content. If that vow is made to one who will keep their side of the oath, then it is secure. If it is made to a liar whose motive is to ruin, then the vow is disastrous.

Evil uses our contempt against ourselves—*I'm at fault because I'm too attractive*—or against others—*Men only want one thing: my body*—to form judgments that produce a vow, or a loyalty commitment. *If I'm at fault because I'm too attractive, then I will never be attractive to a man again.* The vow may then get lived out through gaining weight to hide one's beauty. If men only want "one thing," then the judgment that men are sexually driven egomaniacs may lead to a vow like *I will never give my heart to a man who desires my body.*

A vow can be as simple as *I will never feel again* or as complex as *No one strong or tender can be trusted and I am doomed to only be with people who are weak and cruel.* This kind of vow offers the heart solace and respite. It is an anesthetic that lessens the searing pain. It also serves as a map and a compass to guide the heart in a shattered world where trust and hope are not possible.

This vow—based on lies and contemptuous judgment—links the heart in loyalty to the kingdom of darkness. Is it the same as possession? No, not at all. It is far more like we give the deed of property we own to a squatter. This "giving over" allows evil to have access and authority in that area of our life to do harm with impunity and secrecy.

We mere mortals live with a divided heart. Many sectors are in accord with goodness, but under the surface an occasional eruption occurs that darkens our name. We are used to pulling the pieces together again or moving on from the mayhem without looking at those strongholds that indicate that a rebel presence is influencing our activities. We need to reclaim the deed of the property that is rightfully ours but is falsely claimed by Satan. All vows wittingly or unwittingly made with the prince of darkness bind our heart to the curse of death and ruin. The curse needs to be lifted.

Vow → Curse

I don't understand the power of a curse or how it works; I simply know it exists. A curse calls down wrath and disfavor; it is a desire to see something ruined. Evil works to gain access to our heart through our desire to curse. It wants to reverse the beauty of creation and turn every lovely green garden into a wasteland.

It is not enough for evil to obliterate what we curse; instead, its desire is to mark it as hideous and detestable. This goes beyond the eye roll or sniff of contempt to the intently focused, eye-narrowed hatred. It is what we can imagine in the face of evil when its façade is removed and it is no longer sophisticated but enraged.

A curse opens something in the spiritual, unseen realm against the one who is cursed and the one who curses. It is not an innocuous, unpleasant social interaction or an angry explosion that happens without consequences. It releases darkness. I only know what seems to happen when I am in the presence of people who curse me. It turns up the heat of evil's intent to harm.

On a recent plane trip I sat next to a man who made it clear he owned the armrest. I waited until he reached for a magazine and put my elbow at the back of the armrest. He took all his space when he sat back except for the small portion that I had covered. He looked at me with fury. I was a squatter taking his rightful space. He pushed my arm off the rest and said bluntly, "Move." I smiled. Our faces were inches apart, and I said, "Do you intend to take the entire armrest for the rest of the flight?" He fired back an epithet I'll not repeat. Then he snapped his headphones back on and focused on his magazine.

I went back to writing. But for the next several hours my writing suffered a lack of clarity and depth. I felt like I was swimming in a fog. Could it have been nothing other than the disruptive rise of cortisol? Or that my focus was distracted by the desire for vengeance? Both are true, but I'd argue that my neurochemical disruption and my heart's struggle with revenge opened the door to evil's desire to accuse, mock, distract, and ultimately ruin my time to write. Evil won. I never fully recovered my equilibrium on that trip.

A passing encounter with being cursed like the one I just described bears minuscule impact compared to the power of sexual abuse. It is a hideous condemnation of one's gender, sexuality, and relational and spiritual being. It begins with the failure of a parent's attachment bond and his or her failure to read the substance of a child's trauma. This needs to be said with immense clarity and sensitivity. I have worked with victims of abuse whose parents simply failed to read abuse because they assumed their child was just having normal adjustment or adolescent issues. They read "trouble" but misread its cause. Further, they assumed their child was telling the truth when in fact the child was terrified to divulge the truth. These parents are usually beyond heartbroken and often acknowledge with deep grief their failure to read well.

There is an entirely other class of parents who either defend their innocence or go even darker and blame the child—now an adult—for the abuse. Those who defend themselves take the stance of ignorant innocence. "I simply didn't know and you didn't tell me, so how could I know?" The not-so-subtle accusation is that the victim is at fault for keeping the secret.

This stance is a subtle curse. It takes the ground of neutrality: "I would have acted if I'd known, but I didn't, and my innocence is far, far more important to me than your heartache or anger. I didn't fail in attunement or protection/containment, and you'd better not be putting any responsibility near my door." This is by far the most common response for the clients I have worked with over the last twenty-five years. It is infuriating and heartbreaking. It leaves the adult victim of abuse holding the bag and aware that any conversation is off-limits. Often this is tied to a religious prescription to "forgive and forget." It simply cannot be underscored strongly enough: this is a subtle curse that unleashes immense harm against honest victims trying to address the trajectory of their story in light of their family of origin.

The final group consists of parents whose level of evil is legion. I strongly recommend reading M. Scott Peck's *People of the Lie*. It is the bible for understanding families whose mode of operation sets the child up for abuse. Often the family knows full well that abuse is occurring but gains something to remain ignorant or, far more wickedly, gains power or financial benefit. In a recent Recovery Week workshop for fifteen women, nine had family members who were either mentally ill, vocally hated the victim, or sold the victim to family and friends. This anecdotal data is a growing trend in our work with victims of abuse.

Whether the family of origin curse is elusive and subtle or brazen and direct, the effect is to make the larger story of abuse difficult to discern. There is a haze that makes exposure of the family setup confusing and easily denied. Healing requires that we cut through the fog. As painful as it is to face, many families curse their children. The curse of the family joins the inner curse of the victim, and the combination is lethal.

One client referred to the curse against his body as a "hated protector." Perhaps he was personifying a psychological process. Perhaps he was accurately hearing a "voice" that resonated with deep personal convictions. Perhaps both are true, and he was also hearing the words of a foul spirit that represented the words and voices of family, abuser, and other people who had been inscribed in this man's sexual history. Whatever he was hearing, it was far more than mere "negative scripts" or lies. It was both the prison guard who kept him imprisoned and the bodyguard who stood outside of him and alerted him to those who might use him again. What was even more tragic was how this hated protector sabotaged every interaction that could bring him life and blessing.

Seldom are victims of abuse without curses against their body, often oriented toward specific parts or processes. But if there is a central focus, it is toward the pleasure of the body, especially sexual arousal. One client masturbated several times a day and was sexually active throughout her teens, twenties, and early thirties. She married and soon found marital sex tedious. She remained faithful at home except for occasional one-night flings on business trips. She was highly orgasmic and loved sex. The curse seemed absent until she named her frustration with her husband: "Sex with him is boring and gentle. I like sex with a nameless man who can easily be coaxed into being as rough as I need him to be." The curse wasn't against an orgasm but against any "gentle arousal."

As is often the case, her abuser was a pro. He knew how to intersect immense kindness and eventually perverse degradation. Her husband was "too good a Christian" to participate in demeaning sex, and soon after they were married she grew bored. This is a tragically common story. Her story will seem radically different from that of a man who is not fond of sex. I have a client who knows he "should" want to have sex but often is not aroused. His wife often pled with him to have sex. After ten years of disappointment, she gave up. They have satisfying but obligatory sex about twice a month. When I explored his story, he acknowledged that he often had sexual fantasies about being held by a man. He was not aroused by homosexual fantasies; he simply wanted to feel a man's strong chest and hold an erect penis.

Was he gay? Bisexual? Heterosexual with homosexual fears that caused him to flee from his natural homosexual orientation? These legitimate questions operate with the current political assumption that people like him are LGBTQ: lesbian, gay, bisexual, transgender, and/or queer, and that is enough letters for now. To say that all the letters, including H (heterosexual), are too clean and simple is too confounding for both the left and the right political dispositions. What I have noticed in twenty-five years is immense hatred of something about our sexuality, irrespective of which letter or combination of letters label us.

This man hated the power he had to bring pleasure and joy to his wife. His vow, formed in the crucible of his abuser's dramatic and climactic orgasm, was *I will never bring any human being this kind of pleasure ever again*. Added to this harm was the bind he felt with his mother. She demanded of her son that he succeed at everything he did. She required him to be a docile servant to her wishes and simultaneously a ruthless businessman who made a ton of money. He hated her setup and served her while remaining a thousand miles away in a different part of the country. He hated the drama of his mother and later his abuser. He told me his wife's "demands" for sex were theatrical.

The word made no sense. As he described her legitimate and dignified requests, it became clear that he could not feel her pain or read her heart. He had so deeply cursed his ability to bring pleasure that his vow never to be responsible for anyone else's arousal was an iron curtain.

The work of a good therapist is to cross the boundaries of vows and curses, knowing full well that havoc will ensue. I believe a good therapist is like a gifted thief who cases a house for months, if not years, to know where the most significant family jewels (or better said, vows and/or curses) are hidden. My work is not to steal them but to enlist the homeowner and vow keeper to take me to the vault where they are hidden to discern whether or not keeping them safe is worth ruining or losing one's life. Then I entice the vow maker to break the curses that bind and open the heart to the blessing of God. The work of redemption is to replace curses with blessing, death with life, and ambivalence with joy.

Addressing vows and curses is difficult when the harm against the body is overt and clear. However, it is even harder when the sexual abuse is covert and subtle. The greater the subtlety of abuse, the more the kingdom of darkness is able to camouflage its harm and the crazier the abused person feels.

5

The Damage of Covert Abuse

A portion of the guilt is standard issue for southern boys; our whole lives are convoluted, egregious apologies to our mothers because our fathers have made such flawed husbands. No boy can endure for long the weight and the magnitude of his mother's displaced passions. Yet few boys can resist their mother's solitary and innocently seductive advances. There is such forbidden sweetness in becoming the chaste and secret lover of the father's woman, such triumph in becoming the demon rival who receives the unbearable tender love of fragile women in the shadows of the father's house. There is nothing more erotic on earth than a boy in love with the shape and touch of his mother. It is the most exquisite, most proscribed lust. It is also the most natural and damaging.

Pat Conroy

I can recall reading this passage from *The Prince of Tides* on a flight from Denver to Saskatoon in 1992 and nearly swallowing my cheap airline scotch whole. I had been upgraded to first class and I felt rich. I was now an author and flying to a conference hosted by a seminary tackling the relatively new area of sexual abuse. I was nearly forty. We had recently moved to Denver, and my life felt like it had a trajectory of meaning and goodness. Then I sucked down that scotch and thought I was going to choke to death.

My father had died in August 1991, and I was less than eight months from the loss and all the data his death had brought forth about his broken life. Soon after his death I discovered he had lied about the financial provisions for my mother. He had no savings or life insurance. I was the sole caretaker for my impoverished mother. At the point I read this passage, I was at the highest peak of tending to the complications of my mother's widowhood, and Conroy's words took me down.

I must have reread that passage a dozen times. I don't recall the rest of the flight, the conference, or my return. I don't recall when I picked up the novel again, but it must have been at least a year later. It was another gift from the strong hand of God. Apparently, there was something I did not want to see, and it had to do with subtle, or covert, abuse.

Diana E. H. Russell, in her seminal work *The Secret Trauma: Incest in the Lives of Girls and Women*, addresses three categories of sexual abuse: very severe, severe, and least severe sexual abuse.[1] Very severe includes any form of sexual penetration of mouth, anus, or vagina. Severe includes any digital or oral contact with anus, vagina, or penis, or any digital rubbing or penetration. It also includes touching of breasts without clothing. Least severe involves touch of primary or secondary sexual body parts with clothing on, forced or unforced sexual kissing, and simulated sexual intercourse without penetration.

It is vastly important to understand that abuse is abuse, and all abuse—no matter where it is on the spectrum or how often it occurred—is damaging. All abuse is traumatizing. Nevertheless, the more severe, the longer it lasted, and the closer the person is to the victim are significant factors in determining the extent of the trauma. Abuse that began at a younger age and moved from least severe to very severe, and which is perpetrated by a parent, does more significant harm than abuse that occurred at age twelve involving a touch of the breasts by a slightly older boy, for example. This makes sense, and I have witnessed it in thousands of therapeutic hours. But it is not the full truth.

Adaptability is one of the great gifts that enables us to survive less-than-desirable experiences; it is also the foundation for failing to name an experience, process, or person as traumatic and harmful. We minimize the more subtle experiences of harm by saying, "That's just the way it is"—the expected, the unsurprising, and to some degree the "good." These premises set the trajectory for the remainder of this chapter:

1. The more subtle the abuse (especially in a life with far more overt harm), the more likely it is ignored, denied, or minimized.
2. The devil is not merely in the details but in the subtle, un-addressed, daily pinpricks of abuse that seldom capture our attention.
3. The sweep of subtle abuse is seldom a single event, though it might be remembered in a few scenes; instead, it is like a dark current moving through one's life, with inexorable consequences.

I'll address two forms of subtle sexual abuse: emotional incest and pornography. There are many more, but these two provoke entry into realms that are too often overlooked and provide an opening to consider the other ways subtle sexual abuse occurs.

Emotional Incest

No boy or girl can endure the weight of "displaced passions." Nor can a child resist the seduction into intimacy and sensuality that a parent offers when a child is turned into an adult companion, consort, confidant, or, simply said, lover. A child can become a lover to a parent (and it is not always the opposite-sex parent) when the parent no longer experiences intimacy and joy with their spouse. It is a simple equation: the more there is a loss of intimacy, passion, and purpose with one's spouse, the higher the probability a child will be used as a spousal replacement.

The human heart can't escape the ache for intimacy. Work, busyness, and other distractions can dampen the ache but can't erase it. The "chosen child" serves two primary purposes: he or she relieves some of the parent's ache through their sensitivity, and he or she becomes a powerful symbol of vengeance: *The child is my delight and you are not.* Once a child is chosen as the favorite, all others in the family are put on notice. And the result is increased envy and behind-the-scenes vengeance.

Emotional incest usually involves three key factors: boundary violations, enmeshed intimacy, and resentment from other family members. One key signature of emotional incest is its intrusiveness, both emotionally and physically. One woman said, "I could never close the bathroom or bedroom door." Another man remarked, "I had to divulge all my thoughts and feelings to keep my mom happy. If she felt like I withheld my innermost thoughts, she would feel lonely." A parent might watch a child shower or allow her to wander in and out of the bathroom during use of the shower or toilet. An emotionally abused child doesn't feel like his or her space or inner world is his or her own.

A second factor is a sticky, enmeshed emotional connection. Often this is felt first as a sense of responsibility and power to make a parent happy. The child feels like he or she has to accurately read and responsibly respond, or the parent will not be able to function well. This requires the child to be highly intuitive and sensitive to the nuances of the parent's emotional life. He or she is often the confidant and counselor—encouraging, confronting, and containing.

Finally, everyone in the family knows the score. Behind the back of the needy parent, siblings and the other parent resent the bond. Envy spawns cruelty and mockery. A daughter may have significant power when near the throne, but when she is far from her father,

her mother will find ways to make her pay. Too often I have seen a brother abuse the favored daughter while his mother turns her back to the violation. An emotionally used child is pressured, empowered, ambivalent, and usually unable to name his or her privileged burden.

There are countless other ways that covert sexual abuse can be perpetrated. Clients have told me about how their father's eyes would casually pass over their breasts or their brother would use sexually demeaning language as a nickname. A mother teased her son about how girls were attracted to his body. A grandfather described to a granddaughter in detail how sinful girls masturbate. The list is legion of sexually violating intrusions that at the moment feel "icky" or "weird" and on further reflection are far more than merely inappropriate words or actions. These subtle sexually abusive interactions set victims up to feel like they are making a mountain out of a molehill. The routine becomes the definition of normal.

Just as there is a spectrum to sexual abuse, so there is with emotional incest. There are four forms of interaction that are most common for generating emotional incest: critical and/or demeaning, dependent and/or fragile, sensual and/or sexualizing, and infantilizing and/or hyperprotective.

Critical and/or Demeaning

Murray Bowen, the founder of a systems approach to family psychotherapy, discusses the role of triangles in relationships, or what he calls "triangulation." The tension in the marriage dyad is somehow too dangerous to be engaged directly, therefore a "third" is chosen to both hide the tension and provide an alternative resolution. But this hide-and-seek triangle becomes a sticky and unlivable web, especially for the chosen child.[2]

Bowen argues that an angry, demeaning parent often entangles a child in a network of guilt and performance. The parent idealizes what the child "ought" to be and then critically evaluates the child

91

against this ideal. Often the relationship is fractious and intense and looks like anything but emotional closeness. It is imperative to remember that conflict releases cortisol and opioids that flood the body with both arousal and pleasure even in the midst of a hurtful interaction.

Cathy, a brilliant, gifted hippie-child in her midforties, had floated from one coast to the other, from an ashram to a Christian cult. In our work she talked with both loathing and tender respect for her father. He was a brilliant attorney whose bombast and vitriol were known far and wide. No one crossed him. All her siblings had at least their law degree and acquiesced to their father. Cathy was the only one who was allowed to follow her muse and yell at him with impunity.

Her mother used to send her into his study to get him to come to dinner or to talk him into taking the family out for ice cream. She was the go-between—honored, hated, and used. As conflict-laden as their interactions were, her father respected and idealized her far more than her other obsequious siblings. The power she was allotted and the privileged role of being the only one who could take on their mighty father set her up for both misuse and resentment. Her failures in love and life served to keep her entangled with her narcissistic father.

Dependent and/or Fragile

When a parent is clearly the "underdog" and weak, usually one child will be the wise decision maker and protector. The image one client offered was of a photo when he was four and his mother was wrapped up in an afghan, smoking a cigarette, a light brownish alcoholic drink on the nightstand. The boy was standing legs apart, arms crossed, and he was wearing a Superman costume. I asked if the photo was taken on or near Halloween, and he laughed. "No. I wore that costume every day for nearly a year. It was around the time my dad left us for another woman."

There is immense power in being needed, especially by someone you love. But if this same person is your parent, whom you need, then a setup exists that disrupts your ability to ask for help or admit weakness. *I need to be strong to keep you strong so that I can be a kid, but I can't afford to be a kid if I am supposed to keep you alive.* More often the parent who needs the child also resents the child during those moments when either the child fails or the parent becomes aware of the trap and feels ashamed. This oscillation between being all good or all bad is like walking on eggshells. One hour the child is the scapegoat and the next the hero. One hour the needy parent is gushing and grateful and the next aloof or enraged.

The chosen child often lives between a grandiose sense of power and deflation. The inability to make any real changes in the beloved stirs deep ambivalence. Added to that is the contempt other members in the family hold for both the parent and his or her caregiver. The rest of the family is relieved, of course, that they don't have to tend to Mom or Dad, but there is also envy that the chosen child is getting something from the parent that they don't. Often the child defends against the envy and ambivalence by intensifying a self-righteous commitment to protect and provide, and feeds on the few scraps that come from the fragile parent.

Sensual and/or Sexualizing

This form of triangulation is far more obviously sexually compromising. It is of course possible for a critical or fragile parent to also be sexualizing. But a parent might also sexualize without being demeaning or dependent.

John, a successful entrepreneur, is a genius at thinking quickly and making complex business decisions look clear and simple. His mother often interacted with him as a boy in the context of preparing for the day in her bedroom. Her husband was a workaholic and departed for work early and seldom was home when John went to bed. The "special" interactions with his mom occurred as she was dressing or putting on makeup. Seldom was she fully clothed in these moments. He watched her apply her makeup as he sat idly on the toilet. It was common for him to watch her take off her clothes at the end of the day. Full nudity was uncommon, but the contours of her body and the process of layering herself with makeup and clothing were fascinating to John. She seemed to be aware of his fascination and would turn often to warmly smile and soak in his intrigue.

John occasionally used his mother's makeup. He "grew out of it," but he had a difficult time making love to his wife if she didn't have makeup on. Even in his fifties he struggled with what his attraction to makeup, women's lingerie, and fashion magazines meant about his heterosexuality.

Another client, Jill, had a father who left copious amounts of pornography in his home office. As a little girl, she would wake up and toddle into his office to sit on his lap. His morning routine was to get a cup of coffee and then boot up his computer and watch pornography. She can recall crawling into his lap, looking quickly at whatever scene or photo was on the screen, and then staring off into the distance.

Jill often reported that she felt numb, and as an adult she was seldom able to put words to what her body felt in a particular moment. She reported that the lower half of her body often felt frozen and devoid of sensation. The longer our work progressed, the more she began to feel her body and name pain and arousal. It was during a massage as her lower legs were being worked on that she felt, for the first time, the horrifying sensation of her father's erect penis.

These two scenarios are clearly harmful, but both clients were adamantly defensive against seeing their parent's behavior as sexualized. No adult wants to enter the dark waters of their parent's conscious or unintended sexualizing. It is far too easy to deny intent or even inappropriateness.

For some clients, the sexualizing parent's touch seems utterly normal. A man described how his mother soothed him when he became frustrated doing math problems. She would sit next to him, and when he would tense up she would begin playing with his hair, taking a curl and wrapping it around her finger. He would become calm. She would continue to do so long after he relaxed. He admitted when he told me the story that it felt "weird." Often that word is a code word for feeling awkward and ambivalent.

A young woman told me that when she goes out to eat with her father, he often treats her like a girlfriend. In public he touches her back and arms, escorts her to her chair, and flirts with her. The looks of the wait staff and nearby diners indicate that she is a sugar baby out with her paramour. She remarked, "I often say Dad loudly and often. I can see he is not thrilled being exposed as my father, but he doesn't say anything directly." When I asked her what she experienced in his presence during those moments, she said, "He is just a big boy who never got over the adulation he received in his frat. I guess it is just a weird part of having to get along with my dad." When I asked her about what it felt like to be used as proof of his sexual prowess and desirability, she looked at me as if I were perverse and insane.

Infantilizing and/or Hyperprotective

When the chosen child is seen to be in danger due to real or imagined threats, a protective parent can overstep appropriate care by spinning a suffocating cocoon. Often this shield divides the child from others in the family and binds the "sick," "frightened," or "insecure" child to the absorptive parent. Any effort to release the child from the parent's grip is a threat to both the child and the parent.

Often the child is conditioned to believe that no one understands or will care for him or her like Mother or Father. And that is true. No one will pay as much attention or offer as much single focus as the doting, superprotective parent. The child's impulse toward independence and autonomy is often viewed as a threat to the consuming bond. Success in almost any area of life will take this child away from the parent, and that must be thwarted to keep the child bound with anxiety, at rest only in the presence of the parent.

This pattern falls on a spectrum from the mentally ill mother or father who can barely let the child out of their sight to the helicopter parent who is intimately involved in nearly every detail of their child's life. The so-called stage mother who attends to every element of her child's success and cuts a wide swath to ensure her child's victories fuses her dreams and desires with her child. This bind activates levels of intimacy and arousal, shame and contempt that are profoundly confusing to a child, even into adulthood.

Triangulation and Attachment

Triangulation is often met with abandonment and/or hostility from the other parent. This relational upheaval has profound effects on a child's body and heart. Research in the past twenty-five years has found that the attachment style of our parents has a profound influence on our personality and on how we metabolize trauma.[3]

Attachment is a simple and elegant construct. A securely attached infant has a caregiver or caregivers who can read and respond to the child's face and body with appropriate and compassionate care. A "good" mother knows the various cries of her child and knows how to respond in order to lower stress. A securely attached child also has a sense of containment that provides clear and comforting boundaries. And when there is a breakdown of attunement or containment, the "good enough" mother knows how to restore the break with soothing and play.

A parent who is secure knows how to contain his or her own distress without requiring the child to take it away. In having boundaries for oneself, it is natural to honor and respect the limits and needs of the other. Kindness toward oneself and the other is the core of the ability to bond. Kindness awakens the heart to desire, invites the heart to comfort and soothe, and centers the self to be free to choose goodness.

It has been well documented that early insecure attachment to a primary caregiver makes it more difficult for a person to trust the goodness of relationships. A caregiver who is not attuned to the needs of a child or able to contain the distress of a child does not provide sufficient security to help the child regulate emotions or gain confidence when relating to others.

There are three well-recognized styles of insecure attachment: ambivalent, avoidant, and chaotic. An ambivalent attachment comes as a result of a caregiver misreading or ignoring the cues of distress and then at times being intrusive and controlling. This relationship sets up an internal map of unpredictability and the need for heightened emotion to gain care. This child will often have far less capacity to soothe his or her own inner distress and may oscillate between being demanding and shutting down. An emotionally incestuous parent almost always binds the heart and simultaneously creates uncertainty and abandonment. The result will be a high probability of an insecure-ambivalent attachment.

The insecure-avoidant attachment is formed with a caregiver who is distant, formal, and unavailable. This caregiver is apt to be hard to read and critical of emotional distress. The child learns not to express emotion and, over time, not to ask or want. This child often becomes an adult who is dismissive and contemptuous of both his or her own and others' needs. The triangulated parent far more often forms an insecure-ambivalent attachment, but the other parent is apt to be more distant and critical. The interplay of two different attachment styles is not well researched, but anecdotally I have seen these two parental styles create both immense fear of abandonment and shame.[4]

The final insecure attachment style, chaotic, is formed in the midst of regular bursts of rage, threats, or displays of violence. It is also likely there is an intersection of high levels of addiction, emotional manipulation, and unpredictability. The child in this battle zone will have the need to shut down emotion and desire while simultaneously focusing on every cue that might indicate what is about to happen. This child vacillates between the need for extreme hypervigilance and dissociation. Often this child cannot afford to feel pain, in order to make it easier to endure severe suffering. The inner world of this child can become severely fractured and immune to care.

Research indicates that 65 percent of the population has a secure attachment, but that doesn't preclude abuse or struggles even for those who are securely attached. There is research that indicates that children with a secure attachment suffer less severe consequences from their sexual abuse. A secure attachment makes it easier to engage the stories of one's family of origin and the sexual abuse. But abuse is abuse, and all abuse will require reentry into new relationships that provide secure attachment.

Aftereffects of Emotional Incest

The primary effect of emotional incest is confusion. It feels too subtle to name without overwhelming consequences. When harm is overtly clear, it is difficult to name, but when it is subtle, one is left with nagging doubt that any harm was done.

It feels insane to "blame" the triangulating parent and impossible to find the language to describe any one scene that explains what was felt. As one client said, "If I were to tell my dad how I feel sexually compromised and dirty in his presence, he would be beyond hurt, then passively defend that he didn't know what I was talking about. I would end up feeling like the pervert. It is too easy just to let him touch me the way he does, cringe internally, and later drink to forget."

A reality every triangulated child feels is the tension of being the "favored" child. Everyone in the family knows who is the star, the darling of Mom or Dad. Often the "favorite" is given immense power and influence over family time, money, and energy. This child is then allowed to exercise this authority in a manner that elevates him or her to crown prince or princess. It is pointless to fight against this power directly, but behind the scenes cruelty and contempt rule.

Often the daughter chosen by the weak, insatiable father is made to pay verbally or physically by her angry and envious brothers. Instead of protecting her, her mother ignores the "boys-will-be-boys" rough play and then blames her rival, her daughter, for being too sensitive. The "princess" is safe in the throne room with her father, but when she ventures into the rest of the castle she is a mark for the family's envy and rivalry. Not only is it confusing but it is also lonely.

Perhaps worse than confusing and lonely, it is crazy-making. There are so many inherent contradictions in being the chosen child. One is empowered to bring about life in one's parent, and yet it is a losing game. No one can breathe life into a soul but God. The chosen child is a kind of god, but not God. As fleeting as the power is as it comes and goes, a dark sense of shame remains.

As I read the passage in *The Prince of Tides* I felt the intrusion of memories of a Christmas morning when I was ten years old. My stepfather bought my mother exquisite and expensive gifts: dresses, earrings, shoes, coats. And when each box was slowly, sensually, and dramatically opened, I knew that what it contained would be put on and modeled—first and foremost for me. She would turn to me, and if I didn't respond with enough bravado, she would coo or pout and say that she must look awful. She didn't. She looked fabulous, but I always felt like she should turn first to my stepfather, not to me.

Even as I write this now, I can feel my body tense. I just walked around my office a few times working on the arthritis in my hands. My face feels hot and clammy. I want to go run, swear, or hit something. These are all physical escapes from an abiding sense that it is wrong to tell, wrong to feel her beauty, wrong to be her admirer. It is easier to hide the harm under denial or shrug it off as simply "weird."

To be the chosen one is to be the object of a parent's delight; it is also to feel the shame of arousal, desire, fear, and disgust—none of which can be felt for long without revealing the truth, so it must be wedged into a crack of consciousness and then covered over. The animosity in the family needs to be ignored or explained, so the real issue is obscured and fault is felt as some flaw in the self. Needless to say, the more subtle, crazy-making, shame-inducing, blame-avoiding the harm, the more free evil is to sow seeds that are actually more difficult to address, at times, than overt abuse.

Pornography

I was finally allowed to go up in the tree fort. I was eleven and ecstatic to be able to join my thirteen-year-old brother and our fourteen-year-old neighbor. Normally they would climb up and then pull up the rope, watching me stand below like an alien. But one day, Jimmy, my brother's friend, said, "Hey punk, you can come up if you do what we tell you to do." I wouldn't have cared if I had to eat a worm just for the thrill of being able to join them.

I climbed up, and my brother had to help me make it the last couple of feet on the rope. I was never that big or strong. Once I got up it seemed like a while before they decided to "initiate" me into their club. They whispered. Laughed. I felt scared, but I was finally up in the fort.

Jimmy made me sit next to him, and then he pulled out a magazine and opened it to the middle, and there was a naked woman, like really naked. I could see everything but between her legs. Look, I can't even look at you when I tell you. They pulled out their penises and started to touch themselves and groan. Finally, Jimmy told me to take my dick out and to do the same or he would throw me off the tree fort. I did just what he said. I couldn't get erect, but I kept up touching myself as long as they did. I'd never felt more humiliated. And yeah, I felt like I was taken into the mystery of mysteries even though I didn't understand a thing of what was happening.

Matthew, twenty-nine, married with two young daughters

Matthew remembers playing in the bathtub with his younger sister and knowing something was different when his older brother, Mark, entered the tub. It was a normal childhood process on Saturday night prior to church for the three kids to bathe together. His brother was seven, Matthew was five, and his younger sister was almost three. He doesn't recall any sexual abuse, but he was able to say that his play with his sister felt innocent, whereas when Mark entered the tub the games became more about power and pain. Mark was sinister and scary.

I asked Matthew if the experience in the tub felt at all like being up in the tree fort. He began to weep. Something was stirring in him that he had never connected before: his brother changed every encounter, even as an adult, into an experience of powerlessness and humiliation. Even the brotherly hit on the arm seemed to be a constant reminder: *You are the weaker, younger brother, and I am your master.*

Exposure to pornography happens so regularly that we have come to call it a normal developmental passage for both boys and girls. But to call it normal is not to call it good. It simply happens so often that it can't be viewed as an aberration; instead, it is the primary portal children and young adults use to enter the social conversation on what it means to be sexual.

The ubiquity of pornography on smartphones, computers, tablets, e-readers, and a host of other digital devices is legion. Pornography is being watched and shared on playgrounds and in boardrooms. It is not the fact of pornography that is at issue for the moment; it is how it is used to create a subtle sexually abusive encounter.

There seem to be three primary means by which pornography is delivered: sexual drama, accidental discovery, or haphazard placement.

101

Each provokes a different set of complications for the one who is subjected to images they didn't choose to see.[5]

Sexual Drama

Matthew's experience was an intentionally scripted drama that was likely written and directed by the older neighbor boy and supported and acted out by the brother. The process follows the familiar hazing or grooming setup, eliciting the desire for intimacy that is then used to trap the victim in a sexually evocative encounter.

Pornography is seldom merely "seen"; it is enacted. It intensifies desire and is used as a process to model. In Matthew's case it is impossible to separate the visual encounter with the demand for participatory masturbation. Matthew was too young to be capable of creating an erection and ejaculation, therefore the demand to join his brother and another older boy was to some degree intended to mark the difference in sexual capacity and to humiliate. It did.

Often the drama is also a gateway to more overt abuse. Boys will congregate over pornography and eventually require the youngest or weakest to perform other sexual acts as a reenactment of the visual stimuli. The drama requires prior planning, a powerful director, and usually a number of intermediate actors who serve as the chorus—the ones who watch and attest to the humiliation. The director is sexually sophisticated (compared to the group and the innocent who will be introduced to the pornography) and has the power to condemn or bless. If the innocent child is reluctant or unwilling, the director and then the chorus castigates the "outsider" with accusations of being queer or a "homo." The setup is extreme: *Join us or forever be marked with a label that will follow you throughout your life.*

A mother told me that her ten-year-old son had been at a sleepover at a fellow church member's home. Five boys gathered around a computer and watched porn. When my friend's son deferred and said he didn't want to watch and wanted to go home, he was humiliated and accosted with demeaning words. He ran to the phone to call his mom, and the mother of the house asked what was wrong. He told the truth, and she told him, "Don't be such a wuss. I'll tell them they shouldn't be watching adult movies." The label of being "strange" has followed this young boy for two years now, even in his youth group. It is staggering to see how this scenario is normalized and viewed as just a fact of life. Protest is considered more perverse than participation.

Accidental Discovery

Sandra was twelve when she went to look for something in her dad's closet. She moved a box and found a stack of magazines behind it. On the cover she saw a woman whose legs were spread open, and she picked it up and stared in rapt attention until she heard someone come into the bedroom. She shoved the magazine back and put the box back in front of it. Her mother asked what she was doing, and she said, "Just looking for shoelaces for a school project."

It was no more than a day before she was alone in the house and returned to her father's treasure trove of pornography. She was fascinated by the voluptuous women and even more by what men with erections and whips were doing to the women. She told me that it felt like electricity was surging through her body when she turned the pages. She felt the fear of discovery, and she felt dirty for being intrigued. She reflected on one time she was almost positive her father knew of her interest. He told her at breakfast, "Girls shouldn't look at dirty magazines; it will turn them into lesbians." She had no clue what a dirty magazine or a lesbian was, but she knew by his tone that something was wrong and she was at fault.

She never went into his closet again, but that didn't keep her from incorporating the images into her fantasy life. Further, she began masturbating and practicing some of the images that she had observed. The intertwining of image and reenactment with arousal

103

and shame, addiction and self-contempt, formed the core of her sexual self-identity. She came to therapy with a long and heartbreaking history of sexually dangerous and demeaning relationships. She became inconsolably defensive when I linked her father's pornography addiction to her covertly sexually abusive relationship with him. She saw her struggles with pornography as an entirely separate issue and unrelated to him. I asked her to consider that her father allowed her to discover his stash and then did nothing to remove the "dirty magazines" once he was aware they were being viewed by his daughter. She balked, calling herself a "little perv" to be interested in pornography at such a young age.

As difficult as it is to face, the presence of pornography binds the heart of children not merely to the pictures but also to the one who is clearly aroused by those images. As Sandra was able to say later: "If this is what aroused my father, then I wanted to be what he wanted if I was going to be loved."

Sandra's mother was a sexually squeamish woman. She was harshly cold. Her body was thin and pale. The women in the magazines were ample, tan, and craved pleasure. The contrast was clear to Sandra, and she chose erotic, sensually violent images over the frigidity of her mother. The price was decades of dark internal sexual wars that she had never considered to be related to her father's subtle sexual abuse or her mother's sexual aversion.

Haphazard Placement

In some families pornography is available in ordinary environments. One client had to help her father work on his cars on Saturday mornings. The garage was covered with his favorite pinups, and a stack of magazines was near his bathroom. Her friends loved to look through the pictures when they came to play. She felt awkward but enjoyed their intrigue. Eventually, the magazines became a road map for sexual experimentation with her preadolescent friends. Sex was so normalized by the chronic availability of pornography that no norms or expectations were established other than her mother's dictum, "Just don't get pregnant and think I am going to care for some kid's snotty baby."

My client grew up in a "sexually liberated" home that not only allowed her to experiment sexually but also seemed to encourage it. She was the favorite of her father and could never please her mother. As her body developed, her breasts became equal to, if not larger than, her mother's, and she endured stares and occasional comparisons of her body to her mother's. She was locked in a sexual drama of triangulation, sexual images, and sexual reenactments with her girlfriends and eventually her boyfriends—and she still could not name this milieu as sexually abusive.

The more pornography is available and normalized, the greater likelihood that a sexual drama exists between husband and wife. And this war will never be fought between the marriage dyad alone but will seep into the daily battles with the children. In my client's case, her brothers were free to sexually torment their sister by groping at her and peering in while she took a shower. Her appraisal of her family life was that this behavior was normal.

It may be difficult to comprehend, but few who have lived with the insidious intrusion of pornography—whether through a dramatic encounter, discovery, or daily availability—name these experiences as sexually abusive. The prime strategy of evil is simply to make sexual harm seem common and innocuous. In fact, to raise concern is in and of itself perversely prudish. To address the violation and its setup for other abuse is considered extreme and making a mountain out of a molehill. But nothing could be further from the truth. Pornography is never a matter of merely celebrating the body or sexual pleasure. One only need be aware of the trajectory of pornography from the come-hither allure of so-called soft pornography to the violent and degrading humiliation that a woman endures in far darker sexual dramas. Pornography is not primarily so much about sex as it is about the freedom to offend, to deprive the other of dignity and honor, and to indulge one's dark desire.

Pornography is usually considered to be a men's issue, as if women don't struggle with it. Women do. Men do more. There are countless ways in which men and women struggle similarly with regard to the damage of past abuse, but it is important to consider what is unique for a man as he addresses past sexual harm.

6

Men at War

A final word: Be strong in the Lord and in his mighty power. Put on all of God's armor so that you will be able to stand firm against all strategies of the devil. For we are not fighting against flesh-and-blood enemies, but against evil rulers and authorities of the unseen world, against mighty powers in this dark world, and against evil spirits in the heavenly places.

Ephesians 6:10–12 NLT

One of the dreams I had when I began running our Recovery Weeks in 1988 was to offer at least one week a year for men. We needed ten men to proceed, and it would occasionally take two or three years to get enough men to fill one week. By the early twenty-first century we were averaging about one week every other year. Now we offer about one a year. It breaks my heart. We easily fill all the available slots for fifty to sixty women a year, but it is still a steep uphill battle to get men to engage.

In the early 1980s it was assumed that men were seldom sexually abused, and when it did occur there were few confounding conse-quences. The thought has been that men are primarily, if not almost exclusively, the abusers, and women are the victims of male aggression. A great deal of research still validates that assumption, but there are strong reasons to reconsider this a myth.[1] There is still a lack of research and focus on men's victimization, but few deny the reality that male abuse is underreported and deleterious. And it is not just men who abuse boys; women perpetrate sexual abuse far more than at first considered possible. And men suffer as deeply as women do when they are abused, even if the effects look, at times, different.

What has seldom been engaged is the question: How do the genders of the victim and the perpetrator affect the degree and dimensions of harm resulting from sexual abuse? To consider the effects of abuse on a man requires addressing how men are socialized to be men. Then we need to consider how those cultural ways of being in the world keep men from addressing the harm of the sexual abuse they have suffered.

There are three core socializing currents that are pounded into men: (1) a true man is independent, in control, and masters his world; (2) a true man is eager for and always bent on initiating sex; and (3) a true man is logical, not emotional, and focused on the external world. Those three can be restated as a man is (1) never a victim, (2) always up for sex, and (3) never like a girl.

To address his abuse, a man has to cross into how he felt weak and powerless. Most men who have been abused wonder, *Why was I chosen?* The answer most offered by men who were abused by men is possible effeminacy, or the assumption that the abuser thought the victim was weak or gay. There are enormous relational consequences for what feels like a personal violation of the code of men.

Further, sexual abuse, often the first sexual experience of a boy's life, is mired in shame. If there was arousal then for most men this means that there was no abuse.[2] One man said: "My abuser always talked about the size of my erection. It was said again and again as a compliment, and I know he wanted me to feel like it was proof that I wanted what he did." Whereas a woman's arousal might be slightly hidden or subtle, a man's arousal and orgasm are blatant. A man is almost sure to believe that his arousal must mean that he enjoyed and/or wanted the abuse.

Finally, it is difficult for many men to address the consequences of abuse if they must turn inward and engage their emotions. One man said every time he cried, "I feel weak and stupid, like a little girl." If a "true man" is in control and focused on externally mastering his world, then to feel tears and express pain intensify his sense of alienation and outsider status.

It is a catch-22. The abused man already feels at odds with being a man; to address victimization, arousal, and emotions sets up a condition where the cure feels far worse than the disease. It is much easier to power through the harm, ignore or deny it, and then turn against anyone who exposes the debris. It is not uncommon for abused men to struggle with anger and acting out in a way that alienates others and sets up a long history of reenactment of the abuse drama.

The harm of abuse on men needs to be considered with regard to relationships, sexuality, and struggles with addiction. There will be overlap and intersection for women who engage this chapter as well. We are first human beings made in the image of God, male and female. Gender profoundly shapes our identity and our way of being in the world, but it is foolish to assume that what will be described as the consequences for a man are not similar in some form for a woman.

Relational War

The shadow of abuse clouds men's relationships with other men, especially if the abuser was a man. There will be more defiance, suspicion, and distance that keep an abused man at odds with men in general and even more so with men who have authority.

Men are more apt in our culture to engage in a relationship on the basis of status and competition. When I work with a man as a therapist, there is built-in war with the issue of power. The basis for asking for help is seldom an acknowledgment of loneliness, loss, emptiness, or confusion. Instead, life is not working out. A spouse has betrayed him or he was caught in a sexual sin and his spouse is freaking out. In spite of his best efforts, life is messed up and therapy is often more a punishment than a means to better engage reality.

It is an immense generalization, but for many men, relationships are comprised of a functional social group with an established network of rules related to dress, conversation, and mores. This cultural way of being is immensely powerful and often so deeply assumed that it sets the nature of what is possible without even being factored in as part of a man's choice. Our male cultural milieu is like the water a fish swims in. To violate the unstated is to draw immense scrutiny and suspicion and up the ante of culturally induced shame.

It is unusual for a man to break with his clique unless he already holds significant power both to be in the group and to challenge its unstated rules. The greater the power he holds, the more he can risk his standing by alternative ways of dress, speech, or action. Sometimes I ride a BMW 1200 RT to work, but I often alternate and ride my bicycle. I frequently sit on the ferry with the men I know who ride motorcycles even when I ride my bike. When I am a biker the motorcyclists treat me with more teasing ridicule. When I am a motorcyclist the teasing is far less. When I brought that up in one of our discussions I saw the ripple of incredulity. I had broken the "law" of men: don't tell the truth about how we relate. Men relate, but with little analysis.

I'd like a dollar for every time I have heard a man say, "That's just who I am. She wants to change me." I have seldom heard those words come out of a woman's mouth. The fact is that men are initially more defensive, combative, and suspicious when risk is high. As a rule, women will jump into their internal and relational struggles until the cost of what is being faced is named, and then there is panic and defense. Men, on the other hand, fight first, or withdraw and retreat, and only later begin to engage the real war. The result is it takes a man longer to address his defensiveness as fear rather than a legitimate response to harm.

Many wives and girlfriends find this exhausting. One woman said, "He requires me to crawl down a long, dark, rat-infested corridor just to get access to a small room where he allows me to see what he feels. And after a short time, he disappears and I am supposed to feel good that I got to see his heart." Such emotional constriction is not viewed as related to fear or the abuse; it is what it means to be a man, unless he is acting out anger or rage.

When a woman wants connection and engagement, an abused man typically feels suspicious and defensive.³ Most wives of men who have been abused tell me that if their husband doesn't run, he fumes and spills anger into the fray. Tragically, this not only gives him a sense of control and power but also lowers the stress chemicals, particularly cortisol, adrenaline, and catecholamine. It is a double whammy: power and relief combine, and this feeling state becomes addictive. The man feels calmer and more open to interaction, and his spouse feels scared and withdraws. It is as if a male's wiring is set up to ruin the possibility of being connected, curious, and caring.

Sexual War

There is a dark myriad of sexual struggles that linger like phantoms around a sexually abused man. One man said, "I feel like I am on a merry-go-round ride of sexual issues that rise and fall and go away and come back again and the ride never ends." I asked him to name the different horses that whirled around him. He said, "Compulsion, aversion, perversion, danger, and dysfunction." His categories describe well what I see with many of the men I counsel. Some men cycle through all of these, and others seldom move past one or two, but this client's endless cycle of reenactment had killed all the hope that he could ever change or that a God who loved him would choose to intervene.

Compulsion

Sexual compulsion is far more than merely wanting sex often or thinking about it obsessively. I have worked with men who need sex two to four times a day, every day. Many heterosexual men who have been abused report that not a single interaction with a woman goes by without some sexual thought or feeling. This is far more than merely an obsession; it is how the heart/soul/identity of a man addicted to sex is kept intact. This is true whether the compulsion is connected to online pornography, strip joints, phone sex, massage parlors, prostitutes, voyeurism, fetishism, or several of the above. It is as if the biochemical flow of arousal, anticipation, foreplay, and orgasm is the glue of the soul that puts Humpty Dumpty together again. Without it, fragmentation, usually evidenced in anger/rage, begins to eat away one's self. Anger can also morph into anxiety and find its resolve in hyperfocused OCD-like intensity.

Sexual compulsion or addiction is usually fused with at least one or many other addictive processes. The range includes but is not limited to food, alcohol, drugs, work, pornography, masturbation, video games, and perfectionism. It is like an endless array of escape-ruin opportunities. Every addiction enables us to escape from a world or a moment that bears too much joy or sorrow and find momentary control over the object of our consumption.

The addictive object or process has to hold sufficient danger to warrant our desire, yet in the final moment it leads us to ruin. This is what is often missed in a discussion on addiction: we are fundamentally committed to ruin.

Just as with the man who ruins an interaction with his wife by raging, so every addictive consummation—the orgasm, the second bottle of wine, the final spoonful of dessert after a huge meal—mocks us with the reality that we are still empty, alone, and now full of more shame and pain. Every addict knows, and knows deeply, that this next round of addiction will no more work to resolve the ache than it did the last one thousand times. But for a man who has been sexually abused, the lesser shame of acting out enables him to escape the looming monumental shame that he is committed to escaping. As long as danger or threat of harm is present, the risk itself generates the reward of escaping the emptiness and shame inherent in past abuse. Until the deeper shame is addressed, he will always soothe himself with the lesser shame of compulsive behavior.

Aversion

A wife of an abused man reported, "I don't get it. He wants sex every night for a week and then boom! He isn't interested in sex for a month. I am the one prompting him and he has every excuse in the book that women are normally blamed for." A man's aversion to sex is profoundly confusing for a spouse.

In this phase, men seldom acknowledge their fear or disgust. To do so would violate the rule that a true man is always eager for sex. Instead, aversion is blamed on exhaustion, busyness, or relational tensions. One wife finally named the pattern that seemed to ruin their sex life. In the periods of aversion, her husband picked petty, almost early adolescent fights that turned her against him. He would posture like he wanted sex, but she was too hurt to engage. The one time in the middle of a fight that she reversed herself and pursued sexual intimacy, he panicked and fled.

There are times in lovemaking when a man will be triggered by body sensations, parts of memory, or a full-on flashback and lose an erection. Most partners are kind and supportive, but this usually terrifies and enrages a man because it reminds him of the kindness his abuser may have used while grooming him. Sex is stopped and then fear pervades as to when the intrusion will happen again. For many men, it feels like the only way to regain sexual intimacy with one's spouse is giving his heart over to darkness. The only way to regain a sense of sexual mastery is through the use of alcohol, pornography, masturbation, and degrading images. This works and in turn intensifies shame.

The oscillation of compulsion and aversion is a heartbreaking fight/flight cycle that over time can easily kill the desire for sex. Many men who have been abused settle into hypoactive sexual desire (once called inhibited sexual desire) and live in a sexless marriage.

Perversion

Sexual perversion involves any desire, feeling, or behavior that uses sex to degrade or mar the goodness and beauty of another person or creation. In one sense, all sexual brokenness, including the objectification of another human being, is a form of perversion. This needs to be considered on a spectrum.

Making love with your spouse and fantasizing about another person breaks the bond of intimacy, and no matter how private and concealed, this behavior can't help but lead to division over time. It would be darker to make love to your spouse and imagine the spouse as a younger child or in bondage. It is darker still to demand your spouse dress like a schoolgirl and act out the pedophilic fantasy of sexually abusing a young girl.

Patrick Carnes, a leading researcher in sexual addiction, found early in his work that men involved in sexual addictions, such as exhibitionism, voyeurism, fetishism, and sadomasochism, had preposterously high rates of past sexual abuse. Correlation never proves causation, but the .81 correlation between sexual acting out and sexual abuse is as strong a connection in social research as one can find.

This doesn't mean that every man who has been sexually abused will act out sexually through affairs or that he will secretly prefer sadomasochism instead of body- and soul-honoring sex. It does suggest that every man who has been abused will struggle to some degree with sexual shame. Shame is most often shut down through a movement toward degradation of one's self or partner. What is in the heart will eventually influence the way we relate.

Seldom is it wise to tell your partner about your struggle with degradation. To divulge the degrading images or fantasies to your spouse is to set you up for fear when making love. In most occasions, the confession of sexual perversion is a setup to prove *I am bad*, or that *I can't be trusted and ruin is inevitable.*

Seldom are the fantasies or sexual acting out a direct one-to-one reenactment of the past abuse, but there is undoubtedly contextual and symbolic meaning that must be engaged. Mere will to not feel or be aroused by these images works as well as trying hard not to think of a pink elephant. The effort itself fuses the image(s) into our brain. Instead, we must let a good reader of our story, a wise and experienced guide/therapist, enter our story and invite us to unpack meaning and grieve. Otherwise, the fusion of shame, arousal, and danger will continue.

Danger

For a sexually abused man, danger is both a draw and a terror. He feels compelled to fuse his desire to regain mastery over himself with the possibility of humiliation. Danger is feared and hated; it is also erotically arousing. One must never underestimate the fusion of arousal and danger in the original abuse. It wars against the life and integrity of the body long after the abuse has been denied or forgotten.

There is danger that is alluring and frightening, and then there is other danger that is terrifying and bound to disgust. Many abused men flirt with or consummate affairs to test what they can get away with without getting caught. Others remain overtly faithful but use pornography for both arousal and the danger of being caught. It is also possible to remain entirely internal, with only fantasy providing the increased threat.

One wife complained about how her husband would never change their children's diapers. I asked what he thought was involved in his not helping his wife with that task. He said, "I'm a jerk. I'll do whatever else she needs me to do but just not that." Later, in a private session without his wife, I asked him to reengage the question. He admitted, "I don't know, but I just don't like it and I feel uncomfortable." We stayed with his awkwardness and reluctance, and eventually he looked me in the face with ferocity. "I'd rather kill myself than do anything harmful to one of my kids," he said.

His fear was he would replicate the past harm done to him by a babysitter, an older brother, and an older girl in the neighborhood. There are many men who fear doing sexual harm. Many men have done sexual harm after having been abused. Whether it was reenacting sexual abuse or using another person for sexual spoils, adventurism, or revenge, most men know something of their capacity for sexual violation. Approximately 47 percent of men who abuse have been abused. (This is not saying, of course, that 47 percent of those abused will abuse.)

Add the fear of doing sexual harm to the most common fear for sexually abused men: *Am I gay?*[4] This is a dominant fear irrespective of whether the abuser was a male or female. The abused male wonders if the abuser saw weakness, frailty, and effeminacy in him. These questions are intensified if the abuser was a man. *How do I reconcile the arousal and pleasure felt in the touch of a man with being heterosexual? How do I engage the pleasure that was felt in touching and bringing pleasure to a man?* Even if the victim is gay, the result is seldom different initially; it will be experienced as no less violating.

Mere assurance or comfort only makes the ambivalence and shame worse. It is never enough to remind him he was only ten and it was not his fault. It is sincere and true, but it misses the wound. The wound of arousal is congealed in fury, hatred, and disdain, and that will not surrender to mere aphorisms or good advice. Until he faces the true enemy of his body, which is evil's desire for shame to be bound to pleasure, all our efforts amount to giving an aspirin to someone with cancer.

Dysfunction

Many abused men also war with sexual competency. It is not uncommon for abused men to struggle with premature ejaculation, secondary impotence, an inability to retain an erection, and a lack of knowledge about a woman's body and her arousal process. This in turn can lead to relational tensions, anger, and withdrawal. At least in most cases, it leads a man to feel like a sexual loser: *I am damaged goods and a failure.*

I sat with a man who presented his brief to me like the concluding argument of a prosecutor. He had had an affair. It was the only time he had felt free enough to engage in oral sex and bring his lover to an orgasm. After repeated sexual encounters, he finally initiated sexual intercourse, and though he ejaculated before she had an orgasm, he didn't feel discouraged or full of shame. Over many sexual trials and experiments, he finally came to a point where he could sustain an erection and not ejaculate until he brought his mistress to an orgasm. He could never do this with his wife.

This man didn't need me to tell him he was immoral. He knew he was wrong. He told me his story so that I could act as his Christian jury to pass judgment on him. I refused to play that game.

On the other hand, he also demanded a pass, a reprieve given the brokenness of his life and marriage. He wanted me to exonerate his violence against himself, his mistress, his wife, and God. I also refused to play that game and concede to his self-righteousness.

What was at war in his life and in the lives of many men is that the current sexual debris helped obscure the darker and more fundamental war of betrayal, powerlessness, and shame over arousal of abuse. His unique war was connected to the fury he felt against his sister, who had required him from age eight to thirteen to bring her to an orgasm orally. He hated and feared her. He also resolutely defended her to himself against any accusation of harm. He was the villain, a loser and a pervert.

He married a rigid, aloof, and sexually closed off woman who viewed oral sex as an abomination. Their sexual life was perfunctory and dutiful. He lived with relief that more sex was not required and that he was the moral and functional failure. When his relationship with his mistress began to be exposed, our ongoing work together helped him to see the affair and his choice of a spouse in the light of his refusal to engage the painful reality of the abuse by his sister.

He eventually began to see the level of hatred he had for every woman with whom he was sexually involved. He cut off the affair and began to pursue his wife with integrity. Eventually he addressed his infidelities and his past sexual abuse with his wife. The upheaval almost killed the marriage. The betrayal compelled his wife to seek counseling, and she began a journey with another therapist that took her into her own sexual wars. Both my client and his wife bear deep scars from their suffering, yet their marriage stands against the prevailing assumption that it is better to cut one's losses and move on.

Female Perpetrators

A huge change in the last twenty-five years is the awareness that female abuse of boys is a far greater reality with far more harm than was previously considered. It was at one time deemed inconceivable that a woman would abuse a boy. The research data backed it up, stating that men were twenty-one times more likely to sexually abuse than women. Some of that is due to cultural myths that women can't abuse and that men are essentially more sexual, violent, and abusive.

Another factor that has come to light is the way we ask men while conducting research if they were abused.[5] Men are notorious for not naming abuse even when they know something sexual occurred. When men are asked directly, "Were you sexually abused?" the answer is often no. But when asked to talk about sexual experiences when they were young, stories arise that are unquestionably sexually abusive. The dilemma is a huge cultural barrier shrouding men's sexuality.

The myth is that a man should be grateful for being initiated into sex by an older female child or woman. This myth is propagated by Hollywood films like *The Last Picture Show, Summer of 42, The First Time, The Chapman Report, Class, Private Lessons, Weird Science, The Tin Drum, Murmur of the Heart, Midnight Cowboy, Mishima: A Life in Four Chapters, Little Big Man*, and more recently *The Reader*. In each film an older woman or a mother, sister, or aunt introduces a boy to the wonders and thrill of sex. It is difficult to fight a cultural lie when it is being promoted with almost conspiratorial passion by one of the most powerful mediums shaping culture: film.

In *The Reader*, it is apparent that the protagonist doesn't name the experience of having sex with an older woman as sexual abuse. The trailer begins with the words, "When I was young I had an affair." His life is ruined but the drama is not about the sexual harm; it is about his choice whether or not to speak up for the woman at her trial.

In the film *The Perks of Being a Wallflower*, the teen protagonist and his peers are coming of age, highly sexual, and at odds with their adult world. The flashbacks of sexual abuse resonate and help contextualize the protagonist's reluctance to be more sexual, but it is still not named as abuse or addressed as bearing any consequences other than making him a wallflower.

It takes a radical, countercultural move for a man to say he was sexually abused, and it is an even greater risk to state that what is viewed as an initiatory gift is in fact an unending shadow. But it must be done. The effects of perpetration by a female abuser have only been sparsely researched, but the data available reveal that men who are violent against women were much more likely to have been abused by a female. In one study of sexual aggression against women, women had sexually abused 80 percent of the offenders.[6] This fact needs immediate clarification. It is not saying that the majority of men who are violated by a woman will sexually harm women. It is saying that when male perpetrators are studied, many have a history of being violated by women. What we can draw from this is that, in the lives of some men, direct violence against women is correlated with past female sexual abuse. There is an unaddressed rage that must be engaged.

There are three issues I eventually hear men name as a result of being abused by a woman: feeling used, struggling with inadequacy, and sexual confusion. These issues are difficult for a man to name and are seldom acknowledged without a lot of digging for honesty.

Feeling Used

No matter how much a man enjoys sex, no one enjoys being set up and used. As much as Hollywood wishes to laud female seduction, no human being wants to be manipulated into sex or anything else. The female abuser is not doing the young boy a favor in initiating him into adult sexuality.

Further, the fact of being used means the abuser has power, whereas the boy or young man doesn't. To resist or not fully participate implies that the boy is somehow not sufficiently sexual and/ or is flawed. The only way he can escape the sexual confusion is to fully participate, which makes the abuse seem mutual and equal. But it is not.

This disparity creates shame for having lost the capacity for sexual initiation and choice. What I see as a result is a deep and ugly insistence never to feel sexually weak again. Even mutually sharing power—when each partner is equally involved in desire and touch—still feels like a compromise. Many men need to feel like they are not merely in control but completely in charge. And as contradictory as it may seem, the need for total control sets up many fantasies of not having any control and being at the whim and whip of a vastly more aggressive and humiliating dominatrix.

Struggling with Inadequacy

The disparity in power sets up the boy or young man to be an apprentice to a sexually sophisticated and manipulative older girl or woman. The so-called benefit of sex doesn't compensate for being put in the position of being a neophyte with a master. The abusive woman is not doing the boy a favor as a well-meaning sexual Good Samaritan.

The women I have worked with who have abused boys have eventually named the delicious power and pleasure in being better at something in which men are supposed to excel. Most men admit there was always a degree of failure and frustration in not being able to be as "good" at sex as their abuser. Even the patient and solicitous abuser makes the boy pay for some sexual harm endured by her from a previous abuser. The vast majority of the women I have worked with who have abused a younger boy were abused themselves as children. The vengeance against past abuse is a force that permeates the present perpetration.

One man who was abused by a teacher said he could never get out of his head the tone of her voice as she instructed him on how to please her. He became an expert at oral sex, but even after an orgasm the tone of her voice had the quality of a pat on his head. He hated the sound of her pleasure and the postcoital congratulations on a job well done. He became sophisticated and conquering in his sexual exploits, but he always felt like he was a boy trying to prove he was a man.

Sexual Confusion

Often the man who was abused as a boy by a woman struggles with the same question as the victim who was abused by a man: *Am I gay?* At first it makes little sense, which is why it is even more difficult to address. *How could I question my sexuality when the abuser who chose me is a woman?* As one man said, "You'd think that would be the prize that validated my heterosexuality. It isn't."

The hardest issues to address when the abuse is subtle or perpetrated by a woman are arousal ambivalence and shame. Sex that is culturally viewed as a prize and privilege makes shame more difficult to address. *If it felt good and is considered a prize, then why do I feel used, awkward, and ashamed?* The answer: *Something is wrong with me sexually.* And tragically the next step is the fear of homosexuality. When you add this to the number of men who are abused by men, it is no wonder there is such venom and mockery directed toward homosexuality.

Irrespective of one's views about homosexuality, it is heartbreaking and horrendously wrong when a person's sexuality is spoken about with contempt. The community of God can wrestle and debate this issue, but the presence of disdain or revulsion clouds both care and conversation.[7] The result of this unaddressed fear and shame is more often than not homophobia and hyperindulgence in heterosexuality.

I worked with one man who estimated that he had had over fifty female partners after getting married to a woman who triggered the memories of his early abuse by his sister. It is not sufficient merely to call him a sex addict. His indulgence was vastly more than an uncontrollable craving for sex. It was an intersection of his need to prove his power over women and his need to submerge his sexual doubts. His sexual adventurism was fueled by vengeance and fear. This deadly combination leaves many male abuse victims in the quandary of both needing and hating sex.

The Calling of an Abused Man

What does it mean to be a man? Particularly, what does it mean to be a man whose body is given to holiness and honor after the harm of abuse? As odd as it may at first seem, the strength of a man is seen in his willingness to own his fury against shame. One man said, "Every time I feel sexual I get caught in the web of something I can't see or control. It almost never goes well, and when it does I feel even more angry and scared." His fury, like that of many men, was directed against women and himself. He compared himself to a sexual Samson whose final act of integrity in the midst of massive betrayal and indulgence was to subject himself to death in taking down his Philistine jailers.

No man, obviously, needs to take his own life, but the reality is that there must be a dying to self. This dying is not self-annihilation or merely refusing pleasure, sexual or otherwise. It is a deeper and more difficult surrender. It involves the surrender of one's body and soul to the story of God rather than to living out the indulgences of a safe, vicarious, and manipulative story. A man must have a larger story to honor and serve or he will become a warrior for nothing other than his own pleasure.

When a man serves a smaller story he inevitably repeats that story again and again until the story brings about his death—or he lives into his calling and discovers that death has no final hold over his life. Often it is through our reenactments of our past in our present that we discover the unaddressed story that calls for our care. An abused man can't move forward until he has the courage to return to the burnt ground of his abuse and learn how to grieve.

7

The Drama of Reenactment

I feel like when I walk into a store everyone knows. It doesn't matter how well I try to hide it, it seems like everyone can tell that I am damaged. I know that sounds paranoid and probably is to some degree. But if it is, if I make this stuff up, then how come I end up having men walk up and flash me, about four times since I was twenty? My friends don't have this happen to them, and if they do it is like once. I feel like I have a bull's-eye on my forehead and a beacon to attract every abuser in the city. When I dated, which I don't do anymore, the good men would take about three dates to bed me. The bad boys would try in the first hour. And then the merry-go-round starts up and I'd be back in another abusive relationship. I am getting smarter and I avoid the same old patterns, but avoiding isn't changing me; it's only postponing what feels inevitable, and that is that I am going to crash again.

participant in a recovery group

Whether sexual abuse is overt or subtle, perpetrated on males or females, over time the violations get replayed in the victim's day-to-day life in reenactments of the unaddressed drama of abuse. Reenactment and repetition of past dynamics of harm is one of the deepest struggles for those who have been abused. The past seems to overflow the banks of the present and flood the abused person with hopelessness. The future seems destined to be nothing but a repeat of the past as it becomes superimposed on the present to perpetuate the cycle of harm.

At best (though tragic), the victim of childhood sexual abuse becomes a tough and resilient survivor. At worst a sense of hopelessness leads to exhaustion, indifference, and repetitive reenactments of abuse. Either way, this is not a life of freedom and self-directed power. And it is far more than having an endless cycle of "bad" tapes playing in one's head. It is a reality that changes only when the abused person faces the deep biochemical, relational, and spiritual opposition against him or her.

Recycling Abuse

I have worked for years with women and men who were once involved in prostitution. Many of these friends and clients are involved in ministries that fight human trafficking. The kind of harm they have endured from the Christian community is comparable to, if not at times worse than, the violence they endured in prostitution. The common sentiment they have heard is, "Well, I am heartbroken about human trafficking, but a prostitute could leave any time she wanted. She isn't a victim." Nothing could be further from the truth. Even more inconceivable is what one man told a friend: "I wouldn't give a dime to help a prostitute—she is what Proverbs calls a dog who returns to her own vomit."[1] This is a wicked and soulless statement.

The metaphor is a rough one. It provokes and disturbs. If you read those words and feel accused or demeaned in the midst of your struggles with ongoing issues, then I am grieved that I might be heard as one who stands above you with insolent contempt. I am not. I am often the dog being referred to as I struggle with being foolish enough to return again and again to what I know will not satisfy my soul. Even more disheartening, I often return to what causes my soul to heave.

It is imperative to receive what the Word of God offers: strong medicine. It is even more important to read it in context. What follows the metaphor is something even more devastating than returning to one's vomit. To think we are wise when we are not is even more foolish than returning to our old patterns. Scripture tells us that in our foolishness we repeat patterns; we recycle harm that is as disturbing as a dog devouring the recent contents of its stomach.

How do we understand the struggle of repeating dangerous, risky, and often degrading events? Often those who have been traumatized have a difficult time regulating their emotions in what most would consider even normal or pleasant events. Louis Cozolino, a neuro-psychologist, states:

> A so-called normal life leaves traumatized persons a blank screen onto which their dysregulated psyches can project fearful experiences, keeping them in a state of vigilance and fear. . . . This may motivate the creation of stress, making a traumatized person vulnerable to creating new trauma. The new trauma would, in turn, stimulate the production of endogenous opioids that would lead to an increased sense of calm and well-being. Paradoxically, trauma would lead to a sense of competency and control.[2]

Trauma rewires the brain. It sets up the victim of abuse for arousal in the midst of danger and drama. Obviously, this is not the case with all abuse victims or in all cases of danger. Nevertheless, it is almost certain that every victim of abuse will be aroused to some degree by people, processes, and objects that return the victim to some elements of the abuse experience.

Everyone struggles with repeating destructive patterns—some call this besetting sin. Others call it a repetition compulsion; it is without question a biological remnant of abuse. Whatever it is called, it shows up in some common patterns that include relationships, sexual triggers, and addictions.

Relationships

Relationships with others, whether intimate or casual, almost always have an element of repetition. In fact, if we are honest, almost all of life feels like a series of repetitive dramas with the occasional new character or slant to a recurring story.

One man said, "I started golfing with a friend from work and within a few months I was paying for his lunch, regularly, no really all the time. It is crazy, but I live close to the course we normally play and he lives miles away, but he wants me to pick him up and then drive him home though he owns a car and can afford to drive. He says, 'I love your company.'" When I explored with this client his history of being used, it was shocking to hear how every relationship he had felt like a drain. He didn't have a single relationship with someone who didn't use him.

We may be quite different in the various worlds we inhabit, but there is always something that remains the same. What is that consistency? What are the patterns that make up our way of relating to others? Those patterns not only have meaning in the present but also have a connection to the trauma and abuse of our past. The cause and the consequences may not always be clear, but the issue of reenactment must be explored with sensitivity to how these patterns enabled us to manage an unmanageable inner and outer world.

This drama of reenactment occurs especially in marriage and other partner relationships. There are two fourteen-thousand-foot peaks we need to consider that are surrounded by other large ranges. These two peaks are whom we marry and how we construct barriers to keep risk, hurt, and betrayal at a minimum that over time actually increase our heartache. Unless we struggle with these issues before marriage, there is a high probability that we will pick a spouse who somehow intersects with our abuser, parents, and other authority figures. There are as many possible configurations for this first peak as there are people. A woman might marry a man who is diametrically different from her father, slightly similar to her abuser, and placating to her mother. Her chosen mate might be passive and kind like her father, sexually tender like her abuser, and drive her mother crazy.

It is important to remember that we operate in the world with two hands that are simultaneously inviting and repelling: one hand beckons for someone to hear us and pursue our heart; the other is held either close to our chest, hidden and secretive, or far out in front of us with defiance to warn others not to approach. And this is the key factor in whom we choose as a partner. If we need someone who is going to heed the "come quickly, now, immediately, without hesitation" hand, then we tend to marry someone highly sensitive and often quite weak. They offer care, but their love seems to lack substance. On the other hand, if touch, care, and tenderness are terrifying, we tend to marry someone who is more distant, critical, busy, and independent. What initially attracts us often later repels us.

The second peak, constructing barriers, involves how we live out, over time, the hand that invites intimacy and the hand that demands distance. Prior to marrying my wife I dated a number of highly disturbed, addicted, and unpredictable women. This pattern was a repetition of my relationship with my mother. It led to enough disasters to warrant never dating again. And like many, I swerved to the other side to find stability but often at the cost of silencing a woman's dissent or hurt. This was the pattern I saw my mother live out with my father. He was quiet and seldom, if ever, owned desire.

My wife, Becky, initially fit this arrangement, and we lived out the pattern of Dan (vocal, dominant, and angry) and Becky (quiet, watchful, and struggling with contempt). We were immensely happy until we were not. The bad moments were not frequent but when they arose I did deep harm. I shouted; she stonewalled. I confessed failure; she remained distant. We each retreated then slowly warmed up to each other again until the event was forgotten (but not).

Repetition in marrying a parent and/or an abuser is disturbing enough, but when the pattern leads to some of the same harm from childhood, it is maddening. What occurs is the use of default mechanisms we developed in childhood to survive. Stonewalling was the defense used by my father. I married my father and proceeded to attack the "problem" with emotion, verbiage, and drama, just like my mother did.

When we are engaging at our worst, remnants of our dysfunctional patterns remain alive. It takes immense humility and wisdom to help each other step off the merry-go-round. This is particularly true when one or both partners experience sexual triggers.

Sexual Triggers

A sexual trigger is any event that arouses the senses (a single sense or a combination of touch, sight, smell, taste, or sound) and amplifies the distress related to past sexual harm. Our response is usually involuntary and confusing. Often the person triggered only knows that something strongly disruptive is happening, and it is common for the body/heart to go into shock/dissociation. The body reacts by going into fight, flight, or freeze mode, and this usually happens at lightning speed. It feels bizarre, especially if there is no clear cause of our reaction. More often than not, both partners feel confused.

One's spouse might respond with anger, fear, or contempt simply in order to control a response that feels scary. A client told me that in the middle of intercourse one night, she froze. She couldn't hear or feel touch. She knew something terrible was happening; she thought she was having a stroke. Her husband seemed not to notice and continued on to orgasm. Only afterward, when she was still unable to move, did he note her blank stare and lifeless stillness. He panicked and started to yell at her. She was able eventually to look at him but found it impossible to talk. He began to call 9-1-1 and the words finally came out of her: "I am here. I can't talk. Don't call 9-1-1; I'm not having a stroke."

The event was chalked up to a "weird" experience, and she never debriefed with him or pondered what might have occurred. It happened again five months later, and this time she was aware that prior to penetration her husband had said some endearing words to her. She had no clue why that intensified her anger and terror, but it did. The memory was not forthcoming for a long season, but after many significant conversations she was able to talk about how gentle her father had been when he sexually abused her. He would nestle his face against her neck and intone affirming and tender words before he began intense thrusting. She had not made the connection to her long and deep refusal to receive any tender and complimentary remarks. Whenever someone spoke of her goodness or beauty, she cringed and deferred the compliment. For some tragic reason no one had ever seen the cringe, at least not well enough to engage her in examining her pattern of rejecting delight.

Sometimes the trigger is not as obvious. It is a slight hint of disgust or distance. Often these unseen and unaddressed triggers simply get woven into our way of being and become "who we are." One man found it awkward to undress in front of his wife. He indicated that he preferred to take his work clothes off and shower alone. He locked the bathroom door. His wife found it disturbing but learned to accept his quirks as idiosyncratic.

In fact, he had often been required to take off his clothes, like a striptease, for his two oldest sisters. He remembered in agonizing detail all the abuse but had never made the connection between his awkwardness in undressing in front of his wife and the striptease that preceded his sisters' abuse of him.

Triggers may have a concrete relationship with past abuse or they might be far more symbolic and complex. In either case, it is imperative to listen to "symptoms," not just to figure out how to get rid of them, at first, but far more to listen to them to learn what is involved in the disruption so the root cause can begin to be addressed and healed.

Addictions

The most obvious form of repetition is an addiction. An addiction is by definition a series of self-destructive behaviors that simply don't abate in spite of risk or harm. Whether the addiction is chemically (alcohol), relationally (sexual), or procedurally (perfectionism) oriented, it serves at least two purposes: (1) to satiate emptiness with intense pleasure that turns into numbness or dissociation; (2) to set up dramas that enable the addict to escape even more painful losses and shame. It is the drama of sabotage that is the least addressed dimension of an addiction.

It is said that every addict is running from something. I fully accept that premise. But I'd say it more pointedly: every addict is trying to ruin something. After a few hundred experiences of any addictive substance or process, every addict knows the next time is not going to work any better than the last two hundred times. There is a drive to ruin that subverts the beauty and goodness of the heart.

I see this most clearly when an abuse victim begins to name the darkest part of the damage of abuse: arousal. It is still the least addressed dimension of harm and is often fully ignored or denied by both victims and therapists. Or if it is addressed, it is flown over at such dizzying heights and speeds that it is merely a theoretical construct rather than a topography that is walked in the dirt through ambivalence, shame, and contempt. Addictions are an effort to defeat any attempt to get close to the deep self-hatred.

I worked with a woman who channeled her general hatred for her body into drinking excessive amounts of alcohol. She would combine it with ecstasy and synthetic marijuana, go home with a man she met in a bar, and then wake up aware that her body was sore and often bruised. Her clothes would be on the floor and she wouldn't know the name of the man in her bed.

As obvious as this woman's violence may be, it is no different when we see it in more subtle form. I worked with a woman whose church activities and mission involvement put her in positions where she labored months in a row with no break. Her health deteriorated and her friends urged her to take a break, but she couldn't "afford" to do so. She was addicted not only to ministry but also to the damage that exhaustion allowed her to experience. The more exhausted she became, the less she felt aware of her body, desires, or inner disgust. Her ministry freed her from the occasional bursts of desire for a husband, children, and a "normal life." This destructive obsession with ministry made her appear to be righteous and spiritually passionate; it also provided a winsome excuse for not having time for anything other than superficial relationships. Our early work involved reflecting on her exhaustion and loneliness. This compelled her to begin the hard work of looking at her pattern earlier in life as the primary caretaker for her two younger sisters. Her mother was emotionally unavailable and dumped the burden of mothering on her responsible oldest child. We eventually named that her only relief from her perfectionism came through addictive masturbation.

It is imperative to underscore this reality: sexual abuse survivors seldom struggle with one single addiction. The battles are usually multiple, comorbid, and intersecting. One past therapist had merely worked to assure this woman that everyone masturbated and her shame against a God-given, natural gift was ill-placed. She felt slightly relieved but even more ashamed—not only for masturbating but also for feeling shame for doing so. She never brought it up in therapy again and assured her therapist at a later point that it was no longer an issue. It was.

It is disheartening that many therapists and helpers try to normalize the reenactments of abuse. These repetitions are tackled as life-skill issues; the client simply needs to learn healthier ways to drink, have sex, work, or eat with more self-control. Addictions are, in fact, crucial portals to enter in order to comprehend how the person is attempting to resolve unaddressed trauma. The impulse to repeat destructive behavior is a plea to oneself and to others to hear that there is an unresolved drama that has not come to a satisfying end.

This is particularly true with regard to sexual fantasies and masturbatory narratives. Masturbation for most abuse victims began as a means of self-soothing after having been sexually abused. The genital arousal during abuse is both pleasurable and deeply disturbing. Victims of more subtle abuse, too, will likely dissipate the more ambiguous arousal through sexual activities that defuse the pent-up struggle with the unnamed perpetrator. This can include activities that involve pain and degradation or include masturbation that is more intense and less obviously self-soothing.

The younger the victim of sexual abuse, the more likely this act is reflexive and disconnected from the actual narrative of how the abuse occurred. It is not unusual for eight-year-olds to form a story line that sustains and enhances the masturbatory experience. Certainly, as a victim ages and more and more conversations, movies, television shows, songs, videos, and images illumine the meaning of sexual activity, the story gets more developed and complex.

If the first order of the addictive masturbatory fantasy is for self-soothing and dissociation, its far darker purpose is to ruin. The impulse to ruin is an act of self-degradation that allows the person to sate himself or herself with contempt. This is often seen in the number of times and/or manner of masturbation and in the fantasies that guide the masturbation. Often these erotic narratives are demeaning and degrading, and the more so, the greater the sense of abandon and relief—until orgasm is achieved and the weight of shame descends.

It stands to reason that a person with unaddressed and unresolved sexual abuse issues will suffer countless fantasy reenactments. As a child ages and more and more sexual events occur, the sexual narratives become more and more explicit. If these narratives come up in relationship, it is usually in discussion with a partner who wants access to the stage to join in the drama. It is, in other words, not for the sake of understanding, grief, and transformation but for manipulation. Mostly the sexual images and scenes remain arousing, troubling, and used as a means for dissociation and violence.

Not every victim struggles with violent sexual fantasies, but many do. I have observed three primary structures: (1) Rejection: *No one wants me and I give myself to someone who uses me.* (2) Assault: *Someone violently or seductively takes advantage of me and harms me.* Dreams or narratives of flight, escape, and being caught are included in this category. (3) Perversion: *I am forced or choose to have sex with an animal, with several partners, with a person of a different sexual orientation, or in a manner that violates my sense of decency.* In all three instances, the result is the same shame: arousal is merged with contempt-filled judgment. *There is something deeply wrong, dark, and stained about me that makes me unlovable. This explains why and how I was abused in the first place.*

One victim said, "I am a dirty girl—no wonder he found me and did what he did. I have always been highly sexual and he simply took advantage of who I am." Her words underscore what happens when repetition/reenactment stifles our capacity to choose another path. We instead choose hopelessness, powerlessness, indifference, and exposing ourselves to harm.

Hindering Change

Hopelessness

To feel we can't stop gaining weight or setting ourselves up yet again for another troubled relationship is more than discouraging. It takes the wind out of the sails of life and empties the heart of joy. *What is wrong with me? Others seem to be able to succeed in a job*

135

or find a mate. It is my fault. I am a loser. I don't have what it takes to change this pattern.

Initially, when a victim of abuse starts to see the root of the addictive pattern for the first time, there is a surge of hope. *Finally, now that I understand that I am caught in this cycle, I can rise above it.* Many victims fantasize that going to college, getting married, or finding a new job will "save" them. We all know that a move simply moves our problems from one space to another, yet we hope. But usually, the new insight and hope puddle like a dropped scoop of ice cream on a hot sidewalk. The pattern keeps repeating itself and despair ensues. This despair is actually an attunement to a reservoir of loss and regret.

The fact is that illusions must die; fantasies must hit the wall before the truest dreams can surface. This is one of the reasons that it often takes victims of abuse several decades of "moving on" to realize that not only has their interior not changed but their life is getting worse. In our middle-class culture we give people the time between ages eighteen and twenty-six to play, explore, and train for their future work. The years between twenty-six and thirty-four are about advancing a career and adding the complexities of possible long-term relationships, especially marriage. Once marriage and children arrive, with the addition of a new home and the exhaustion of work, church, friends, and an aging body, it is easy to ignore the growing angst. It seems that many finally start the hard work of facing disillusionment in their midthirties to forties. It is in this context that the loss of hope is most present.

Powerlessness

Hopelessness spirals slowly downward into deeper despair to the degree that change is attempted with few positive results. Like yo-yo dieters, many make changes only to find soon after that more helplessness settles in. But we seldom quit easily. We try another self-help book, guru, or church. There is always the newest new thing. It feels manic—the rise of hope and then the plummeting into reality. We return again to compartmentalize the problem, to shelve what is truly under the surface. Compartmentalization serves to cut our losses and focuses us on what brings momentary satisfaction. This works fairly well—until a reenactment of the abuse begins to disrupt even the areas where we seem to have control.

An acquaintance of mine handled his rotting marriage by running five miles every other day. His marriage was faltering because he refused to seek help. He lived out the same patterns that enabled him not to be budged by his weak father or his even weaker mother. In his family, he was the star who kept their hearts afloat by success in school and athletics. He kept his distance from them as if they carried the plague. They did. They were toxic.

His aloof, distancing coolness worked brilliantly in his field as a physician, but it was killing his marriage. And as you might expect, his deteriorating marriage was infringing on all the other areas of his life. He was losing power and capacity as the decay spread. Then he encountered a new level of powerlessness when he blew out his Achilles on a run. His source of power dried up and he had to address what he had been literally running to escape.

Indifference

Indifference is a tragic mark of past victimization. It is a shrug of the heart and empty, lifeless eyes that say, *Who cares? Whatever!* The eyes and face register the inner lifelessness with a shallow, cynical presence that alerts others that little to nothing matters. The indifferent heart may feel passion through anger, but even that feels like too big a weight to carry. An occasional burst of rage might restore momentum for a few hours, but it fades like any cortisol high.

Once the high wears off, in its place is an even darker commitment to not commit, care, or have compassion. *Why bother? What will desire bring other than more pain and trouble?*

A pastor I know has lost his heart for the ministry, but he says, "I am too old to start over." He preaches, meets with folks, and tops off his day with a few shots of vodka and cranberry juice. He functions just enough to get by. He has learned to survive with a C+ in life. He told me, "When I wake up, I feel sick. In the hour before I fall asleep, I feel sick. But in between I just feel numb because I keep telling myself, 'Who cares? Just survive. Put in a few more years and retire.'"

His story is tragic, but especially so because it is the same deadness that drowned his desire after his older brother sexually abused him. He willed himself not to care. After coming to Christ in college, his zeal and joy returned and he entered seminary and the pastorate. But after several decades of trauma and abuse in churches that brought him more betrayal and grief than he remembered even with the original abuse, he found himself returning to the same patterns of indifference, or soul suicide, that enabled him to survive as a boy.

Indifference is a refusal to desire, a refusal to risk disappointment. It can be seen in a passivity that allows others to make most choices, or it can be fueled by chronic anxiety that is only quelled by not caring what happens as long as the threat goes away. Indifference is a stance against hope. It is a way of allowing hope to be deferred without feeling loss. Normally, deferred desire leads to an inner sickness, but indifference allows the heart to stop caring. The result is always more harm.

Exposure to Harm

It is heartbreaking to see victims of abuse revictimized. It will sound to some like I am putting the blame for sexual or relational harm on the shoulders of the victim. I am not. If a woman drinks or wears clothes that some might say are too revealing, is she the cause of a sexual assault? If she hadn't been drunk or worn provocative clothing, would she have escaped sexual harm?

138

These are slippery questions, but let's be clear: a woman is never responsible for a man's lust or choice to sexually violate. She could be naked on the street, utterly drunk, and still any sexual violation is the full responsibility of the person who perpetrates the crime. On the other hand, the choice to put oneself in the path of harm is likely an issue of reenactment of past harm. It is not merely dangerous or lacking wisdom; it is a setup for muggers, sexual abusers, spiritual bullies, and conscienceless bosses to read if the woman is likely to say no to violation. Her inability to do so makes the probability higher that abuse will occur.

Is the victim of childhood abuse in any way, shape, or form responsible? Absolutely not, but what about the victim of abuse whose reenactment patterns since childhood have set them up for repeated violations? The answer is not as unequivocal; it is more nuanced. The adult who was abused as a child is like the person who ate mostly fat, sugar, and junk food as a kid. This not only sets up unhealthy habits but also reinforces structures in the brain that register fullness and contentment with food associated with self-harm. Is it impossible to change? Change is unquestionably possible, but it is likely there will always be proclivities to fat and sugar that will cause even the person who eats well to crave the addictive high.

After considering the pervasive harm of reenactments it is easy to feel hopeless, but there is always possibility for transformation. It is now our task to consider what must happen for the pattern of repetition to relent and for healing to take place. What is ahead for some victims of abuse may feel like too much hope too soon. For others, the promise that change will come might not come soon enough. Hope for healing is far more terrifying than most reckon at first. But to engage the harm of abuse without hope is not only empty but also a denial of the resurrection. The hope for the sexually abused man or woman is that sexual abuse, like death, never has the final word.

Part Two

The Healing Path

8

The Power of Kindness

Like our ancestors, we have sinned. We have done wrong! We have acted wick-edly! Our ancestors in Egypt were not impressed by the LORD's miraculous deeds. They soon forgot his many acts of kindness to them.

Psalm 106:6–7 NLT

Never let loyalty and kindness leave you! Tie them around your neck as a reminder. Write them deep within your heart.

Proverbs 3:3 NLT

Your kindness will reward you, but your cruelty will destroy you.

Proverbs 11:17 NLT

Do you show contempt for the riches of his kindness, forbearance and patience, not realizing that God's kindness is intended to lead you to repentance?

Romans 2:4

A sexually abused person is usually ambivalent about kind-ness. Because 91 percent of abusers are known to their victim, it is highly likely the abuser used kindness and sensitive reading of the victim to create access and trust. Grooming ruins the childlike desire to trust. A kind person will be read with great suspicion. *What do you want? What is required to keep your care?*

But kindness is the instrument God uses to open the heart and begin its renovation. It is the means God uses to transform fear, hardness, cruelty, and despair. Without kindness, a heart will be bound to the repetition of past trauma in the present.

Kindness, unfortunately, gets lumped in with niceness. A kind person, by this definition, is pleasant, eager to please, and not a fighter. In our world it is akin to being a good Boy Scout—admirable, but not enviable. It will not get you ahead in a dog-eat-dog world. Sharing the armrest may make for a good seatmate on a plane, but it is hardly a quality we look for in leaders or movers and shakers. However, the Bible considers kindness God's impetus for change. It is the thing that we are to bind around our neck and write deeply into our heart. To fail to do so is to end up like the Israelites who forgot the signs and wonders of the Exodus and rebelled against God.

There are three key qualities to kindness: it deeply touches the heart, it is unexpected, and it is undeserved. One victim of abuse described her current pastor as "formidably kind." She described him as not easily pushed away nor blind to her efforts to hide. What unnerved her was his relentless commitment to name her flight, fight, and freeze without requiring her to change. She felt seen, known, and pursued without demand. He remained attuned and honored her boundaries and his own. He established an attachment with attunement and containment that enabled her to hear things from him that she wouldn't hear from anyone else. She said, "He sets a table for me every time we talk and sometimes what he serves is not sweet, but I eat knowing it is all good food."

The heart of kindness is hospitality. Good hospitality welcomes with open arms, receives with pleasure, and honors the other with goodness. It is how we are meant to make space for the stranger, whether a guest in our home or a memory of ourselves at age twelve. How do we handle the part of us that reenacts by looking at pornography again? Overeats and feels sickened by our lack of control? Accepts another project on top of what already can't be done in a sane manner? How do we welcome, receive, and honor a memory that is fragmented and diffuse but indicates that a neighbor may have abused us?

How we offer hospitality to our estranged self and our memories will eventually determine how we care for others. Kindness begins the healing process as it soothes ambivalence, engages our heart, and calls our soul to wholeness.

Soothing the Ambivalent Heart

We are not meant to enter the dark waters of memory without the presence of comfort and care. Kindness involves learning to trust our body and our stories in the presence of another person. Receiving kindness from another in the midst of the distress of narrating our stories begins to form a bond of trust.

Every time we are stressed our brain produces biochemicals that ramp up our ability to run from a tiger, fight off an enemy, or freeze against a bigger foe. Soothing is our primary means to lower distress. An attuned mother distinguishes the cries of her baby and responds in a manner consistent with what the child is experiencing, whether pain, fear, discomfort, or irritation. She reads the cry with the child's needs foremost in her mind. As any parent or grandparent knows, soothing a child can't be done with criticism or command. It is slow, kind comfort that dials down fear and rage. Over time a child will internalize a parent's comfort and find ways to soothe himself or herself. At first, a baby needs another human being to help regulate distress, but the internalized image of the mother or the memory of comfort becomes the basis for self-soothing. A child who is rocked to sleep may mimic the movement with imperceptible swaying. A child who had his or her hair stroked may take a strand of hair and twirl it. Sucking on a thumb replaces a mother's nipple. A warm, cuddly blanket symbolizes a mother's warm and comforting presence.

Not a day goes by that we don't need soothing. As I write I am typing at a standing desk where I can move forward and side to side. I usually have a pen or an unlit pipe in my mouth. I am wearing soft, comfortable clothes. I often light candles, have music playing quietly in the background, and enjoy the scent of aromatherapy. We all need comfort and soothing. Without it we simply ramp up higher and higher in response to the stress of the day.

Imagine the kind of stress involved in being sexually violated as a child. It is an inconceivable assault against the brain, body, and heart, and it comes at a time when a child has not fully developed the means or structures to self-soothe. No wonder masturbation is often chosen, though with the consequence that it heightens a child's erotic focus and intensifies shame.

The majority of an abused person's repetitious reenactments are an effort to soothe both heart and body and cover shame. The tragedy is that the means of self-soothing often create more complications and heartache. As a child ages, the most available means for self-soothing include food, television, video games, alcohol, and sex. There are fewer and fewer ways to self-soothe without shame. A child who rocks in a classroom will be thought to be on the autistic spectrum. A child who needs touch from an adult will be viewed as dependent and clingy. We socialize children not to need comfort. Imagine how this plays out in victims of sexual abuse. As they have more distress to soothe and simply repeat their default mechanisms, they end up harming themselves—at times for longer, and in more convoluted ways, than the original abuse. Kindness disrupts this cycle.

I met with a student whose life was rife with sexual harm. Her way of interacting with others was distant and often contentious. I was to meet with her at noon, but another student was waiting at my office for an appointment. I had apparently made a mistake and double-booked. I spoke first with the student with whom I thought I had made the first appointment. Then after that meeting was finished, the second student came in. She glared at me as she sat across the room, and it was apparent she was angry for having to wait.

Before I could apologize, she said, "What I need to ask you about really can't be done in a twenty-minute appointment, whether you screwed up or not." It would have been easy for me to apologize or simply offer to reschedule. Most of us think that kindness is merely being pleasant and avoiding conflict, but I said, "I am honored that you'd desire to speak about difficult matters with me, and it is clear that I have lost your trust." Her response was self-contemptuous: "I'm sorry I'm such a drama queen. I didn't mean to ruin what time we have." Her anger toward me was defensive, but when I didn't respond either to apologize or defend myself, she turned on herself.

Kindness upends contempt not by trying to soothe it or take it away but by engaging it with honesty and honor. I said to her, "Your contempt moves fluidly from anger at me to a harsh judgment of yourself. What is the war you are fighting as you swing back and forth between other-centered and self-contempt?"

Her face softened and she admitted, "I don't want you to care or know that what you say matters to me. I am too used to having Christian leaders see me as a nuisance and a troublemaker." Her heart felt comfort as she was able to name both what she desired and what she feared, given her history of many unpleasant interactions with other male authority figures.

When the heart can name its inner conflict without fear of retribution, the struggle does not go away but ambivalence is lessened. A kind response enabled my student to name what she feared and eventually what she wanted. Kindness awakens us to what we are meant to know: engagement and delight.

Engaging the Dismissive Heart

In the exhaustion and hopelessness of reenactment, the abused person's heart gives up; it becomes bound to the relief of shutting down emotion and keeping desire afar. Over time this internal "deadness" becomes a nearly impermeable shield that keeps people at bay and desire dismissed. The disappointed heart accepts that nothing is going to change, and survival depends on the ability to look at heartache from a distance.

One client told me about how she routinely had to wait on a good friend who was perpetually late to their get-togethers. The closer we got to her buried and frozen desire, the more her irritation and testiness rose. Our conversation looked like this:

Dan: "Your friend left you waiting at the coffee shop for thirty minutes later than she said?"

Client: "She does that often. I know if I am going to meet her to take a book."

Dan: "You are resourceful and there is little that you will let trouble you."

Client: "What is the point of letting little irritations get to you? She is late to everything. She will be late to her own funeral."

Dan: "If I go the route of inviting you to consider how rude that is or inconvenient, I think I know how you will dismiss my irritation with your friend. But I am glad you were more irritated with me a month ago when I was ten minutes late to our appointment. At least I know that tardiness sometimes bothers you."

Client: "I pay you. I don't pay her to be on time."

Dan: "Can you feel your face tighten and your voice become more brittle?"

148

Client: "And what is your point?"

She was never outright combative, merely impatient with any interaction that invited her to feel the weight of her heartache. She sloughed it off and looked at me with polite disdain. She became more entrenched while considering the impact of others on her heart, but the fact that she had been miffed with me for being late to an appointment in the past was a small indication that her dismissive stance toward others was not as strong as she claimed. Movement into her cool, distant heart required naming her dismissive response without requiring her to change.

A kind heart pursues without the need to corner or catch. To demand in any way is to replace kindness with coercion. It is a complex and holy paradox. If I pursue, I normally want to catch the subject of my labor. But the intention to offer kindness is closer to the mindset of a nature photographer than that of a hunter. The "shot" requires I get close, but I don't need to take down my subject. I only need to get close and then prepare for a battle with their ambivalence and shame. Kindness is not initially comforting; instead, it arouses some of the deepest contempt.

The apostle Paul asks a profound question: "Why do you treat the kindness of God with contempt?" (see Rom. 2:4). We defend against kindness. It is too unnerving merely to accept kindness, even if it is one of our deepest desires. We are made for delight and honor—anything less in any moment is an insult to creation and the Creator.

I believe the last sentence somewhere in my being, but the fact is that true delight and honor are so infrequent that if I measure every interaction by that dictum, I will be at a loss in almost every relationship. It can't be true. If it is, then it requires far more ability to hold disappointment than we normally have in order to live well with others. It seems far easier to lower our expectations and live with what is rather than to desire what was meant to be.

The variety of ways people discount and dismiss heartache is just on the border of infinite. Listen to two examples:

Client #1: "Life is just what it is and nothing more. I don't expect anyone to come through at this point. You have to buck up and rely on yourself because no one has the time anymore to help."

Client #2: "My mom just doesn't get it. She seems never to hear what I am saying. She just didn't grow up in a time when relationships were that important."

Both statements serve to limit desire, defend against hurt, and distance the heart from disappointment. If that kind of armor is allowed to remain undisturbed, as if it were part of the person's personality, then there will be profound loss for all.

Kindness, unlike niceness, is not afraid to plunge into the matters of the heart. This requires two skills: discernment and risk. Therefore, any word that depersonalizes and/or diminishes heartache must be at least noted, and in due season engaged. It is not uncommon for an abuse victim to spread a minefield between himself or herself and others. To simply wander across the terrain will lead to explosions. One must be able to see, feel, sense, and intuit the slightly roughed-up ground and begin the process to disarm each mine.

To engage the dismissive heart requires that we offer ballast and comfort and not be easily threatened or put on the defensive. A kind heart doesn't corner or demand; instead, it patiently and confidently waits for the repeated dismissals to fall to the ground.

This can be maddening. A dismissive person can shrug, roll his or her eyes, or simply say, "No, you're wrong," and end the discussion. The dismissive person is often unaware he or she is being dismissive. When asked what he or she feels, a dismissive person might say, "Nothing. I feel fine." There is often a lack of internal dialogue or openness to being questioned.

This can easily degenerate into a fight or indifference on the part of the one asking for engagement. What difference does it make if I ask how you are feeling, since I never seem to get anything back other than anger or contempt? But kindness is not fooled. When kindness is also wise, it pursues not only the dismissive person's refusal to engage but also, much more importantly, the story that bent the person to take a dismissive stance in the first place.

Calling Forth Wholeness

We are called to live as whole beings with full hearts in the beauty and brokenness of this world. Though this may sound highly spiritual and removed from day-to-day existence, it is, in fact, the height of what it means to be human. As human beings, we are meant to live each moment of our life, in every activity and in all relationships, with a heart ready and able to receive and to give.

The fact that this is rare doesn't make it a single bit less true or less important. The scarcity of people on the earth who live full, deep, rich lives open to heartache and simultaneously embracing joy makes it that much more crucial to intend to do so on one's own behalf, and even more for the sake of those we love.

I have often described myself as a lazy therapist. I am willing to put an inordinate amount of hours into projects or tasks but I am less willing to do so with people. One of the reasons I find myself preferring to work with abused men and women is simple: this population doesn't need to be convinced that life is broken. Heartache has seeped into almost every sinew and cell. What is deeply questioned is whether or not there is really goodness, love, truth, beauty, and wisdom in trusting again.

It is painful work to enter the stories of death, but it is not hard work. Hard work is trying to open the door to the self-righteous, the optimists, and the turn-the-lemons-into-lemonade self-doers to help them see that all their work, wisdom, and strength will not put Humpty Dumpty back together again.

Kindness disrupts the soul and calls it from death to life. When we let go of attempting to protect and provide for ourselves, we discover that God was our truest desire all along. Kindness has the power to lead us to repentance. Repentance involves a turn from the path of self-righteousness to trusting the righteous death of Jesus as sufficient to cover our shame.

I spoke with a friend whose marriage is in turmoil because his wife discovered his pornographic files. He is thick in remorse and self-loathing. He hates the pain he has caused his wife and adult children. He is broken and his sorrow stings like salt in a wound. As is predictable when shame rules, there was no hint of rest or relief in his sorrow. I told him that if he continued to indulge shame, the return to pornography, as inconceivable as it would seem now, was assured. Shame is the fertile ground where all addictions grow.

We talked about the forgiveness of God. He said, "Even if God forgives me, I don't know if I will ever be able to forgive myself." The fact is that he is a profoundly gifted man, rich with wisdom, competence, and skill in his profession and life, but he is also a man who has long eschewed his need for kindness and delight.

He has a lengthy and troubled history of an entangled and emotionally incestuous relationship with his mother that is only beginning to be engaged. He is far more comfortable with holding his life in contempt and then working to restore his losses through backbreaking labor. But this breakage can't be fixed by sincere and faithful restoration. It will only come through kindness. As we talked, he said, "I can't believe God looks at me with kindness, let alone delight. It is too hard to believe. It is too good to believe."

If the core war with kindness is the battle with hope, then it makes sense that God's kindness is not merely surprising; it is offensive. His kindness comes in the most unexpected moments, when we have forgotten he exists or denied that he could possibly be kind after all we have done. We know that we do not deserve the joy we see in his eyes. We deserve judgment—we receive care. Kindness calls the heavy heart to struggle honestly with the Creator, with all the heartache and doubt that resides in our heart. God can bear our questions and rage and doesn't turn away in either fear or disgust. Rather he moves toward us, without overtaking us or intruding, and offers a kindness that sings life to our heart.

The singular quality of a full heart is the capacity to take in both grief and joy and to offer to others tears and laughter. To laugh with those who know joy and to weep with those who suffer sorrow is the height of what it means to be human. This giving and receiving increase desire and intimacy whenever they are enacted. And in turn, they break down every other enactment that compromises love. As simple as it may sound, love heals the heart and every dimension of life to which it flows.

A heart open to suffering and to receiving and offering blessing will know joy. Joy is not the absence of heartache but the capacity to know that death never has the final word. Joy begins with receiving goodness and in turn offering kindness that transforms both the one who gives and the one who receives. As hard as it is to believe, there is joy ahead for those who have been abused.

9

The Promise of Joy

For all who rely on the works of the law are under a curse, as it is written: "Cursed is everyone who does not continue to do everything written in the Book of the Law." Clearly no one who relies on the law is justified before God, because "the righteous will live by faith." The law is not based on faith; on the contrary, it says, "The person who does these things will live by them." Christ redeemed us from the curse of the law by becoming a curse for us, for it is written: "Cursed is everyone who is hung on a pole." He redeemed us in order that the blessing given to Abraham might come to the Gentiles through Christ Jesus, so that by faith we might receive the promise of the Spirit.

Galatians 3:10–14

The hardest interview I have done in the past twenty-five years was with two Christian radio jocks who took the topic of sexual abuse as seriously as drunk frat boys. Within the first minute, one of the dudes said, "Is this show about how to do it or get over it?" I asked him directly, "Are you nuts?"

There was a tittering of laughter on their part—none on mine. They straightened up, then, and did the interview. I never stopped wanting to hurt them. I cursed them in my heart. I am called to bless my enemy, but at the time I didn't want to bless, let alone did I have the wisdom to know what that would look like or how to do so.

I have since learned to bless my enemies, a little, at times, including my father, who asked me after *The Wounded Heart* was published why I had written a "dirty" book. The issues of sexual abuse have been the basis of the loss of friendships and professional relationships. There has been a legion of debris that has come to my life and family as a result of this work.

But what is truer than these things is that I have been blessed tens of thousands of times beyond what I have deserved, given the harm I have done to family, friends, clients, students, colleagues, mentors, and a long list of assorted strangers. What I am most aware of is that cursing will not win; blessing will prevail. All violence will one day fade in the light of unbounded love.

But the current struggle, arising out of the damage of abuse, is what we will do with the lingering and at times pervasive curse over our life. Humanity was never cursed after Adam and Eve tasted the fruit of the knowledge of good and evil. The serpent was cursed to crawl. The ground was cursed to bear thorns and thistles. Humanity bears the effects of the curse indirectly through desire that feels too desperate to birth and futility that seems too pointless to work against. We live in a bloodstained, curse-bound world. There is an endless cycle of hunger-fueled, empty violence that devours the weak of every genus and species.

This cycle would be an endless circle of reenactment of predator-prey violence—except for the incarnation, crucifixion, resurrection, and ascension of Christ Jesus. The gospel story nudges all other stories toward a different trajectory. It parallels and intersects our story without eclipsing our suffering or joy. The gospel doesn't replace our story; it actually gives it even greater meaning. His story is mine and my story is his, and all the stories in the world are ours—all for the sake of blessing what is to be blessed and cursing what God despises.

All change regarding the harm of abuse begins with the awareness that someone must bear the curse with me and, far more, take my curse from me. Jesus suffered the trauma and abuse of a creation set against its Creator and endured the unrighteous setup, harm, contempt, and mockery of the seen and unseen realms. He did so in order to free us from the curse of sin and evil and bondage to its power of accusation.

From the outset it needs to be underscored that this process of healing is not an event or the completion of an established sequence of steps. Let me contrast what I am suggesting with many models I have encountered that offer help to those who have been abused. I don't believe in quick, methodological cures, whether that cure is a series of EMDR sessions, healing prayer, theophostic therapy, or spiritual warfare. For example, I have worked with a legion of men and women who have had a significant experience of having Jesus brought to their imagination as a source of comfort and solace during the experience of sexual abuse. "Imagine Jesus sitting next to you as your father is abusing you. Look at his face, his kindness. Turn from your self-hatred and let his face bring you comfort." And though it may seem contradictory to my argument, significant change often does come from these interventions. The underlying assumption, however, is that once cured the work is finished. The wound is resolved, forgiveness completed—tidy and complete. This sets up a vicious cycle of hiding new layers of abuse that become exposed once the "cure" is finished. Or perhaps even worse, it serves as the self-righteous claim that "I have been healed and you can be too if you follow the same path that I chose."

The truth is sexual abuse, like all trauma, must be engaged again and again as the heart matures and has new awareness, insight, and freedom. The scars never go away, but their meaning and power can grow as new freedom and choice provide access to even deeper understanding. I can only move out of myself to bless if there has been a movement inward to receive blessing. As well, I can only receive blessing to the degree that I desire to give it away.

No wonder evil works so hard to curse the heart's and body's joy in receiving and giving pleasure. Once this reciprocal movement is marred, the entire process of loving, blessing, and celebrating life is marred. It is therefore through blessing that God reconciles our wounded heart and restores the joy that is our birthright.

Blessing Desire through Awe

Blessing involves using the authority God gave us to name something as beautiful, good, and true. One morning, I watched from my lakeside hotel window as an older man appeared. He walked slowly and with pain. He took out of a shed a paddle and a life jacket. He then walked to a kayak and bent over with difficulty to pull the boat to the water. It took time, but he finally situated himself in the boat and began to paddle out onto the water. My back aches, and it is easy to sit and write and not exercise. I felt initially nothing more than curiosity and slight envy. But I found myself vocalizing a blessing over this man's tenacious commitment to enter the chilly waters early in the morning.

Blessing first names goodness. Do we know beauty when we see it? Courage? Honor? Perseverance? Resilience? Kindness? Generosity? I saw the man and I spoke out loud my admiration of him for not being limited by his aging body.

The second element of blessing is a desire to see, taste, touch, smell, hear—in other words, to sensually encounter the goodness so we can become more of what we bless. As I blessed him I realized I too could move. Blessing is not an abstract wish, something hidden in the heart that passes like a whim. It is articulate and draws the one who blesses to participate in the blessing itself. After I blessed that older man, I stopped writing and took an hour to exercise and work on the tight muscles constricting my back.

Desire is the impetus God uses to draw us to himself. Not all desires bear goodness and honor, but desire, even at its darkest, can't escape the imprint of the Creator. Even the desire to destroy God reveals that one's heart is being lived toward him, and all efforts to annihilate God leave us emptier and angrier. We simply can't annihilate desire even through suicide. Desire can't be destroyed. It is to be blessed through awe.

One of the deepest wars for an abused person is to bless the desire that was wickedly read by the abuser and used to make entry into the heart. A man told me how his mother would take him to a babysitter, and he would cry and occasionally vomit before he got out of the car. His mother called him a "drama queen." He was flamboyant and full of passion, and it made him difficult for his mother to control.

My client hated to go every day to his sitter, yet it was in relationship with an older, mentally disadvantaged predator that he found the sweetness of a delight he seldom experienced at home. His father was distant and critical. His mother was demanding and occasionally present and concerned, but more often irritated. He learned to hold wretched anxiety and disgust and delight. It was a toxic drink.

When I asked him to tell me what it was like to put on shows and entertain his abuser with skits, songs, and comedy, he lit up for a brief moment and then a shudder of contempt covered his face. I caught it. I named what I had experienced with him: artistry in his language. He smiled and turned away. He could not bear being seen for what had bonded him more deeply with his abuser.

We were at a critical point. I asked him what he saw when he pictured the little boy staging a theatrical presentation. He described the boy in detail, and then with a snarl at the end he said, "The little drama queen." He cursed the boy. He cursed his gifts and desire.

I asked him what it would cost him to see that little boy as clever, bold, and artistic. His look could have turned Medusa into harder stone. "I'd have to grieve that no one but my mentally retarded abuser saw those gifts and delighted in me." The cost was naming even more deeply the loss of life and the setup for abuse in his relationship with his mother and father. It was too much. It would likely cost his current relationship with them, which had been patched together because he was now a rich man and his family was far poorer and needed his help.

His stance toward the boy was to curse; my ground was, and is, to bless. And we were at loggerheads for months. He brought me data weekly of his selfishness and drama queen reactivity. But the boy was never far away and occasionally came to peek out from the back of the stage to see if I was mocking him or was truly sincere.

We are meant to be in awe of the Creator and his creation. We are meant to be captured by the wonder of a waterfall and a deep cavern. If we are to be in awe of creation, then we must be in awe as well of how we are fearfully and wonderfully made. And that includes our gifts, character, way of being in the world, and the ways we attempted to address and resolve the agonies of abuse. If we are not in awe of the little boy or girl we once were, we will not be in awe of who we have become as a result of our struggle. We are meant to be in awe of who we were, who we are becoming, and the new heart that we have been given.

Blessing Arousal through Gratitude

Evil means for the arousal associated with sexual abuse to drive shame deep into our heart and silence us. Evil intends for the pitched battle to become a civil war that ruins the integrity of our body and heart. In my life, evil accomplished this through addictions and drug dealing. The use of drugs and the power to make considerable sums of money while dealing were a salve to stories I could not bear to remember. Then evil planned to use the war to cover its tracks as it seduced me to harm others and myself, while I unwittingly served its kingdom. It almost won. The harm I did is immeasurable, but by God's mercy Jesus turned my heart toward him and began a major process of renovation and transformation.

I am not now nor will I ever be grateful for being abused—no more than I am grateful that I too harmed many others in the wake of the abuse. I grieve my sin; I am sickened and heartbroken about what every abuse victim has endured. But I am also aware that evil despises gratitude even more than exposure. It can't bear how, as Luther said, "Evil has taken me more often to the cross than even my friends."

Gratitude is one of the strongest weapons we have against the work of evil. And it is not a silly positivity that finds good in all sorts of harm. The turn-lemons-into-lemonade strategy may be helpful for dealing with a missed flight, but it is not robust enough to engage the kind of tragedies this book is addressing. We need a meatier gratitude that can stand up to the most hideous harm known to humanity. This is the gratitude for life itself, for the pleasure of breathing and moving. For the pleasure of watching a sunset and hearing the coo of a turtledove. If we can't drink in the wonders of this earth and bless the pleasure of light, rain, touch, and bread, then we have given our heart over to death. And many have.

For an abuse victim the hardest labor is to bless the body for the pulse of pleasure in the touch of hair, the stroking of an arm, or the erection that brought the clitoris or penis to the point of heightened arousal, whether there was an orgasm or not. To bless the pleasure, as one client said, "feels like I am letting my abuser win." But in fact, to hate the body's capacity for arousal and plea-sure is not only letting the abuser win but also falling into the arms of the evil one.

We are called to bless what God blesses. And he blesses sexual and genital arousal. Can you feel the abused person's natural repulsion to this last sentence? We want to scream, "No! I will never bless what I felt with the abuser!" This refusal makes it impossible to enter the memories of abuse, because as we do so we will feel remnants of the arousal we felt with the abuser. It not only secures that we will not enter our memory but often forces us to turn against that arousal with swift and harsh judgment. We turn from our shame in the past to contempt in the present. There are some who think they can bless their sexuality today and hate it when they were eight. The fact is if we hate our arousal at eight, it will bleed into disgust for it today. Pollution of the river at its wellspring will flow through all its tributaries.

Others are willing to bless their arousal but refuse to enter the memories with depth and detail. Remember a core principle: we change at the level we are willing to enter reality. If that reality is entered at thirty thousand feet, then change will occur at that altitude and it will be too high to affect what the body and heart feel down in the dirt of reality.

I worked with a woman who told me that she had read *The Wounded Heart* and it had helped her, except in terms of nightmares and a profound hatred of sex. When we talked in greater detail, she told me that she hated sleep because it was filled with dreams of sexual perversion and degradation. The dreams were primarily about a faceless man using her sexually and occasionally performing oral sex. The combination of the sexual arousal and the experience of oral sex in her dreams was enough to make her feel like a shameless pervert. When I told her that her dreams were sad and involved emotional violence and misuse but were not perverse, she was incensed. I was told I was likely a misogynistic sex addict.

She remained in therapy, and we continued to talk about her use of *The Wounded Heart*. She informed me she would stay in the conversation because she appreciated the book in spite of my misunderstanding of her dreams. Eventually she told me that she could not get within a universe of remembering the abuse because to do so caused her to feel anxious and nauseated. She let it slip that when she got close to the memories her body began to "tingle." I asked what it felt like and she dropped her eyes. "It feels like my body wants what I know is evil to want."

More exploration brought us to this boundary: her body had felt alive and simultaneously terrified when the abuser would begin to take her clothes off. Before all her clothes were off she would disappear and go numb in her mind and body. She didn't recall what happened or remember anything she felt during the abuse.

I asked her a simple question: "What do you think the body of an eight-year-old girl would feel if she suffers oral sex?" In this case, the word *suffer* was the key that unlocked the door. She burst into tears and said, "I did suffer. I know I suffered and he was so gentle and took so much time to make me feel good." She was as surprised by her words as I was. She now was at a profound moral juncture: Would she curse that little girl's vaginal pleasure, or would she bless the pleasure and her vagina's capacity for arousal, as well as acknowledge and honor the nausea and terror?

It is when we enter the story's deepest well of shame—the moment or moments when evil has whispered its greatest accusations and contempt—that we are most empowered to stand against the plot of darkness and embrace the grief of God. It is in those darkest moments when our brain is experiencing the memory in the present that we can turn to embrace the God-given gift of arousal.

Blessing arousal is, at its core, blessing the way God has wired our genitals to experience pleasure and arousal. It is not blessing what happened. This is the conundrum that trips up many. *I can bless what I felt without blessing how the feeling came to be.* By blessing the arousal, we are standing against the accusations that we "wanted it" and that we are culpable because we were a coparticipant in the arousal. *I wanted what the abuser offered through grooming, but I didn't know that I was being groomed or what the grooming was setting me up to suffer.*

We bless when we are grateful that our body bears the capacity for arousal that bonds our heart and body to another human being. We are meant to be bonded and to express and experience through our body the delight of love. Sadly, what occurs in abuse is not bonding but bondage. We must loosen the bondage through forgiveness.

Blessing Freedom through Forgiveness

We are told not to let the sun go down on unaddressed anger. The reason for this warning is that bitterness, rage, slander, and every form of malice open our heart to evil, allowing it to take ground, or a foothold, in our heart (see Eph. 4:26–27). The apostle Paul is not saying that all anger is wrong—only anger that seethes and condenses into a fermented fury that makes us refuse to work toward healing and transformation.

It is a dark and hideous reality: the more hatred we have for those who do us harm, the more bondage we enter into, not only with the person we hate but also with the one who is the father of lies and hatred. And we fool no one, especially evil, when we take the stance of indifference: *I don't hate him; I simply never want anything to do with him or to ever think about him.* Indifference is simply hatred with a blank face.

Jesus tells us that we have power to bind and loosen on this earth what will be bound and loosened in heaven (see Matt. 16:19; 18:18). We are not to be bound to deceit, lies, and contempt; we are to loosen our heart from every judgment, accusation, and the mockery of evil. Blessing our body and sexuality with awe and gratitude brings a huge change in our heart.

But something more is needed: the bondage to evil's accusations and authority needs to be shattered. It has likely gained a stronghold through hatred of self, the abuser, authorities who failed to act with integrity, and parents who failed to provide what the abuser offered through his or her grooming. There is hatred, and it has to be addressed as both a psychological and a spiritual issue.

A stronghold implies that evil has gained access to some of the topography of our heart. We must address the squatter(s) who inhabit(s) our land and property as if it were their own. Every vow and agreement we make with evil gives it access to another portion of our heart. While our heart is fully under the authority of Christ Jesus when we give our life to him, apparently we can give portions of our heart back to evil as we harbor hatred and find succor in contempt.

The last thing I wish to be heard saying is that an abuse victim should be hounded or confronted into forgiving. The desire to forgive is acquired through honest grieving and caring for the wounds that exist. Quick forgiveness, like any fight-or-flight oriented behavior, only reinforces the harm and doesn't bring about healing.

However, Jesus gives us authority over powers, authorities, and principalities through prayer. We are to loosen every form of bondage, whether it is sexual, psychological, spiritual, physical, systemic, political, economic, or ecological. We are to stand against evil and speak: "Hell, no." We are to be clothed in the armaments of God in order to expose the schemes of the devil (see Eph. 6:12–17). We are to resist the devil and he will flee (see James 4:7).

However scary this might sound, or how preposterous it might seem to a mind given to denying the unseen spiritual world, it is imperative that we use the authority given us to loosen the bondage that weds us to our abuser through resentment and contempt. As we forgive those who have done us harm, we cut through the tentacles that bind us to the abuser, and far more to the kingdom of darkness. God desires that we, instead of binding ourselves to judgment and contempt, bind every enemy through participating in the wonder of forgiveness.

The woman I worked with who hated arousal and the capacity of her vagina to bring pleasure eventually acknowledged that evil had invited her to curse her body, especially with a gentle man. Sadly, she had married a man who was harsh and critical. She could relax with his contempt and escape her terror of kindness.

She was willing to open her heart to more awe and gratitude. She entered many torturous moments of past arousal and began imagining what she would have felt as a young girl in the arms of her abuser. The deeper she entered her story, the more she sensed an external darkness and mockery that felt relentless and cruel. She felt haunted, at times, by a presence that felt eerily like being with her abuser. She said, "I feel like I am being pursued by something that is not in me." We talked about vows and agreements, the plan of evil, and its capacity to take footholds in our heart.

It didn't take long before she said she wanted to reclaim those sectors of her heart. We prayed against two of her vows:

1. *No gentle and kind man will ever have access to my heart and body again.*
2. *Every sexual pleasure I experience only proves again that what happened with my abuser was just as much my fault as it was his.*

She broke both of those vows. The result was freedom to forgive her body for having felt pleasure and in turn to forgive her abuser for violating her. But I reiterate: it is not magic. These vows were broken only after she did immense personal work in facing the debris of her life, telling the stories of abuse with immense particularity, and pursuing Jesus and hearing from him the desires of his heart.

None of this took away her relational struggles, but it did give her more energy and courage to deal with her angry husband. She asked him to stop demeaning her when she felt sorrow. She named his contempt and offered him kindness and space to wrestle with his failure of her. Eventually, she began to invite him to touch her with kindness and sensuality. It took a long time, but her stance to loosen the bondage of resentment through forgiveness increased her desire to forgive her abuser.

Like my client, I know I have countless more vows and agreements to break from over six decades on this earth. There is much more healing for me, especially as I age and can't use my retinue of schemes to escape from reality. But we don't need to operate with fear regarding the vows that are unaddressed in our heart. In due season, the goodness of God will make clear what needs to be addressed next. As each vow is broken, our heart will open to receive new gifts from Jesus. Jesus loves to give gifts, and he is utterly unpredictable and generous in his offer of delight.

Blessing Delight through Play

When Jesus ascended to the right hand of the Father, he disposed a kingdom onto his disciples and gave gifts. Jesus is a gift-giving, delightful presence. Any voice masquerading as Jesus that is critical, belittling, or demeaning is not Jesus. His sheep know his voice, and he is consistently calling every human being to his love. When portions of our heart are given back to him, he delights in giving gifts, just as his Father, through the story of the prodigal son, gave the boy new clothes, a ring, and sandals. Those gifts were marks of honor. Each gift bears new privilege and indicates full and complete restoration.

A man I worked with, who had told Jesus he was done with him and refused to pray or engage in any past activity of faith, began to address his abuse. His story involved being abused by a coach who pushed him hard to succeed, and when he achieved beyond expectation, the coach took him to get an ice-cream float. Amid the celebration his coach began to touch him and led him to mutual masturbation. The craft of this abuser was so supreme that my client remembered actually being the one to make the first touch. After a few conversations he remembered how often the coach had talked about masturbation and normalized an orgasm as the finish to any great victory.

He also remembered feeling woozy and exhausted the night he first touched his coach. The sensation of being drugged occurred about a half hour after drinking the float. His eyes flared with rage. "The bastard not only groomed me, he drugged me after I was the happiest I had ever been up to that minute."

Rage enabled him to name the genius of the abuser in picking his happiest moment to begin what would be a three-year abusive relationship. He was heartbroken that he had failed to see both the setup and that the shared responsibility for the supposed "affair" was in fact planned and brilliantly executed sexual abuse. But he also began to see that he had come to hate any celebration or anyone who enjoyed him. He named and broke the vow that he would hate anyone who delighted in him.

Later that day he ended up in a mall, and as he entered the door, he heard Jesus say to him, "I want to go shopping with you. Will you let me join you?" He laughed out loud and figured he was having a near psychotic moment. He said, "Sure. Where do you want to go?" Jesus knew this man was a fabulous chef, and he said, "Let's go to a cooking store." So the man wandered through the store, and eventually he discovered a saltbox. He quickly decided to buy it and then he heard Jesus ask him, "Do you really like the color?" He laughed out loud. He replied, "No, it is dull and ugly blue." He heard laughter. Jesus then said, "Let's keep looking."

They talked, laughed, and played with each other. My client said he kept pinching himself to make sure he was not drugged or crazy. It was simply beyond weird to interact with Jesus after never hearing his voice directly and wishing for over a year not to be at all involved with him.

At another store that appeared to have some cooking supplies, he asked the clerk if he had any saltboxes. He smiled and said, "Oh, do I! Follow me." He led him to the back of the store and said, "These just came in yesterday." He waved his hand across shelves that held more than eighty saltboxes. My client simply knew it was all for him.

It pains me to know that there are many who read this and say, "Why not me? When I turned from God I heard nothing but static and saw only a cold, pale sky." I can't predict when or how gifts will come, but I know and have seen in a myriad of lives the presence of the gift-giving Jesus who loves to shower his children with delight. The fact that he does so each time the sun rises often goes without notice. Often his gifts are deflected or ignored because of the deep vows we have made that stuff our ears with cotton or shield our eyes with blinders. But when we open our heart to delight and play, we are tuned in to the frequency he uses to speak. When we begin to bless the young child who was abused, enter the narrative where shame is lodged, and do the hard work of excavating our heart, joy comes.

10

Caring for Another's Story

To mourn and wonder, that is what the spirit yearns for when it stands in the midst of trauma and breathes in the truth of grace. Mourning and wonder— neither one answers the question that trauma poses to grace. They are, instead, states of mind that, if nurtured, open us to the experience of God's coming into torn flesh, and to love's arrival amid violent ruptures.

Serene Jones

If stories come to you, care for them. And learn to give them away where they are needed. Sometimes a person needs a story more than food to stay alive.

Barry Lopez

The privilege of being given access to the story of a victim of sexual abuse is holy. It is a gift few on this earth are honored to receive. It is difficult terrain to enter, but healing requires the submission of one's story to the heart and mind of a guide and a community of pilgrims whose passion is set on the kingdom of God. The harm of sexual abuse was done in relationship, and it is only through relationship that victims regain the vision to live in freedom.

An abuse story told, no matter how difficult it is for the one telling it, is merely an announcement that a crime has taken place in their mansion. The story acknowledges, to some degree, why the mansion is in such disrepair, while making it clear that there are many locked rooms, barricaded wings, and trashed hallways that in due season will need to be engaged, but only when and if the person is ready. An abuse story must be heard not as the telling of an event but as an entry into a journey. The telling must be received with one's shoes off and hands open to take in all that is said. It is as though the listener is being given a tour of a large, aristocratic mansion that has fallen into disarray over decades. A trusted hearer is given access to the rooms most lived in, but there are many locked doors entered only by the owner, and vast wings of the mansion are off-limits to everyone, including the teller of the story.

Whether the listener is a therapist, minister, spouse, or friend, the announcement of abuse can't be presumed to be an offer to enter the home. One must ask for permission. To care well for the victim of sexual abuse, there can't be a rudeness or demand to enter stories of heartache and shame. One can't command, will, or teach shame away. It must be entered and inhabited. It must be accepted as the terrain we are called to walk. We may wish the road were paved, but it is not. We may wish we didn't have to pass through briars and thick underbrush, but we do. Those who want prepackaged tours with wild animals viewed through a two-inch-thick pane of glass and gourmet meals promptly and professionally served at 9, 12, and 6 ought to remain home.

Entering the domain of abuse sounds scary—and it is. No wonder many view this terrain as too dangerous to walk unless they are an experienced therapist. The fear of doing harm is legitimate. But if the person who is sharing trusts the listener enough to offer their story, the caring friend will do more harm by trying to defer.

There are many ways to become a better caregiver for abuse stories, but only two things are required to begin: humility and courage. Skill will eventually follow.

Resist Superficial Cures

Sexual abuse is so deeply disturbing that most good-hearted people ache to help and resolve the suffering. Who in their right mind would choose to go swimming in the sordid waters of sexual darkness, violence, betrayal, rage, confusion, suspicion, and a legion of other toxic harm? Most caring people stand on the bank of these waters that seem to be diseased and dangerous, far enough away from the melee to not get polluted. Who can blame them for wanting to offer sincere, albeit superficial, cures?

Most often the story is first told to a trusted friend or therapist. It is told not to engage and explore the story but to see how the telling will be received. Abused persons fear that their anger will be condemned. For that reason, many are reluctant to be angry or allow their anger to be seen. *How will the hearer respond? How will I bear having the story heard by someone else? Will I believe the story I told if the hearer denounces my story or my feelings?* These questions are far more at the surface than the story itself.

The majority of the sexual abuse clients I work with profess to be Christians. It is my opinion that Christians have more resources than most to engage trauma both past and present, but sadly, many abused men and women have been told, overtly or subtly, that if they are stuck with symptoms, memories, and heartache, it is proof that they are failing to believe.

The most sincere believers are, by far, the most likely to feel guilty for struggling.

> *If only I could keep my eyes on Jesus, then I would not be so bound to my past.*

If only I could forgive, then I'd be free.
If only I believed the gospel, I wouldn't be suffering.

The assumption is that the resurrection overcomes sin, death, and suffering once and for all in the here and now. This is bad theology, and if the listener voices this view, it is cruel.

A healing community desperately needs to be courageous enough to enter the realm of shame and arousal without spiritualizing or cutting off the engagement through a cheap trick of quick healing. This process is not going to be finished by one prayer, confession, or renewal of the Spirit. It comes when the war is truly faced and fought. When the enemy is clearer and the bondage is named with appropriate grief and desire for liberation, the Spirit of the Holy God can take broken and courageous survivors of sexual abuse on the journey of their lives.

What is needed is a view of the resurrection that is not the immediate resolution of the story but the inciting basis to enter the waters of death—with the promise that death will not have the final word. In her brilliant work *Spirit and Trauma: A Theology of Remaining*, Shelly Rambo writes, "Theology must account for the excess, or remainder, of death in life that is central to trauma. This reconfiguration of death and life, viewed through the lens of trauma, unearths a distinctive theology that can witness the realities of the aftermath of trauma."[1] She warns, "Insofar as resurrection is proclaimed as life conquering or life victorious over death, it does not speak to the realities of traumatic suffering. In fact, one must recognize the ways in which resurrection proclamations may gloss over and negate the difficult experience of life in the aftermath of trauma."[2]

Rambo disrupts a Christian triumphalism that obscures human suffering by raising resurrection Sunday as a panacea rather than as the courageous hope to enter the humiliation of abuse Friday and the despair of hell Saturday. The truth is, trauma is an encounter with the unspeakable. It disrupts the victim's sense of self, of time, and of meaning. It slurs his or her memory and forces his or her speech to stumble. Any effort to hear his or her story must be done with a theology that does not see Friday (death), Saturday (hell), and Sunday (resurrection) as linear and finished; instead we must allow Sunday to offer us the courage to enter the humiliation and violence of Friday and the utter silent emptiness of Saturday. The promise of the resurrection enables us to go further into his or her suffering.

Few stories are engaged well in the first hearing. The normal stance of a listener is to wait until the full story has been told and then interact. Because an abuse story is full of so much heartache, most listeners feel overwhelmed and offer little but sympathy. "I am so sorry for all that you have endured. I don't know how you have lived with this harm for so long alone. Thank you for sharing." Imagine what this offers to the victim who has finished and now looks at the listener. The burden is back on the victim to speak, and likely any sense of relief is mixed with shame, fear, gratitude, numbness, and intense body sensations. In most occasions the story ends, the conversation shifts, and tragically the hearer succumbs to offering advice: "Have you thought of seeing a therapist?" "Have you forgiven the abuser?" Or the hearer lauds the teller and remarks, "You are so brave. I could never share what you just did."

These kinds of responses, though tempting in their avoidance of another's overwhelming grief and anger, will only enable both hearer and teller to maintain a thirty-thousand-foot view of the debris. Mere empathy is sweet but simply validates the story without opening the door to deeper exploration. Greater healing requires greater entry into the story of harm.

Every human being is desperate to be known, to be heard; every human being is also terrified, and often contemptuous, of being pursued and indwelled. We are ambivalent. Or, more concretely stated, we have one hand up, saying, "Keep your distance," and the other hand gesturing, saying, "Come, come, please don't leave me alone." It is this universal bind that keeps most conversations, even in marriage and close friendships, pleasant and distant. We sacrifice the depth of indwelling for the comfortable distance of pleasantness. We glide against the surface of the other and refuse to do harm by creating offense, confusion, or more pain. The desire to do no harm, honorable as it is, precludes the ability to step into the dark, cold, and fast waters of shame. What must we do instead?

Be Prepared to Meet the Guards at the Door

Stories fused with shame are told with sleight of hand. It is like watching a carnival worker playing the shell game; a pea is put under a shell and then with lightning speed the shells are whisked in a mesmerizing dance that blurs the eyes. Soon we see only what the teller of the story wants us to see. This is not usually a consciously intended deception; it is a natural defense intended to keep both the teller and the hearer from having to plunge into the dark waters.

As I listen to a story I let my imagination see what is happening. Where does the story get fuzzy? Where are details, context, character development, plot, and process told quickly? Where does the story fail to elicit image and sight? I don't merely hear words; I let words create scenes and images. It is like reading good fiction. You don't merely read words; you conjure in your mind the hero: how he or she looks, speaks, moves, laughs, and fights. When an action scene arises you can feel your heart rate increase and your muscles tighten as danger is engaged. The dilemma for many is that this evokes too many emotions.

Perhaps it is clear why this natural skill is not often utilized in hearing a story of abuse. The teller doesn't want to bring his or her body to the story and feel what was felt during the abuse; the hearer doesn't want to feel the terror, fury, confusion, or arousal that is an inevitable part of the process of telling. We anesthetize the impact of the story by distancing ourselves. But this approach will always create gaps and contradictions.

We need to stumble into these gaps and trip over the apparent contradictions. Yet we shouldn't ask a person to fill in an incomplete story or explain an apparent contradiction. We don't ask for more detail. We don't ask a person to plunge into waters that he or she is unready or unwilling to enter. Rather, our task is merely to offer to the other our awareness that certain portions of the story have been passed over, are vague, or have been told with emotional sleight of hand. This gives the teller the right to privacy and the freedom to enter the untold terrain if he or she chooses. Pushing the teller forward before he or she is ready is to increase his or her shame rather than to offer to dwell with him or her in the darkness.

Shame boils to the surface in the form of contempt when we are closest to the deepest desires of the heart. Where there is hidden shame, contempt will surface. Skillfully listening for shame and contempt is like having a diviner's rod—a special divided stick that, when held by a sensitive reader of the terrain, will point to underground water. Contempt, when read well, always takes the hearer of the story to the storage vats of shame.

Some forms of self-contempt are as discernible as the scent downwind from a turkey farm. These individuals have a way of being in the world that is a relentless undermining of themselves. Other forms of self-contempt are more sophisticated and difficult to read. They may be so infused in the way a person lives that they are indistinguishable from his or her personality. At times self-contempt masquerades as humility, but more often it is evidence of a strong commitment not to require anything of others.

Or consider the role of other-centered contempt: this manner of relating to others is fueled by a relentless suspicion and sarcasm, an antagonizing strength that alienates and distances whenever the heart feels too vulnerable. In either case, self- or other-centered contempt has the same goal: distance from shame.

I will never allow a person to tell me a story of abuse unless I have confidence the teller can remain present in the telling.[3] This requires

177

some history of knowing how emotionally attuned he or she is with stories that bear less heartache and shame than the darkest stories of abuse. What happens when a person feels overwhelmed by emotion? Is he or she able to stop and care for the disrupted self, or does he or she shut down and keep telling the story without being present? Is he or she able to remain kind in the telling, or does contempt rise in a growing fury against one's self or the other?

The first telling has often been practiced, as a person conceptualizes what he or she can tell. It usually includes a context, or setting, an account of the process of how the abuse began, something about the abuser, and a statement about what happened after the initial abuse. It is usually diffuse and vague. There is more often than not a preponderance of shame, a high level of anxiety, and a disconnection from what is felt in the body. At worst it is an itinerary of an abusive event told in the dispassionate tone of a reporter. For the abuse victim it is agonizing; even with emotions blunted with dissociation, it feels like jumping out of a plane without a parachute.

Research indicates that the way the story is told often depends on the nature of a person's attachment structure.[4] It was found that when asked to talk about their parents and what it was like to grow up in their family, people with secure attachment were honest, balanced, detailed, and coherent in their storytelling. There was a significant difference with those who were insecurely attached. Ambivalent-attached storytellers tended to have "excessive, poorly organized verbal output that lacked boundaries between past and present. They appeared preoccupied, pressured, and had difficulty keeping the perspective of the listener in mind."[5] Avoidant- or dismissive-attached persons tended to have little recall of their past, and what they did remember was distant and less coherent. They were far more dismissive and defensive as the stories were told. It stands to reason that our attachment style, which affects how our brain is dispatched to metabolize trauma, would influence how we tell stories of our past abuse.

Trauma steals the ability to speak with depth and clarity about what happened to us. There is simply no point in listening to a story of abuse that is hurried, adrenaline driven, or emotionless. The result will likely be an intense rise of stress and dissociation in the teller, along with an intensification of the sense of harm. One must engage the story only if the storyteller is aware of his or her body and its connection to the story as the story is being told.

Hearing a story of abuse well is similar to watching a nonrunner buy the gear to run a half marathon, come home, put the gear on, and go out to run 13.1 miles; no one with wisdom would allow a friend to do so. But this happens all the time with inexperienced listeners. If a person begins to tell a story of abuse, it is wise to stop them and say, "I am honored to hear your story, but I need to ask you some questions:

1. If during the telling of your story I sense you emotionally leave or turn toward contempt for yourself, may I stop you and tell you what I hear?
2. If you can't tell any more without being absent or unkind, is it okay with you if that is where we stop until your heart can reengage?"

There is always the possibility of retraumatization if the teller is not present and capable of self-soothing kindness. Countless victims have said to me, "I have told this story again and again to friends and other caregivers, and each time I feel worse." More often than not, the person has not learned how to do self-care, especially during intimate exchanges, because the pain is too severe.

As basic as this may seem, we long, to our core, to be honored and delighted in. For an abused person, however, the prospect of this kind of intimacy is more than he or she can bear. The desire related to delight is more frightening than death itself. If this sounds extreme, consider the fact that every addict who dies of alcoholism, workaholism, perfectionism, or self-righteousness died in the bitterness, resentment, and fear related to the absence of delight. The same emotions accompany the abuse victim, and he or she will do anything to guard his or her heart. A good listener must always be prepared to meet the guards at the door as well as to help the teller move through his or her story without causing more self-harm.

Recognize the Dark Enemy

As I have written in earlier chapters, I believe we inhabit a complex story world where the seen and unseen intersect. Seldom is the intersection between the two realms unmistakably clear. Evil works far more often with the cloak of invisibility. It simply wants to destroy our life and then make us presume that it was entirely our own act or the observable harm of others that has caused our suffering. Denial of the true cause of the abuse can be ferocious.

Notice the parts of the abused person's story that seem off-limits or vague; when the person is engaged something arises that seems different from his or her interactions in other normal conversations. I had a proverbial church lady, a demure "good girl," look me fiercely in the eye and say, "My father was a good man. He didn't know about the abuse. Period. Discussion closed." I am not saying a demon took over and spoke. I am not saying a demon was not involved. But I believe I encountered a guard that was both a psychological defense mechanism and a dark spiritual warrior.

The woman turned hard and defensive, expecting me to back off or to try to take down her defenses. Again, it is not my task to remove the guard, whether it involves a spiritual presence or a psychological process or both; my only task is to name what I experience and offer the storyteller the data as to what I suspect, in general, may be behind the door and what will need to happen to open the door.

I said to her, "Your face has turned fierce and hard. The change is dramatic. You told me that you wanted to face what is true, but when you gave me data about your father's failure of love, you would rather have taken my head off than look at where you were failed. How do you want to proceed?"

She looked startled. As intimidating as she had become, she was only slightly aware of the bind she was creating. By acknowledging that she both wanted the truth and didn't, I gave her the choice as to how she proceeded into her story.

As a therapist, I knock on plenty of doors that many fear to approach. From the moment I meet a client, I am involved in a process of discernment, sensing and assessing what strongmen I am encountering. The more intelligence I can garner through listening to the Spirit of God, the better I am at knowing what will be involved in gaining entry into the heart. Entry is not given merely for the asking; instead, one must learn how to gain access through knocking with snakelike wisdom and childlike innocence.

To respond to an angry person who is drawing a line in the sand requires the ability not to flee or fight. Instead, it is a gift of innocence to remain present to the anger and not react to the fear (unless there is the threat of physical violence). Remaining present requires bringing both strength and kindness in equal force.

Follow the Yellow-Brick Theme

Every life is more than an anthology of stories, yet in a sense our life is one overarching story. Over a lifetime seemingly disparate and wildly divergent stories carry an uncanny thematic unity. We are ourselves, no matter when, where, or how. And certain patterns or traits remain at play irrespective of context. Even more, we are written by God to reveal something distinctive and unprecedented about his heart and way of relating to his creation. No one can reveal what I am meant to tell about God in the way that I am most uniquely meant to offer.

Years ago, in the midst of a major decision to start a new graduate school in Seattle, I also had the opportunity to take a job at an excellent theological school instead. Becky and I wrestled with a pro and con list, and the negatives for starting a new school clearly outweighed the positives. When a decision needed to be made, I said to my wife that it seemed obvious we ought to take the more reasonable option that had vastly more positives attached. Becky responded, "You have never in your life chosen the sensible option; why are you starting now?" I was stopped in my tracks. What a minute before had seemed inevitable was now being questioned on the basis of my wife reading the themes of my life story.

She then recounted my decision not to remain in the pastorate, the path I took to work in the area of sexual abuse, and a host of other odd and broken decisions. I was stunned. She was more than right; she was prophetic. She read my life, my stories, and discerned that I had seldom chosen the "smart" path; instead, it was a path more akin to the nomadic life of a prophet than the predictability of a priest or the formality of a king. That day we chose the "foolish" option, because my wife followed the yellow-brick road of my story.

It is never enough merely to follow the details of a story. The good listener is always looking to see the narrative arc and what the theme seems to offer as a window into the meaning of the story. My wife read not only the unique situation we were in but also my long history of being part of stories that didn't make a great deal of sense at the moment. She reminded me that God had been writing my "themes" well before I was old enough to make decisions.

A friend of mine is a successful entrepreneur. Nearly everything he has touched financially has flourished. He is popular, handsome, and was voted most likely to succeed in high school, college, and graduate school. It would be easy to look at his life and say he has the "golden touch." But this misses the point that our stories are meant to reveal the character of God. My friend was recently diagnosed with inoperable cancer. He told me, "I thought I was going to live a charmed life, and now I know that I get to live a few months that will be full of suffering and deterioration. Rather than having a charmed life, I get to live a life bound up with the real story of Jesus."

Christ's story has the narrative arc of suffering, death, resurrection, and taking on all authority and rule through his ascension. My friend will live his final months not charmed with the blessing of a happy story but with the depth of a bigger story written uniquely for him to live.

The gift he gave me in our final time together was knowledge of how I had brought him the courage to bless his last few months on earth. The gifts I gave him were my tears and my pursuit of his heart in the midst of dying. He said, "Few want to talk about death with me. They want me to hold on to a faint hope that the physicians or God will come up with a cure. I want that too. But I want to talk about dying and who I am to be in this story."

This is true for the abused person. Far too long the story has been hidden. When it finally surfaces, well-meaning people want to blow the acrid heartache away with platitudes. But we gift others when we live in their stories long enough to see the bricks that indicate a path. If we follow those themes long enough, they will take us to the brokenness and debris of the work of evil as well as the beauty of God's plan. What is most stunning, when one follows the path long enough, is to see the redemptive reversal of evil in the master craftsmanship of God.

Understand the Function of Memory

Every pastor, therapist, spouse, or friend who attempts to help faces the powerful barrier of smoothed over, largely erased, ignored, denied, or forgotten memories that are guarded by self-loathing or other-centered contempt. Here is the bind: as long as the memories remain vague, detached, ignored, and unexplored, the boy or girl is trapped behind the door as the guard fiercely defends against entry.

There is a way in, but it is only through the power of a story well engaged.

When victims of abuse begin to tell their stories later in life, the stories are usually told with a dark bias and with fear and shame. They are often told with the anticipation of being disbelieved or blamed. For a victim of sexual abuse, the fact that he or she trusted and opened his or her heart to an abuser is more than unforgivable. It is a shame that blights the heart and leaves trust of any sort nearly impossible. Further, it leaves the heart guarded against memory and any reentry into what could arouse the heart to what it once desired and embraced in the careful reading and pursuit of the abuser. Life depends on keeping the reality of the abuse far from consciousness.

The victim of sexual abuse remembers too much and too little.[6] Sexual abuse shatters reality into pieces. The abuser, whether through one act of falsity or thousands, rearranges reality by requiring the victim to live in a parallel universe. It is as if the abused is at least two separate persons—one who is known to all persons and another who is known only by the abuser.

This profound division in the mind, heart, and body of the abuse victim is hemispheric: left and right hemispheres of the brain are at odds, and the internal structure of memory, the interplay of the amygdala and hippocampus, are not in harmony.[7] The result is a disruption in memory and compromised capacity to tell the story. One study found that 38 percent of those who had been abused, even though the abuse had been documented at the time of the harm, had no memories of the event.[8]

Nevertheless, these memories are harbored in the body. We are flooded with oxytocin, the biochemical that is most pivotal in bonding. When a mother meets her child for the first time, there is a surge of oxytocin.[9] The same is true when a grandfather first gets to hold his grandson or granddaughter. It is the same with a crafty abuser. In offering something the child craves, a profound connection is established. The wiring in our brain doesn't allow us to truly forget.

Once we have bonded with someone, there is always the memory of that connection emblazoned on the brain.

I have heard victims of sexual abuse say they can't get rid of the abuser in their most intimate moments and deepest sorrows and joys. One said, "He haunts me. At my most vulnerable times of loneliness, I see his face. At the times of my most ecstatic sexual pleasure, he is there. When I am honored for an achievement or suffering the pangs of a failure, he is always with me. I read that Jesus is always with me, but the fact is my abuser is always more present to me than God."

It is not hard to fathom why the omnipresence of the abuser feels oppressive and consuming. Further, it makes sense why the abused person works ceaselessly to distance the abuser from his or her heart. Tragically, this distancing demands keen attention, even if the object of thought is ignored or denied. Even when the victim has turned against the abuser and the memory with bitter rage or hatred, he or she is actually reinforcing the bond with more intensity. It is as if the energy required to keep the abuser far inevitably brings him or her near, therefore requiring even more internal division to create a parallel world where the abuse and abuser don't exist.

A forty-two-year-old participant in a recovery group said:

Nights were the worst. During the day I knew who I was. I was a fourth grader in Mrs. McConnell's class. I wasn't the brightest and the one she smiled at when I went to the board, but I was smart enough to get an occasional, "Good job, Sandra." I was Sandy to everyone else, but she said my name like she meant it. I felt like I existed and knew my place in the world. It was as if I forgot my other world, until I was getting on the bus. Timmy, who sat behind me, would play with my hair, or ask me if I was wearing a bra yet. I ignored him, but he signaled that I was going home to my other life. The one that came with the creaking sounds of a silent moving shadow. I never knew who it was. Okay, I knew all along it was my dad. But you know it has taken nearly three decades since the last time he crawled into bed to know, like really know, it was him. All along I only thought of the shadow that smelled

185

a lot like my father's cologne, cigarettes, and cheap beer. He got into bed and then things happened that I still don't remember. I just know that I didn't feel my body, or look through my eyes, or hear the sounds that swirled around me. If I held my breath and did math problems it would all be over and I could look forward to waking up and going back to school. I got to be one person in the daylight and then I got to be no one at night. It is how I survived until the shadow divorced my mother. Then I don't remember being alive during the day or night.

The labor involved in this rewriting of reality is beyond exhausting; it is bone wearying. The damage of such broken trust is an utter inability to rest. Jesus said that his yoke is easy and his burden light (see Matt. 11:28–30). But the idea that a yoke could be easy or light doesn't seem true for those who have been abused. Instead, their yoke of bondage feels insurmountable and their burden ceaseless. No wonder the abused person spends so much time attempting to smooth over the shards of memory to lessen the bondage. The relentless energy this takes may over time dull the sharp edge, but it does nothing to erase the bulk of the rock.

The effect of broken memory on present-day relationships is profound. The inner world of traumatic emotion and thought and the external world of relationships need to be kept distant and unaddressed at all costs. Otherwise, the fear, anger, and shame will overwhelm and drown rather than merely seep through the crevices. Further, the double life must be hidden or someone might discover the secret—and then another kind of hell will ensue. Any effort to eradicate the memories only creates a deeper bondage. The signatures of this internal war are elusive gaps, disrupted integration, unaddressed implications, and an antagonistic bias against oneself.

Elusive Gaps

We tell stories mostly to serve a point or purpose, and that purpose is as important if not more so than the story itself. Sometimes the purpose is as clear as a person saying, "I know what I did was wrong, but I need your input to know what to do next time." Other times the wisest of interpreters can't fathom the labyrinth-like, convoluted purpose of a story that rambles on interminably. But we are always listening to a story with a "so what?" interpretive ear—*What do you want me to feel, think, or do as a result of you telling me this story?* Often there are multiple purposes in the telling of the story that can only be discovered through multiple hearings.

An interruptive question often invites the storyteller to offer greater depth and clarity. The question itself breaks into the story and calls for a telling that is not what the teller planned. It is a disruption that brings sediment to the surface that expands the meaning of the story.

Normally, a question that interrupts the flow of a "normal" story seldom causes difficulty. When a story hides shame, however, an interruptive question provokes distress or confusion. There is a sense that the entry to certain hidden or unseen data is either off-limits or simply unknown. Often a client will go blank and say, "I don't have a clue what happened next." It is common for abused men and women to declare, "I simply don't recall and I don't want to make it up." It is for that reason many therapists resort to attempting to find a way to get behind the firewall by using hypnosis or other regressive techniques to get the client to remember.

This leads to a high probability of false memories or data that a client feels obligated to believe. Research indicates that what we remember about most events is not first and foremost what really happened but rather how we "tell" the story. We remember the original event through the lens of the telling. If we have told the story truthfully and completely the first time, then we are able to hone and edit down to what is most salient in the telling. But if we tell the story while cutting away the shameful and heartbreaking bits, then what we remember is largely a mixture of truth and diversion.

A woman told me, "My father sexually abused me in a hotel room as soon as I walked out of the bathroom after I got ready for bed." When I asked her if the abuse happened the instant she walked through the door, she replied, "Of course not." I sat there, waiting for her to reply. She said, "He abused me when I got into bed." I asked again, "Did the abuse start the instant you got into bed?" She laughed roughly and offered, "No, of course not. He built up to it." I waited for her to address how the abuse progressed. She sat silently looking down at the floor. After a few minutes her head snapped up, and she nearly shouted, "Do you want me to tell you the details? Is that what you are asking? If so, what kind of sick bastard are you?"

Stories only have power to heal if we allow the salient details, the particularity that holds our shame and hatred, to surface in the conversation with a person who knows how to use those doorways to enter the deeper terrain of the heart. With a less skilled listener, we remain distant storytellers.

The key to good listening to stories of abuse is to listen to the intersection of shame and contempt. Contempt is always a cover-up for shame. Whether the contempt is directed toward the self or others, it is a strong indicator that deep hurt is infected with shame. The wound needs to be addressed with comfort and kindness. Shame can't be wished or willed away. It must be entered—to the point where the wound is exposed and the hatred directed against the body for what was felt during the abuse is revealed. This again requires more than mere courage; it requires that good listeners know for themselves the kindness of God through facing their own shame and contempt.

Disrupted Integration

I was interacting with a man whose story of trauma was long and convoluted. He was beaten regularly by his father and then comforted and given solace by his mother. His oldest sister, who was aligned with the father and given power to do in the family whatever she wanted, began sexually abusing my client when she was fourteen and he was eight. She had a highly contentious relationship with her mother, and whenever the mother comforted her brother, the oldest daughter would soon thereafter come to his room and hold him and soothe him, similarly to how the mother would publicly. Then she would begin to genitally arouse him and demand he do the same for her. The abuse would end after she had an orgasm, and then she would devise some means of sexual humiliation that ended the episode.

My client remembered the abuse all his life but had severe difficulty seeing how his story moved from one event to the next. Each bit of his life seemed severed from what preceded or followed. He described it as a lightning strike that suddenly lit up the night and then everything returned to stark darkness. He saw the terrain for a second but then was unable to see anything. He could describe in detail the ground he was on, but he was unable to link the trauma with anything else.

The limbic brain has two primary memory structures. As we have described before, the brain is not a mechanism that can be easily delineated. Memory seems to be held in many portions of the brain in a manner that showers images, thoughts, and feelings like overlapping sprinklers that soak a lawn in a variety of patterns rather than in a single streamlined flow. Nevertheless, these two primary structures seem to be operating in a complex interplay.

One system is related to the amygdala. Its primary purpose is to warn of danger. It operates without context or a sense of time. For example, every time you see a power cord on the floor, your amygdala shouts, *Snake!* Thankfully this always-on warning system doesn't need to be turned on or off—it is constantly screening danger and sending out signals. But it needs a buffer to keep us from constantly being on high alert.

The second memory structure is formed around the hippocampus. The hippocampus regulates the amygdala by bringing to bear context, time, past learning experiences, and the capacity to intuit, or infer meaning based on relatively few present cues. The hippocampus calms and restrains the constantly alert amygdala by reminding the brain that what you see is a power cord and that very few dangerous snakes are white and ultrathin. The problem is that trauma often shrinks the hippocampus. In one study the hippocampus was found to be 12 percent smaller in a group of sexual abuse survivors than in a control group with no history of past abuse.[10] This implies that the regulatory systems built to slow down and contextualize the amygdala are not operating at the same level of strength for those who have been abused.

Abuse and trauma seem to create a brain divide, or split, between disruptive effect (amygdala) and narrative process (hippocampus). Abuse victims will often have little or no narrative memory but instead have strong feelings, reactions, and triggers that have little or no context or plot, let alone details. Others will have discursive memory, rich in context, detail, and plot, but emotion is absent or minimal compared to what occurred.

My client whose complex story felt like lightning strikes described the beatings from his father and the later sexual humiliation inflicted by his sister in a matter-of-fact, nonchalant tone. His emotion was estranged from the story. Further, he had never considered how the violence was related to his father's envy of the son's relationship with his mother. He had never looked at how his sister served her father by arousing and humiliating him. The network of relationships in the family had no connection or meaning to him.

When I asked him to consider how his sister comforted him similarly to her hated mother, he was shocked. He never considered he was set up by his father to be punished by his sister. He began for the first time to see that his sister's sexual abuse was related to her desire to align with her father and destroy anything her mother loved. As we began to look at how his mother failed to protect him and further set him up for more harm, he was furious at me and incredulous that such evil could exist. He had never made the linkage between events and therefore had never looked at the meaning of what he had endured.

This split between amygdala and hippocampus seems to disrupt the integration of one's story as a progressive plot with clear detail and appropriate emotional depth. Consequently, for many abused men and women, memory feels disconnected, piecemeal, and void of emotional meaning. A skilled listener knows that only the Spirit of God can weave emotion and story together. It is not a technique or a methodology to be practiced. It requires desiring healing enough to keep dismantling every obstacle, defense, and seduction to remain divided. The good listener simply keeps naming the impediments, exposing the ambivalence to move forward while giving the teller opportunity to return to the story that seems to divide his or her heart and brain.

Unaddressed Implications

Usually we make meaning of our experience so naturally that we don't even realize we are doing so. We simply flow from one experience to the next, and the implications are a given. That remains true—until a disruption occurs.

I can easily flow from one event to the next on my scheduling calendar: student appointment, class, phone call to donor, meeting regarding a future conference, more student appointments, next class, walk to the ferry, ferry ride home, bus ride, walk home, dinner. The meaning is given because it is my routine for the day throughout most of the year. But if something disrupts the day—for example, I awaken early in the morning on that day and I am stricken with vertigo and can barely stand—the meaning must now be renegotiated. Questions need to be answered that are not part of my normal routine: *Can I get to school? If not, do I cancel classes or can someone else cover for me? If no one can cover for me and I cancel, then when can I make up the class? Whom should I contact first?*

Just as we seldom explore the purpose or meaning of a day, we rarely ponder the outworking of such implicational thinking. We seldom think about our thinking process; instead, we just work out plans, assess contingencies, and choose a path that seems most sensible. We seldom do a meta-analysis of how we think—unless it becomes clear that our thinking is out of kilter.

For the abused man or woman, implicational thinking may be natural and easy in some areas of life, but seldom is that true with regard to memories of abuse. The client whose sister abused him after he received comfort from their mother following a physical assault by their father had not considered the meaning of the process. The process had not been seen to be a pattern, a repeated form with few variations over extended experiences. Patterns demand that we ask the question, "So what?" *What am I to make of this process or problem? What is its outcome? What happens if one portion of the pattern is changed? What will be the effect?*

Implicational thinking enables us to vary our response to a pattern and infer what the result may be so that we have more influence over the outcome. If I know that I don't have a single date left in the calendar year to offer a missed class, then I have to assess whether I can get to class without driving and teach as much of the class as possible given my vertigo. Decisions are made with a "best guess" quality that serves the most desired goal.

My client had never named that his sister hated him. She had continued over decades to undermine and ruin his relationships, jobs, and connections with his parents. She gossiped, told half-truths, and blamed him for much of the unhappiness in the family. He simply would not add up the data and come to a "So what?" regarding his sister. When I invited him to name her as his "enemy," he balked and accused me of hyperbole. Thankfully, I had heard his countless stories, which had yet to be plumbed for implications. I retold story upon story back to him, and I asked him to consider what the data told him.

The trajectory of the stories put the sister in the role of securing her power, doing harm, and then blaming him for her contempt. The cost of naming his sister as cruel, his father as complicit, and his mother as manipulative and weak was facing that his family hated him. He was/is an orphan, and everyone in the family used him as a scapegoat. He endured repeated failures not only because it was his role but also because through doing so he gained the only "value" his family offered for him to enjoy.

The implications of these patterns had never been considered with his family of origin or with his wife and children, let alone in his work life and walk with God. Good therapeutic work requires the story caregiver to see, name, and explore the patterns that have not been faced and then consider the implications of these patterns for life as a whole.

Antagonistic Bias

Often an abused person's memory is spotty, vague, divided, and unsure. The absence of meaning due to unaddressed memories and implications of abuse often leads to unwise decisions, especially when there are triggering events that involve relational vulnerability. It is as if the original abuse set up a flaw in the algorithm that inevitably results in a wrong conclusion. This is especially true in regard to judgments about oneself. More often than not, the abused person bears strong contempt for some aspect of his or her body or self.

Let it be said that this is not unique to those who have suffered childhood sexual abuse. It seems to be endemic to all humanity, sparing only those who suffer an absence of conscience. We all struggle with a vastly inaccurate perspective of our self in relation to others. Further, we all have an inflated view of how others see our idiosyncrasies and failures. But the central bias is against something in us that lies so deep it is inaccessible.

I often encounter abuse victims whose global judgment is extreme and pervasive. One man said of himself, "I am a loser in every dimension of my life." He was a successful businessman who had made considerable sums of money. He had a good marriage of twenty-six years; two loving, mature daughters; and a ton of respect as a leader in his church and community. I brought him the data from his life, not to marshal an argument against his judgment but only to discover how he interpreted what others would view as the fruit of a successful life.

His face was patient in quiet condescension. I could tell he viewed my effort as pitiable. He finally interrupted. "I am aware of my life, but what you are not saying is that you know that I am a good fake and apparently people are more gullible than I am honest. I am tired of my marriage, my money feels like a noose, and people will respect anyone who will take responsibility for a problem whether they know what they are doing or not. I am a liar and a fake and apparently a good actor." His bias against himself was invincible.

His world unraveled as we entered into memories with his baseball coach—the first man who tutored, cared for, and celebrated this young man's efforts to hit a curveball. The coach was a master abuser and groomed this young man for years, from advanced youth leagues to early high school. On an away trip, due to a supposed scheduling error, my client had to share a room with his coach. The touch that occurred, only once, after an exhausting day of endless play and supportive interactions with his mentor, seared his heart shut. The guard outside the door carried a thick oak bat, and he virtually dared anyone to try to make entry.

The boy inside was shattered and recalled little of the event. He could only say that his coach told him that his shoulders looked tighter than a drum and that he should lie facedown and he would loosen his rock-hard back. Then something happened. He only knew it seemed to last forever, but he couldn't recall anything other than going blank and feeling like he fell asleep. He awakened at three o'clock that morning and choked back the vomit. The feeling of bile in his chest and stomach had never fully gone away. Instead, it

194

remained contained because the door was well guarded and entry or exit was impossible.

Antagonistic bias doesn't relent to sincere comfort or intense confrontation. It seems like trying to take off a barnacle with your fingers. What is required is again the ability to name the dark fury directed against the body and self. It needs to be exposed and the deeper wound of shame engaged. For the abused man or woman, the shame will always reside in the hatred of having been groomed and fooled, and then touched and aroused. Until these particular memories are addressed and the infection treated, the war of bias will only be temporarily dispatched.

For many, the cost of entering the story of harm feels overwhelming. There are so many ways to fail and fall. It seems like the listener will likely do more harm than good. But the greater harm is always to refuse to enter the burnt ground.

11

Restoring the
Marriage Relationship

Nothing I have ever done or faced was harder than telling my wife about what I experienced with my abuser. It was not the telling; it was her tears. Her eyes were so kind and fierce. I never thought I would experience anything so holy, terrifying, and beautiful in my life.

participant in a recovery group

I asked myself, why do I love, and what is the power of beauty, and I understood that each and every instance of beauty is a promise and example, in miniature, of life that can end in balance, with symmetry, purpose, and hope—even if without explanation. Beauty has no explanation, but its right perfection elicits love.

Mark Helprin

Will the person I married ever come back?" This is the question I am asked most often by the non-abused (or at least the one who has not yet addressed abuse in their past) spouse. Often it is followed by a wave of resentment that he or she was deceived. "I had no idea of her past. She didn't tell me, and if she had, I don't know if I would have married her." "I feel like I don't even know him anymore. I had no clue of the baggage this was going to bring into our lives."

The debris of past sexual abuse brings immense heartache into a marriage. It is one thing to address harm in one's past; it is an entirely more complex process when it directly and intimately affects another person. Only one partner may have been sexually abused, but both persons in a marriage are victims of the abuser—one directly and the other indirectly.[1]

It should be obvious that every marriage is unique. Recall Tolstoy's first line in *Anna Karenina*: "All happy families resemble one another, each unhappy family is unhappy in its own way." There are many marriages that are highly successful even though they bear the mark of sexual abuse; however, when abuse is directly addressed the marriage will face unique challenges. For most couples it seems like the foundation of trust has been shattered. Sexual abuse is a shadow that darkens one's capacity for loyalty, conflict resolution, and pleasure, and almost without exception there will be issues of trust, loss of emotional and sexual intimacy, confusing extremes and unpredictability, helplessness, and hopelessness.

Loyalty

Even if our partner knew of the abuse and its implications beforehand, which most don't, there is a profound though understandable struggle to remain loyal. We make an oath "to have and to hold from this day forward for better or worse, for richer or for poorer, in sickness and health, to love and to cherish till death do us part." "In sickness" includes all physical, spiritual, and psychological struggles. But how do we remain loyal when the foundation of the relationship feels cracked?

It is imperative to honor a sense of loss—she used to laugh at your jokes, delight in your smile, and was proud to be your spouse. The wounds of marriage tear off the mask of illusion and reveal how hard it is to love. Disillusionment also reveals how much we need to be loved when love seems impossible. It should be obvious how much we need the love of God to enter these difficult waters.

What our spouse needs more than any gift is the promise, the vow, that we will not merely survive as a couple but also grow together. Often the one who begins this process becomes the designated problem: she is the one who was sexually abused, and she needs to recover and get well. This sets up the dynamic that one partner is well and the other is sick. The well spouse is then supposed to be supportive and understanding and put his needs aside while the other gets well. This may appear noble, but it is a failure of honor. It sets up resentment and pressure.

The truth is that one person often needs more focus and care during this process. The supportive spouse, however, is not merely there to endure the turmoil and provide stability during the times the wind is a howling gale or create movement when the marriage sits in the doldrums. Instead, it is a time for both husband and wife to be transformed. One person may be more focused on the path toward healing, but both partners must be open to deep change.

A further truth is that spouses choose each other to some degree because their way of being in the world complements their spouse's. Angry wives find passive husbands. Controlling husbands find compliant wives. We find a partner who doesn't threaten us or disrupt the attachment history we have learned to unconsciously manage. This is what must change for both spouses. The gift of this disruptive process is that the status quo can no longer work.

As much as it may hurt, the process calls us to walk through the valley of the shadow of death so that we might give up illusions, false gods, and self-deception. It is a hard discipline.

We are told in Genesis 2 that we are to leave our mother and father to unite with our spouse. I understand this to mean we are to leave all our past loyalties in order to forge a new bond of trust. We must break with the past in order to bring ourselves, naked and open, to our spouse to establish a brand-new kingdom.

This is not done solely through a change in geography or financial independence. Instead, it is accomplished through a commitment to one another that supersedes all other loyalties to family, job, hobbies, ideology, or assumptions. It also calls us to relinquish all patterns of life that work against joy with our spouse. This is not a single, one-time event; it is a lifetime process that says no to all loyalties that interfere with our marriage. No one is finished—we all bear ongoing idolatry that is not meant to rule our heart, let alone our marriage. What is required first and foremost is the ability to name those influences and how they shape our present.

Becky and I grew up in homes where touch was either absent or complicated. Becky was seldom touched. I was touched, but with the requirement to soothe my mother. We can often go lengthy periods and not hug or hold hands. I say I love to touch my wife, but I don't touch her easily. It is true that I love touching her, but it took decades for me to admit the unease I felt when I did. It had nothing to do with her and everything to do with a failure to address the issues related to my mom's use of me as a surrogate spouse.

It is inevitable that we will reenact the patterns that enabled us to survive our family of origin, especially the war of sexual abuse. To be loyal to my wife requires that I own up to, name, and take hold of the patterns that disrupt our ability to be one. Our deepest loyalty must be to being formed in the image of Christ, to become the person we are most deeply created to be. This exceeds the legitimate desire for happiness; it must prevail against every inclination to seek safety, an absence of pain, or false comfort. It must be a priority over golf, a glass of wine, or finishing a business project. It is our highest calling to love our spouse like Christ loves the church and in so doing become our truest self.

Conflict Resolution

We are called by God to mimic his union with creation. We are to be united with our spouse through a communion of words and actions. This requires us to enter our disparity of desire. It is rare for both spouses to share the exact same intensity of desire related to anything—shopping, football, food, travel, sleep, windows open/closed, room cold/hot, not to mention sex. How we deal with desire will set the stage for how we enter conflict.

Conflict is always about regulating and/or achieving desire. I want to write to achieve the goal of finishing this chapter. My wife wants to go to a Filipino dance celebrating a new friend. She is frustrated with my work schedule. I am behind on my deadline. Our desires are at war and I don't want to disappoint her, but it is also raining and I'm already tired of our winter weather. I want to take a walk but I don't want to put on rain gear. I don't want to go outside. I am a labyrinth of conflicting and contradictory desires. It is easier just to do what she wants. However, when I simply comply with others' desires, as I often did as a child, I usually withdraw and refuse to be fully present. I will go, but I won't have fun.

Becky can easily let me stay home and write, but later she will stonewall and simply get busy with projects, and when we do have time together she will be silent and cold. We can give in to the other without giving our heart. When we fight, I am the loudest and most verbal. I command words like a general setting up the battlefield to win. She fights by shutting down and refusing to offer thoughts or desire since I will only pounce on her. We each use contempt to mobilize our troops and war against the other.

Nothing mars union like contempt. And contempt for oneself and the other is the number one strategy an abuse survivor has mastered to defend against all the harm of abuse. It is more natural than breathing and harder to give up than one's heartbeat. Yet it is the biggest issue in conflict resolution. In fact, overcoming contempt is the most important thing that must occur if the harm of abuse is ever to be addressed in a marriage.

Most abuse victims are brilliant at provoking contempt. This needs to be read carefully or it will be used to intensify contempt rather than address it with kindness. As a victim of abuse, I have used contempt to escape the heartache of betrayal, the swirl of powerlessness, and the nausea of ambivalence. It is easier to shield myself or provoke contempt from others than to enter the war of my heart.

It is imperative to recall what happens to the brain in the midst of relational stress or trauma. Broca's area, the portion of our brain that regulates speech, goes offline during the traumatic event or when that event is triggered by any current relational threat. It causes the abuse victim to move between confusion and paranoia. Notice the times you or your spouse have moved initially from being self-contemptuous (confused, scattered, fragmented) to being contemptuous of the other (tunnel vision, angry, paranoid). The self-contemptuous movement begins with uncertainty and then moves to having thoughts that jump around. If it progresses, it may move to broken sentences or disconnected phrases. This style of relating is more apt to be self-critical for the one unable to think clearly or articulate desire. The other-centered contemptuous progression goes from high, singular focus to becoming angry with the other, and eventually finds control through a cynical or paranoid perspective. Usually a marriage is made up of one person who is more comfortable with self-contempt, while the other more regularly uses other-centered contempt. Indeed, one can be caught in both cycles and move from confusion through anger and paranoia.

As one partner finds it hard to speak of desire, the other pushes to get clarity. The pressure is felt as traumatic stress, and language becomes harder to find. As irritation grows, focus is demanded, and fear and hurt are funneled into greater anger. The concluding crescendo of anger fragments and the meltdown is complete.

This pattern can happen for my wife, Becky, and me over something as simple as picking a restaurant. I am usually vocal and clear about what I want. She is less certain and less verbal. If she hesitates I am apt to offer suggestions that I know she would enjoy. Even when my desire is to please her, she feels frustrated. If she shuts down, I can get more verbal and "helpfully" intrusive. This can lead to a meltdown for us both.

If a marriage is to weather the storms of past sexual abuse in one or both partners, there must be a loyal commitment to a zero-contempt relationship. No matter the issue, no matter its importance, contempt must be viewed as dangerous as lighting a match to look into a gas tank. Contempt, self- or other-centered, is a mechanism to flee or fight against heartache and fear. What must happen is the hurt and/or fear must be cared for through kindness first before any movement can be made to address the problem. Any other approach, including bullying or throwing in the towel to avoid the conflict, will lead to disaster and a replication of the past abuse.

The non-abused spouse didn't start the war caused by sexual abuse, but tragically, due to a failure of care, he or she has often added a reservoir of fuel to keep the harm lit for a lifetime. If that is true with regard to conflict, it is even truer with regard to sex.

Sexual Pleasure

Sex is the canary in the coal mine: its health indicates when there is toxicity in the air, though I have worked with a number of couples who have a disloyal and contemptuous marriage but have great sex. Often it is a couple in which both partners were abused, and intense, aggressive sex (especially after fights) keeps them bonded together and lowers the triggering effects of cortisol. More often, however, if both partners have been abused I find that they have conspired to have an irregular, almost nonexistent sex life.

The most common pattern in a marriage marred by childhood sexual abuse is that one partner wants sex more than the other, and tension, disappointment, and contempt seep into the marriage. In this scenario one partner endures sex in an obligatory fashion that is rote. The other is grateful for any sex but will also feel angry and eventually disconnected from any awareness of whether his or her partner is present and feeling pleasure. Sex in this case is dissociated and empty, and replicates what was often felt during the original sexual abuse.

Often I find abused men prefer masturbation and pornography to real sex. This is disturbing to the spouse who feels like her husband is not sexual, at least not with her, yet is aroused by pornography. The fact is that singular sex is an escape from sexual failure while still being able to control the orgasmic fantasy.

Sex may be consensual and still reenact the past abuse when arousal is cut off through contempt and dissociation. Good sex is not first and foremost about one or both partners having an orgasm. Good sex is about being fully present to both one's own and the other's pleasure for the sake of growing in delight for the Creator and his creation. To be fully present and delighting in one's own and the other's pleasure will bring not only orgasm but also intimacy and joy.

Our sexuality is but one aspect of our capacity to play, but seldom is sex considered in the light of play. Play requires an investment of time and energy and a willingness to experiment and practice. Just as one visualizes and works on one's golf swing or ponders Sudoku patterns, sex requires discipline to grow. The discipline is not primarily learning and practicing sex; instead, it involves growing in the areas of loyalty and communication that make sex better.

A couple will never grow sexually unless there is a willingness to leave one's parents and past—that is, to begin to name and own the influence of the past over the present and see how the intersection of both lives creates the necessity for change. And that change requires a new investment in conversation. There can be little to no sexual joy without the capacity to enter conflict well. Mere avoidance of conflict is not sufficient ground to reclaim the harm to the body.

For many couples, there is not sufficient commitment from both partners to do this work. But the flight of one spouse from commitment should never stop the one most committed to growth from moving forward. The spouse most aware of the war must avoid returning to the patterns of harm that have typified the marriage. One can leave past loyalties even if the other spouse refuses to do so. One can refuse to pretend all is well when it is not. It is not necessary to join in contempt or despair. While it is agonizing to stand on the rim of the pit and throw down a rope when the other demands you sink into the mire alone—yes, this is as confusing and contradictory as it sounds—one doesn't need to drown in the mud to love; in fact, it is dishonorable to do so.

Nevertheless, it is easier to remain in reenactment ruts, even when they are lifeless, than it is to risk the uncertainty of a new way of being. In the last twenty-five years I have witnessed many relationships in which one spouse changes and the other spouse turns against the transformation with hatred. The quiet spouse who discovers her voice takes away some of the godless power of her shaming husband. The frightened husband who becomes more courageous upends the control of his critical wife. When this occurs, marriages that at one point appeared to be stable become shaky.

Sadly, many blame the spouse who is finally choosing to love rather than the spouse who is committed to the status quo. I have seen pastors and well-meaning Christian leaders challenge the spouse calling for change to "forgive and forget" the past abuse and/or the current disappointments in the marriage and to move on. Usually this is conveniently tied to false notions of submission, which silence the legitimate issues that need to be addressed.

By no means am I advocating a lessening of commitment to one's covenantal vow of fidelity. In fact, I am asking for that commitment to be so high that one is more committed to one's partner as an individual than to the marriage. The apostle Paul wrote: "Dear friends, never take revenge. Leave that to the righteous anger of God. For the Scriptures say, 'I will take revenge; I will pay them back,' says the LORD. Instead, 'If your enemies are hungry, feed them. If they are thirsty, give them something to drink. In doing this, you will heap burning coals of shame on their heads'" (Rom. 12:19–20 NLT). What this requires is doing "good" by living in a way that exposes the failure of love through bold and playful kindness. The apostle Paul used this metaphor to expose the shame that is at work in the one you are called to love. Unaddressed shame always works against intimacy. It turns the heart inevitably to contempt.

To change this pattern, something more than good intentions is required. Deep change can't occur for most couples until they begin a process that is intentional and disruptive, and this usually requires seeking outside help. It is difficult to fix a faulty airplane engine while it is in flight. This kind of relationship change requires the disruptive work of submitting one's way of being—past, present, and future—to the engagement of a wise and experienced guide.

The Journey toward Restoration

Most couples can't afford two individual therapists and a marriage therapist working simultaneously to address all the issues that arise. Even if it were financially possible, most people wouldn't be able to metabolize all that comes up with that much intensity. Instead, another process will need to occur.

The one who is addressing past abuse needs to see an individual therapist who is at least trained to deal with sexual trauma and its spiritual, relational, and internal debris. This process needs a spouse who is an ally and a partner in healing. It demands active participation through growing in knowledge and understanding to address the disruptions of ambivalence, numbing, triggers, blaming, and sabotage.

There is no greater gift to an abused spouse who is engaging the heartache of abuse than to grow in wisdom and understanding about the devastating consequences of his or her childhood harm. There are countless men and women who will pay for lessons and more gear for a beloved sport but find putting time into understanding abuse intrusive or beyond their grasp. The non-abused spouse's willingness to read, reflect, and enter the terrain of abuse is a sacrifice of love. There will be a number of issues that he or she must face.

Ambivalence and Shame

Contempt arises like smoke from the fire of shame. The partners in a zero-contempt marriage make a vow to address ambivalence and shame directly. Marriage is a relationship that is intended to be a place where we are "naked and know no shame." In a fallen world, we will always struggle to some degree with shame, but marriage is the place where our past shame is most exposed and available for healing. Tragically, many marriage relationships deepen past shame rather than heal it.

The sexually abused spouse needs to see a therapist who allows the stories of their life to be explored and engaged in a manner unlike any past experience. No doubt the non-abused spouse has heard some of his or her spouse's stories, but seldom have they been entered into and the implications considered as deeply as they will be with a good guide.

It is easy to feel resentful of the time, cost, and intrusion of another person into a spouse's life. Or the non-abused spouse may feel guilty that he or she has not been a better listener or story reader. On the other hand, initially it is a relief that someone else is helping, especially if he or she has felt overwhelmed. The experience of both resentment and relief is one of ambivalence. The abused spouse will feel that as well.

There is no resolution for ambivalence other than to own it and bless the truth on both sides of the battle. The worst that one can do is to try to deny or ignore one side of the internal conflict. The things the abused spouse will begin to address, even after a few sessions, will ramp up this internal war. Therapy doesn't resolve the inner conflict; it intensifies the covert war fought just below the surface and lets it come to the forefront. There is one truth that must be embraced: the process of therapy stirs up what has been hidden.

The abused spouse needs the non-abused spouse to be grounded in God and aware of his or her own war with shame and contempt. These experiences come with being human and living in a fallen world as a sinner. The more we ponder, write, and talk about these issues, the greater the common ground. The non-abused spouse needs to find a person or a small group to help begin and support this conversation.

A group for spouses of abused men or women would be an ideal place to start. Unfortunately, at this point these seldom exist anywhere in the world. The next best thing would be a group oriented around the book *To Be Told*.[2] This book helps spouses consider the importance of their own stories and provides direction for how to hear and tell that story to others.

If nothing like that exists in your area, then a group of men or women who are committed to asking the question, "How has our past influenced our present?" needs to be formed to explore the core issues of family of origin and the effects of trauma in our lives. It will likely not be the same level of intensity or depth as working with an experienced guide, but such a group will allow both partners to grow in empathy and understanding together.

Numbing

The further the abused spouse enters his or her story, the more likely there will be greater periods of numbing. This psychological process is a form of dissociation or flight from feeling. It is not wrong nor is it an indication of not doing good work. For most, it is a mild form of shock that allows the body and soul to regain composure when there is too much to process.

For many spouses, however, it provokes loneliness or helplessness. One husband said, "I feel cut off. In those times I feel invisible and like a nuisance she wants to get rid of." Many have said it feels like their spouse is a robot, merely going through the routine of life with no sense of presence or desire. For some, this is when both spouses go to separate rooms, activities, and lives. Distance soothes the fears of abandonment or distress. Other couples let this growing numbness become the basis of a slowly moving conflict that explodes into contempt. At least the blowup feels more alive than the cold suffocation of living in a freezer.

What is needed here is grounding that comes from the ability to name the ambivalence. The non-abused spouse needs to say, "I know you are not here. I don't know where you are, but I know whatever has taken you away is big enough that it will take time for you to come back." Don't expect the abused spouse to be forthcoming about what is going on or even appreciative of such grounding. Often numbing feels like the only way to survive when so much is going on internally and externally. He or she needs comfort, care, and soothing.

The mere invitation to sit and drink a cup of peppermint tea is a gift. Or the offer to do the dishes may allow the abused spouse to sit and feel rather than keeping busy to escape what is going on. Numbing is not wrong, but it is a stopgap measure rather than the best entry into what is causing the body to be overwhelmed. Eventually, the numb spouse needs to find more enlivening ways to engage what is provoking his or her fear, hurt, or shame. And in due season, it will be safer for him or her to engage in those internal wars more directly with his or her spouse.

Triggers

One of the effects of post-traumatic stress is intense and at times extreme responses to things that don't seem that big of a deal to others. The extreme response is usually framed in fear/flight or anger/ fight. The response from others is often incredulity or irritation that leads to a dismissal of the "problem." This response of minimization may seem helpful to the one offering it, but it is at best patronizing and, far worse, demeaning. It implies the response to a trigger is a choice. It is not. And it will not amend to mere will.

Because it feels out of control for both the one triggered and the one who is present, the strategy most utilized is either logic or avoidance. I met with a couple who struggled whenever the wife felt her husband no longer wanted to be with her. She would feel abandoned and jealous of other women. He loved her and would protest that he had no heart for anyone other than her. She then felt dismissed and didn't trust him because he often failed to tell her the full truth in order to avoid conflict. His efforts to affirm and provide a rationale for her triggers only increased the conflict until she withdrew.

Logic and affirmation didn't work, and in the end they would isolate. After a few hours, she would feel sufficient shame to admit she was wrong and apologize; he accepted and was happy the tension had passed. But this kind of "resolution" not only doesn't work but actually reinforces the power of the trigger. Here is the bind: direct engagement with the triggering moment intensifies the fear/anger, but not addressing it does the same thing, only indirectly.

These are the kinds of binds that cause spouses to throw up their hands and say, "I can't win. So why bother?" This is a vow that needs to be broken and the roots of our war with powerlessness exposed. We can't let this bind increase a sense of failure or blame—in our self or our spouse.

The abused spouse needs grounding, soothing kindness, and a willingness to hold the tension and volatility without fear or demand for resolve. The husband needs to say to his wife, "I know you fear my betrayal, and I am willing to hear you out without trying to talk you out of it." And when calm returns, the couple needs to reenter the experience she suffered and explore the context that might have been the basis of the trigger. The goal is not to find an explanation for or control over the trigger but to be better able to care for the aftermath of the upheaval.

Triggers are not something that logic or rational argument will resolve. In time, triggers that are understood and engaged with tender care will lessen in severity, even if some remain for a lifetime.

Blaming

One woman, whose husband was abused by a female cousin, told me, "Anytime we have sex and I have an orgasm, I know I will pay in the next several hours in some way. I try to orgasm as quietly as possible so as not to trigger him." He was required to perform oral sex on his cousin, who regularly climaxed with immense pleasure. Even as an eight-year-old, he was highly aroused and disgusted by the pleasure he was able to create for her.

His wife offered this analysis: "I don't know what happens, but for a few hours afterward he treats me similarly to how he related to his cousin. He is cautious and watchful and tries to stay out of my way, until I do something that angers him and then I get it. He explodes and I am at fault for every bit of unhappiness in his life."

Often the supportive spouse is accused or is treated like the abuser. It is a deeply painful part of being married to an abuse victim. Frequently the supportive spouse will come to feel intense anger toward the abuser and the family of origin that enabled the abuser to do harm. However, it is almost a rule of thumb that the one harmed protects the family of origin and the abuser from confrontation or even disclosure of the abuse. This puts the supportive spouse in the position of holding a family secret and having to pretend all is well when interacting with the family they are angry with. This bifurcated reality is nearly impossible to hold well. The tension that occurs before or after a visit spawns a host of destructive marital patterns. How does it get displaced? Tragically, the answer is often through blaming. The non-abused spouse becomes the abuser and gets accused of some infraction, failure, or omission that takes on titanic importance.

I worked with a couple who went into a two-week spiral after nearly every encounter with her family. Her brother had abused her when she was eight to twelve years old, and it had been dismissed by her family as "boys will be boys." As a result, she considered the abuse to be normal childhood play even though it had been perpetrated by a brother four years older and sometimes also involved her brother's friends. There was significant sexual debris in the marriage related to the past abuse, but she dismissed the struggles as nothing other than normal male and female differences.

Her husband despised the superficiality and pretense of her family. Whenever he refused to play the game she became enraged and blamed him for trying to destroy her family. He would attempt to name the hypocrisy and she would refuse to talk with him for days. This became a demilitarized zone where both learned that any attempt to talk led to chaos and it seemed better not to talk at all.

Naturally, the response most often offered when one is blamed is defense. But to say "I am not your abuser" only increases the victim's paranoia and shuts down the conversation. Trying to prove or defend against the blaming pours fuel on the fire. Again, the next obvious response for the non-abused spouse is to shut down, throw his or her hands in the air, and walk away. This is also a disastrous response. One must enter the bind and remain in the wind's fury if redemption is to grow over time.

What is required of the supportive spouse is to own whatever truth is actually being named in the blaming. As difficult as it is, one must turn to address the log in one's own eye rather than address what appears to be a forest in the eye of the accuser (see Matt. 7:3–5). It doesn't mean merely to apologize. It means taking a stance of openness, curiosity, and exploration of the perceived harm. Usually there is something true in every accusation. A wise spouse will own it, consider its effect on his or her spouse, and then grieve the harm done.

The husband whose wife drove him crazy by covering over the profound denial of her family finally admitted he was exasperated. He named his anger and desire to drag her kicking and screaming into the truth, even at the risk of triggering an avalanche of turmoil in her family. At first his confession allowed her to blame him even more for the unhappiness that resulted when they visited her family. He didn't deny or defend himself against her accusation. After an extended period, he asked for help in knowing how to respond when her mother radically distorted data or outright lied about a situation. As difficult as it was not to argue, he took a posture of kindness and honor that didn't back off from the truth or demand his view of the truth be preeminent. After months had passed his wife slowly acknowledged her frustration that certain stories could not be told, or if told had to be rewritten to be acceptable to her parents. Her husband's willingness to name his own contribution to his wife's anger eventually opened the door to her willingness to consider his view.

At first owning the log in one's own eye will not lead to peace but to more turmoil. The blaming is not intended for the supportive spouse's good; instead, it is designed to help the abused spouse manage his or her inner world by melting his or her shame and ambivalence into an undifferentiated rage. To own and address the failure that becomes the basis of an accusation exposes the reality that war, not peace, is desired. This can't be exposed if the non-abused spouse defends and tries to explain that his or her intentions are good. Sometimes the abused spouse will be so angry that he or she simply needs to know the supportive spouse won't back away or turn against him or her. On the other hand, the abused spouse needs to know that the non-abused spouse is not weak and capitulating merely to avoid conflict. He or she again needs grounding, kindness, a willingness to hold tension, and ownership of what he or she perceives to be the non-abused spouse's failure.

Sabotage

When the disruption of the rage occurs through an intersection of humility and strength, expect sabotage. Sabotage is any act that is designed to threaten, discourage, or tear down the marriage by harm directed against property, self, or the other. It can include but is not limited to drinking or eating to excess, sexual acting out, throwing or breaking objects, out of context disclosures/major confessions, ripping clothes, pulling out hair, screaming until hoarse, public humiliation, domestic violence, repetitive accidents, bouts of procrastination, and putting oneself into dangerous situations. Sabotage is far more than an adult temper tantrum; it is the fusion of the impulses to kill and mar. It is prompted by the taunting internal and external voices, which merge into a cacophony of shame. The amygdala is flooding the brain with a torrent of cortisol. This is not a rational, chosen act. It is a limbic storm. One client called it "the nuclear option."

Sabotage by the abused spouse is a profoundly disruptive act that makes returning to normalcy almost impossible for a long season. A common issue for the supportive spouse is deep confusion. As one man said, "I feel like the better we are doing for a period of time, the more likely she is going to eventually explode. It seems like we do better if I treat her poorly."

Sabotage by a spouse who has been abused is by far one of the most difficult parts of a victimized marriage. The saboteur eventually melts down in shame. The victim of the sabotage feels confused, hurt, and fed up. A huge sinkhole swallows what was a good or at least better period.

This confusion wanes when both partners better understand the catastrophic war of shame due to pleasure. Pleasure—relational intimacy and sexual arousal in particular—is the impetus for the magma of sabotage to flow. Understanding sets the context for healing through what is most needed: grief and strength. The saboteur relinquishes the power of harm only if he or she feels his or her grief. He or she must open his or her heart to the sorrow of Jesus and receive from him his tears and delight. It is then that sabotage can be sabotaged.

This requires the presence of a strong man or woman who knows how to set boundaries and limit even greater harm. This doesn't usually require direct intervention; instead, what is most helpful is the ability to remain calm, aware, and not add to the frenzy. To set boundaries is to contain the harm and let natural consequences play out until calm is restored. Once the storm subsides, and it will, there are downed limbs and uprooted trees. That is when grief on the part of the supportive spouse—not shame, withdrawal, or counsel—can enable the abused spouse to discover his or her capacity to feel sorrow and compassion for the part of himself or herself that could find control only by losing it. For the abused spouse to reverse the tendency to self-harm, he or she must not only see how he or she is using harm to escape desire but also ask Jesus to stand against the curse he or she has set against himself or herself. This process may not resolve the consequences, but it ensures that sabotage doesn't work by fusing shame with rage. It divides the power of shame and contempt and gives the saboteur a context to grieve well.

There are two questions every supportive spouse asks: (1) How am I supposed to do this and not fail? and (2) How long will this take? The answer to the first is unequivocal. We can't engage without failing. Sometimes the clearer we are of what we want to do, the more severely we will fail. For this reason the love of God for those who fail is not merely needed; it is crucial.

The second question is harder: I don't know. I promise it won't go on for years if good work is being done with a good guide. But it will go on far longer than we think we have the capacity to endure. I am often reminded of those who fought in World War II. How long did they think they would be at war? Did they have a clue what they were going to face and endure? How did they remain faithful in the war? At one level, they had no choice. The war simply had to be fought. At another level, they fought not primarily to win the war but for the sake of their buddy in the next foxhole.

What can we trust will happen in our marriages if we fight long and well? The deepest marriages, like the relationships that come out of war, are ones in which spouses have fought, bled, suffered, and sometimes died together. Not only is there the bonding that comes from suffering but far more is there the celebration of the gift that *we are waking up together having lived through another day.*

The fruit of this labor will not merely be our own healing. A renewed and revitalized marriage is one of the greatest weapons God has to do war against the kingdom of darkness.

12

Steps to Transformation

*What am I getting into if I say yes to what you are asking me to do? How long
will this take? What am I going to have to face to make progress? What is the
ground ahead and do you really think I have the gear to survive, let alone
succeed with what is ahead? I don't care that God told Abram and Sarai to
leave without clarity of where they were going. I need to know, what is the
topography of change?*

participant in a recovery group

I loved this man's rapid-fire, cortisol-clipped, intense, and insistent
questions. I had recently returned from a dangerous fishing trip
into the Bob Marshall wilderness, where I had fallen down a
steep embankment and punctured my hand on a fallen pine tree, and
so I felt somewhat equipped to tell him what was ahead.

I told him we would be on a long, dusty trail going up and down a
path that paralleled an inaccessible river. Eventually we would enter
dark woods that eclipsed the river and hid the trail. If we survived
we would come out somewhere higher up than when we began.
When we glimpsed the river again, we would slide down a mountain

embankment that was strewn with shale, downed trees, and hidden critters that could eat us. Once we got down, we would need to cross a river that could sweep us away in a second and send us careening into submerged boulders. If we were not crushed, we would need to fight not to drown. Once we were on the other side, we could fish, but we would eventually need to climb out and return to camp.

He smiled. I loved his smile. He asked if I knew the path well enough to guide him. I said, "No. I know my path. And all I know about yours is that there are parallels, but what is ahead will always be unique."

No one's path is the same, but the terrain is similar. How long will the journey take? I have no clue, but the best answer is far longer than a single year and likely less than many years. In one sense we are never done, and this particular journey requires a commitment to go longer and farther than seems possible or desirable.

The end can't be assured; it can only be trusted. Faith grows to the degree that we do what seems counterintuitive: open our heart to remember, grieve, and ask God to engage our anguish with tenderness. What is required is far more than merely acknowledging we were sexually abused, though no change can come until we do. Even more, we need to go beyond merely knowing that it was not our fault. We must allow God to open up the festering wound to expose the infection and begin to address the curse(s) against our body and heart. We must bless what God blesses and curse what he curses. We must stand against the seduction and rampaging hatred of evil and discern how our trust in its solace has shaped our personhood.

This is not a journey taken by many. It is a healing path that seems, at first, worse than the disease. It is not. It is life-giving, freeing, and empowering.

I have coded this journey into seven stages that walk victims of sexual abuse toward transformation and participation in God's redemptive plan for healing. However, the fact is there are as likely to be thirty stages as there are seven. No one number best describes all that needs to occur, nor can anyone assure the traveler that the sequence is the same for everyone. The journey is ultimately designed by God and not by man. Nevertheless, over the past twenty-five years I have found that the topography of change is similar for all who walk toward healing, no matter how haltingly or slow.

Stage One: Going into Exile

The first steps of this journey begin when we name that we were sexually abused. This is a courageous act. But it requires that we take the next step: owning up to the reality that the past abuse has harmed us and is affecting our present life. Further, we must recognize that if we don't address the abuse it will shadow and darken our future.

Seldom does anyone start this journey by choice. It is not a planned trip that moves from pleasant attractions to cozy bed and breakfasts. It is usually a crisis and/or trauma that sets the pilgrim on the path of healing. Trauma awakens trauma. A marriage is coming to an end. A child has rebelled. A job is lost. Depression deepens. The ground has become like water. Often panic and confusion cloud the sensible decisions of the day, and mere survival feels unsure. Still, this often is not enough to propel intentional movement. The beginning of change is usually more tenuous and subtle.

Most victims of sexual abuse begin to seek help by hinting. They acknowledge to a friend that they are not doing well. They ask a pastor to pray for them. Their lives start a precipitous slide downward. But it takes time to feel the thud of hitting bottom.

I wish I knew what truly brought my clients to my door. When asked, few really know why. They simply know that it's time. They can't continue on the routine course. Life is unraveling and they are desperate to get it under control. The presence of desperation may be hidden underneath blaming one's spouse or planning the next step to resolve the problem, but there is a quiet terror that says,

There is no way back through the gate to Eden. Nothing will ever be the same again.

At first this is resisted and solace is sought, counsel solicited, and new plans made. Usually none of these work. The problem is not a failed marriage, a troubled teen, job uncertainty, or a biological disposition to depression—those are merely symptoms of a life on the run. One can only hope that the pilgrim doesn't find a therapist, friend, minister, or stranger who offers the false hope of a quick fix.

I have worked with many men and women whose journey has been derailed by such a resolve. *Here is the plan: simply do this and your struggle will fade into a forgotten past. Sing this song. Receive this Spirit. Pray this prayer. Trust this process. Just do something and you will be better.*

A good friend went to a conference offered by a well-respected teacher. She found the material helpful and went to pray with one of the conference staff. He prayed over her and told her that God was confirming her desire to be free of a deep and profound wound from the past. He said, "God simply wants you to stop working on it and let him heal you in his time."

She did just as the man told her to do. She stopped counseling and reflecting on her life in order to let God do the work. For a season, her life improved greatly and she felt "healed." The dilemma was that the triggers related to her past abuse didn't go away. The residual issues that disrupted her relationships didn't disappear. It was only when her nightmares returned that she realized putting aside the work had only brought the temporary relief of flight, not true healing.

What propels us on the journey toward deeper transformation is reflected in these words: "I believe, help my unbelief" (see Mark 9:24). *I am broken and I believe there is hope, but my hope is so shattered that I can't live like I have lived any longer.* It is the conundrum of hoping against hope. A willingness to ask for help that goes beyond the presenting problem to the deepest issues of the heart prompts a wise person to seek out a good guide.

Stage Two: Wandering

At first, addressing sexual abuse feels like wandering lost in the woods. There is so much to face in the present, past, and future. There is an overwhelming array of issues to grapple with, including anxiety, depression, addictions, relational tensions, and triggers that prompt dissociation. It is important to allow time to wander and bump into the many issues that will need to be named.

Any good guide, usually a therapist in the case of the complexities of sexual abuse, is going to spend the first few times together hearing about the current context that prompted the collision with helplessness. There are characters and context to fathom. Every character in a drama is living out a role, a set of themes, and a way of being in the world. As a counselor I need to hear not merely what occurred but also how it came to be. I need to hear the conversation. The breakup. The firing. The rage. The confusion. I need to hear it to the degree that I can begin to see the actors and listen to the dialogue. It is not a matter of hearing so I can help; it is hearing so I can understand and begin to help the client to do the same.

This stage is called wandering because it involves covering ground that is not always clearly related to the past abuse. Most people want to "get it over with" and figure that the best way to do so is to jump straight into their memories of abuse. This is seldom helpful. The journey has begun, but the direct work with abuse needs a period on the trail for the victim to strengthen muscles, develop a rhythm, and prepare the heart for what is ahead.

The key to this stage is awareness of patterns that are reenactments of how the client likely managed the trauma, stress, and complex emotions and bodily states that go along with abuse. Seldom do people make a link between how they handle current crises and struggles and the manner in which they coped with past abuse. It is too long ago and usually involved a radically different set of people. And the abused person has changed over the years, at least on the surface, making it difficult for them to see how deep patterns often remain the same.

I met with a young woman, twenty-six years old, who in the midst of navigating the complex relationship with her mother told me what a big deal her mother made of a sexual event that occurred when my client was sixteen. A friend of her older brother, who was twenty-one, got her drunk during a Christmas break and taught her to French kiss and fondled her while the family was upstairs wrapping gifts and getting ready for a Christmas Eve church service. Her brother walked into the bedroom when the abuse was occurring, laughed, and told his friend not to make so much noise. My client did not name this event as sexual abuse; it was just a "weird" way to be sexual.

Her mother found out about the event several days later and barred the friend from the house, raged at her daughter, and proceeded to get sloppy drunk. She also divulged to her daughter her own past sexual abuse. Nearly a decade later my client still hated to go home for Christmas because it triggered her mother to drink and rage, and the result was crazy behavior that brought shame to the whole family. She asked me to talk with her about how to handle the drama that Christmas evoked in her.

When I asked her how she viewed the sexual "event," she was protective of her brother and his friend. She could name her brother's failure to protect her as a betrayal, but she stopped short of naming what he and his friend did as sexually abusive. She was also unable to name her mother's behavior as an extension of the abuse she suffered from her brother and his friend.

I am still stunned by how many clients who have been in therapy for years remain unable to talk about their repetitive thematic reenactments or open their heart to the question, *Why do I repeat the same patterns again and again?* It is as if the therapist has failed to hold a mirror up to their faces so they can see their fear, grimaces, suspicion, dissociation, self-loathing, and fury. My job is to read their faces and to help my clients who have been sexually abused experience what their faces are saying as they tell their stories. This invites them to begin learning and experiencing their bodies. We seldom, if ever, feel our body in the presence of another and talk about it until there is a connection, a response that says, *I feel what I am feeling and it is related not only to the surface trigger but also to deeper matters.*

What happens in this process is twofold: trust is developed and an attachment bond is formed. The client is learning to name and engage his or her body's emotion with curiosity and perhaps the first fledging steps of kindness. We can't go further on this journey until the client grows in his or her capacity to be present and not turn immediately cruel or dissociative.

There are of course countless issues and stories that come up every week regarding whatever drove the victim of abuse to seek help, but all the events that arise provide greater flesh to the bare bones of his or her initial understanding. He or she always insists on help in knowing what to do regarding a marriage, children, finances, sexuality, job, and so forth, but unless the issues are nearly a matter of life or death, I seldom offer direction or advice. What I offer is exploration of how his or her usual way of engaging the problem has obviously not worked and what he or she would like to do now. There will be no change unless desire for change increases.

When I asked the woman who regularly chose to return home at Christmas to an abusive and degrading family, "What would you like to bring to this scenario that might alter the outcome this time?" she couldn't think of a single thing. Her pattern was to get flooded, shut down, and then let the people around her choose to run her life. When I named what was happening, she became enraged. She demanded I tell her what to do or not charge her for the hour. I let her know there would be a charge, and the best I could offer was to help her imagine another option in how she related to her family.

She glared and then spat, "I suppose I could get a hotel room if my mother gets mean." I smiled; she was now repeating another pattern: come to a decision and then attack the person who failed to help. The more we engaged her reenactments, the more she began to feel her fury and terror. As she moved beyond her anger, her grief began to swallow her. She then developed the ability to regulate her breathing and soothe herself by stroking her arm. As she did so, she came to be present, take ownership of her decision to visit her family, and be empowered to do things differently. Her simple decision to admit that she didn't need answers and didn't have to remain locked in the ugly drama of her family dynamic allowed her to address the real issue: she was fearfully and idolatrously bound to the whims and will of her mother. This helped her begin to explore her life in a new way and make decisions that were based in hope and freedom. Her progress and movement were phenomenal. But it was only the beginning. The next stage of her journey would be treacherous and costly.

Stage Three: Entering the Dark Woods

This stage is far longer and harder than most people anticipate. For most of my clients, this stage feels superfluous to the real work of dealing with the memories of abuse. It is not. It is an entry into the relational context that gives form to how they were set up and groomed. This stage compels us to enter the domain of our family of origin and our attachment history. For victims of abuse, nothing is more difficult. We may know the ways in which we have been failed by our parents, siblings, and extended family, but we often approach these issues while chanting, "They did their best. They didn't mean to harm me. They had no clue what was happening; if they did they would have protected me. No one spoke of abuse in the family, culture, or church. I have done just as much harm, if not more."

There is something honorable about looking for the best in people, but I have sat with victims of unquestionable evil who work just as hard as children of good parents to defend and excuse their primary caregivers for all sorts of damaging behavior. We are called neither to blame nor vilify; instead, we simply need to tell the truth and allow the heartache to be engaged.

There is always a staggering toll initially for telling the truth, especially about family. The pushback from the spiritual realm and from relatives proclaims that the victim of abuse who speaks up is now an alien and a stranger and will never have a home again. But it presses him or her that much more to ask questions such as, *How did my character and my style of relating get formed in the midst of trauma and sin? How did I metabolize the warfare in my family? How was I used by my mom to prove she was a good mom? How was I used by my dad to fill his insecurity and validate he was not a failure?*

Every parent needs to be studied. Every marriage must be truthfully pondered. One's role among siblings needs to be comprehended. This is not being critical; it is studying the landscape to make one's way through the dark woods of past harm. We are formed in the midst of the crucible of attachment and the tensions of our family of origin. We can't even begin to understand our character until we better understand the role we played in relationship to every member of our immediate family.

This will unquestionably bring up stories of harm. It is imperative to note how we enter those stories. We bring our flight, fight, and freeze trauma response to our stories of origin. Do we freeze internally as we tell our stories? Do we remember up to the point that the harm became intense and then dissociate? Do we allow confusion and uncertainty to keep us from seeing the themes of the story? Do we use rage to provoke others to flee?

The goal is not to tell our stories to get over them, or even to gain insight. Instead, we must enter the stories for the sake of grief, anger, and forgiveness. Grief opens the heart to receive comfort. Anger moves the heart to stand against injustice. Forgiveness frees the heart from resentment and the accusations of evil.

Almost everyone wants to forgive too quickly. But forgiveness does not require that we refuse to enter the dark woods of abuse. When forgiveness provides justification for avoiding entry into the heartache of our stories, it is a form of cheap grace. We must allow the stories of our childhood to come forth one by one and then offer grace, care, and healing to the broken child within. We are meant to receive the care of heaven and stand against the darkness of hell in our own life, family, and world.

When we remember past harm we are accessing some of the neurons marred by the trauma. It is not that we merely remember; we experience some of the synaptic, biochemical, and muscle memory consequences of those moments. The more concrete and particular a memory, the more likely the body will experience the intensity of the harm. And each blow, touch, seduction, abandonment, fit of rage, or desperate plea will send aftershocks through our body. The questions are, *Will I be kind, offer comfort, and find the strength not to return to sabotage or dissociation? In due season, will I explore and dismantle some of the self-protecting vows I made during these episodes?*

Breaking through the woods usually requires setting new boundaries in relationships that are shrouded in reenactment drama. We must clarify what we can carry and what we must discard. Often this means limiting access to people who are committed to harm. The bossy sister needs to be thanked for her advice and told that it is not currently helpful. The intrusive friend who insists on knowing all that we feel needs to be told that those issues are being addressed with a counselor and no longer with her. The abuser who pretends that nothing happened and wants us to act normal needs to know that we are not going to glide back into the status quo. The abuser may need to interact in accord with the desires of the victim. By his or her behavior the abuser has lost the right to determine how the relationship will proceed.

This stage begins to put flesh to the bones of our life and intensifies a lot of the heartache and internal war related to our abuse.

The changes provoked by the journey will disrupt most of our core relationships. We may feel as if we are in a freefall. This is particularly true when marriages are full of chaos and friendships seem to be stalled in midflight. Everything is a mess, and if it were possible we would levitate ourselves back to the tame path and return to base camp. The problem is that we can't go back and we are terrified to go forward.

There are two keys to progress in this stage: honesty and kindness. It is brutally difficult to be honest about the failures of our families, especially our parents. It opens the door to past disappointment and often disrupts current interactions. It is equally difficult (or more so) to be honest about how our past abuse shaped the way we currently relate to others, including our spouse and children. Honesty will not only help us admit the truth but will also begin to move us closer and closer to the particularity of our story. It is often said that the devil is in the details. However, in the arena of sexual abuse, the living God is in the details. It is in the details that we feel the deepest levels of loss, fear, anger, and shame, as well as faith, hope, and love. If we remain aloof and enter our story as if it were merely facts or conjectures to be reported, there will be little change.

The second goal during this stage is to grow in kindness. This is not merely being nicer or less harsh. Kindness is the key to redemption and to transformation. The kinder we are to our story, heart, body, and relationships, the more profoundly different our life will be. And our need for kindness will increase exponentially as we move into the raging waters of shame.

Stage Four: Crossing the River

Moving toward the river is to face a slope that seems insane to descend. A radically steep decline has little vegetation to use as handholds to get down. Descent requires a willingness to fall and slide when there is little to hold on to for safety. It is dirty, painful, and slow—very slow. It requires planning and risk, trial and error. We must go slowly.

Seldom do we come to our story of shame quickly. Often it takes more than a year to tell the truth about our family of origin and current relationships, and make even small, stumbling moves to re-create our world. The kingdom of darkness doesn't want us to engage our story of shame, fearing, of course, that we will find greater freedom. It seems like a legion of issues and problems forestalls entry into the river. More skills, insight, and strength are needed to cross more dangerous topography.

No doubt many are saying, "Enough. Stop. No more." But the river crossing is the real work—the beginning of the end. There is exhaustion but also the interlacing of truth and kindness. There is openness to the mystery of the way God works and wonder that one is alive and freer than at any other time in life. There is a distinct sense that we are ready to enter the fast-moving waters ahead.

Often portions of our story will already have been told, but without depth, detail, or presence. Most people test the waters, walk in up to their calves, and wait to see how it feels. If the guide merely listens and offers condolences or trite solutions, no other portions of the story will be revealed. But if shame is met with grief and honor, then in due season the next chapter of even greater shame will surface. This process is sometimes interrupted by months as a person weathers the exhaustion and integrates the freedom.

Shame that is relinquished and further renounced in the breaking of vows prepares the heart to receive even more deeply the resounding delight of God. Delight is what our heart most desires, but it also triggers our deepest terror: that it is all a ruse, a setup. We are not loved. We are not courageous. This process is all a bad joke, costing immense time and money, and it is about nothing. The level of warfare that comes when shame is challenged, at least for some, validates the fact that we have an enemy that is relentless and cruel.

The struggle with sabotage intensifies, and travelers often return to self-harm, sexual darkness, or addictions.

As we have discussed, the most sickening shame lingers in the moments when we felt most complicit and alive in pleasure. The apex of shame is when there is a fusion of harm and pleasure. It is when we heard our abuser moan in ecstasy. It is when we had an orgasm even though we worked hard to withhold it. It is the gentle touch of the face when being raped. That touch gave us a tiny taste of being human during the bestial violence, and for that pleasure we have condemned and despised our body, our humanity. And evil has joined the harm, if not prompted the curse, and further seduced us to give it power to condemn.

But if we persevere in crossing the river, a time will come when it becomes clear to our spirit that we can continue to curse and kill or we can choose to bless and live. We can bless the twelve-year-old boy whose body was just coming into the first phases of sexual maturity, who was awkward, scared, confused, and alive with lust. And we can grieve how he was set up and maneuvered into a position to be abused. We can bless how his heart and body came alive in being pursued. We can hold as both precious and cruel our specific memories of receiving delight and joy from the abuser; there is no longer a need to split off one memory in order to hold on to a false innocence. We can approach the memory of where we felt most alive and shame-bound, and the curse of contempt can be broken. We can come as an adult to grieve and honor the little child.

When our story is dismantled in the face of kindness and strength, the power of shame can't prevail. Kindness wins. Love triumphs. And eventually sabotage begins to be predicted and our sabotage is sabotaged. The river has been forded. There may be many more stories of shame, but the darkest currents have been crossed and the rest of the journey is now about living out the freedom of blessing.

It is in this context that Jesus delights to give gifts. Some of the most exquisite fishing I have ever done has been after making my way across rivers I thought might kill me. It is the kindness of Jesus that he pours out unexpected goodness on those whose hearts are set on pilgrimage. As shame abates, it is time to sit on the opposite bank, reflect on the goodness and the agony of the journey, and prepare for the arduous climb out of the valley.

Stage Five: Climbing out of the Valley

Once major stories of shame have been engaged again and again over the period of river crossing, there is the need to consolidate. This must become a period of remembering and not anticipating. The simplest question needs to be asked often: *How do I live well given what I now know?* True hope is in knowing and choosing the next right thing, trusting that several thousand small steps will take us out of the valley.

What is ahead is a trudge up the side of a very steep incline. There is no path and no handholds to begin the trek. There are just boulders and huge trees that have been tossed around like matchsticks by the spring runoff. In some ways it is similar to the terror of descending toward the river, only now the work is climbing out. Once one begins to make the yard-by-yard climb, there is always the prospect of falling backward and losing ground. In fact, losing ground is a certainty. It is all too easy to forget the victories of the crossing during the upward climb.

Climbing out of the valley requires slow, tedious, deliberate movement without looking ahead more than twenty yards. To look up the side of the mountain that we need to climb is pointless and defeating. There is enough work within sight. We must sustain our focus, move forward, bless the need to rest, and drink a ton of water.

This is often the period when evil takes its last dramatic shot to prevent us from proceeding on. We will climb out, no matter what, because our life depends on getting out of the valley. But evil wants to mock and mar all we have done by creating an exasperating sense of futility, failure, and frustration along the way.

This is often the period when marriages that have survived and sometimes grown now face immense challenges. Spouses ask, *When is it going to get better?* The survivor of abuse is different—*Shouldn't the marriage be different and better? Shouldn't there be a new wind at my back and greater ease in life?* No. This is, in fact, where the struggles with hope intensify. This is the period when spouses and friends are prone to become more aware of their own disappointment or demands. The closer we get to the summit, the harder it is to sustain progress without sabotage. Impatience and impulsivity are enemies in this stage. This period is a time to return to breathing, staying grounded, and remembering.

As I worked with one couple in this period, we began a long process of recollecting the dangers and near disasters on the journey. We spoke of the failure and agony. Many of the relational challenges were still unresolved, but the couple had to grieve their mutual failure together. There was no need to make it all better or find resolve. And there was much charred ground to face.

In remembering, however, their hearts were woven together with greater awareness of all they had endured and suffered with, for, and against one another. There were tears and laughter. There was a sense of being both overwhelmed and strengthened. They had been through a war together, and their mutual suffering had bonded them more deeply than mere victory or resolution. Step by step, we moved to look slightly ahead at their broken sexual relationship, their failure to fight well, and the temptation to return to addiction and dissociation.

As their terrain just ahead was named and engaged together, they experienced occasional moments of exhausted exaltation. They had undermined evil's design to discourage and overwhelm their hearts with the long journey. Together they had named and broken a host of lingering vows regarding their marriage. And the day came when the husband of my client said, "We are not cured or finished, but it is getting clearer and clearer. Janet is not the so-called problem in our marriage; I am too. I need to step into my own story. Who do I see to get going?" They had reached level ground and now could make real progress in redefining their relationship.

Stage Six: Walking on Level Ground

At this stage, one might think there would be an exhausted collapse and a hunkering down for a long respite. But that is not usually true. Rather, there is a new energy and an expectation that life is truly meant to be engaged in all its sorrow, joy, and power. What is also new in this stage is that shame is no longer easily used by evil to shut us down.

This time is life-giving, fruitful, and volatile. There will be immense change in due season, but the task in the early portion of this stage is to make an accounting of what is central and needs to be engaged immediately and what can wait. Who needs our primary focus, and in what form and time frame? This is not the time to make major decisions about ending relationships, changing jobs, or moving to another part of the country. This season can have such freshness and newness that it is easy to run on mania. My role in this period is to help people walk on level ground and not run off too fast without dampening their wonder and gratitude.

The journey up to this point has required saying no to some demands and expectations from others; otherwise one can't progress on this pilgrimage. But now it is time to ask, *How do I want to say yes and maybe?* I find this to be a stage of refinement. *What foods do I really like? Who do I really want to spend time with? What do I want to do with the years remaining in my life?* Our "yes" may be as simple as taking up an exercise class or starting school. Whenever we say yes to what gives us joy and a sense of purpose, we are living out God's calling for us. "Maybe" gives the opportunity to try out and taste and over time see how our desires are being reconfigured, especially sexually. This is a period in which the triggers of the past are slowly eroding so that new sexual pleasure can be engaged without us resorting as quickly to dissociation or harm. Walking on level ground is saying yes to the next right thing that is linked to the immense privilege of living for the kingdom of God.

One of the significant assaults of evil in this period is to try to triumph through regret. It is easy to survey all that might have been and grieve that it has taken so long to savor and delight in life. Add to this the desire to remove all the debris we have brought into the lives of our children, friends, and family, and it is easy to feel terrible and work frantically to restore all that is broken. We must resist this seduction. Grief is freeing, but regret is the cul-de-sac of despair.

Stage Seven: Following Your Kingdom Calling

Let me tell you a secret: there is no final stage. Deep in our heart we have known this from the very first steps of our pilgrimage. We are not finished. The good news is we get to recapitulate without the exhaustion of reenactment. Reenactment is the repetition of the story to reconfirm doom. Recapitulation involves returning to the story to reengage and open our heart to more healing.

This stage is a declaration of goodness and blessing. We allow ourselves to announce, "I am gifted. I am called. My life matters and I will live my life for the glory of the kingdom of God." It is a season of blessing the scars of abuse, not the abuse itself. Our blessing acknowledges that we are warriors and we have been given gifts, weapons to be used for eternal good.

John Eldredge says, "I am not the hero of this story." This sentence summarizes all that I wish to say. The labor of this pilgrimage is not to gain freedom or joy as much as it is to be captured by the story of Jesus and his death, resurrection, and ascension. But we don't do so by forgetting or ignoring our story. We do so by entering into our own death, resurrection, and ascension in order to learn his story and to live out his story through our own.

As we do so, we will form alliances with those whose stories position them on the same battle lines. These resources and friendships will call us, together, to cry out for redemption and to develop the passion, wisdom, and skills to fight even more beautifully for matters of eternity.

13

Thy Kingdom Come

Each of you is to take up a stone on his shoulder, according to the number of the tribes of the Israelites, to serve as a sign among you. In the future, when your children ask you, "What do these stones mean?" tell them that the flow of the Jordan was cut off before the ark of the covenant of the LORD. When it crossed the Jordan, the waters of the Jordan were cut off. These stones are to be a memorial to the people of Israel forever.

Joshua 4:5–7

When he came near the place where the road goes down the Mount of Olives, the whole crowd of disciples began joyfully to praise God in loud voices for all the miracles they had seen:

"Blessed is the king who comes in the name of the Lord!"

"Peace in heaven and glory in the highest!"

Some of the Pharisees in the crowd said to Jesus, "Teacher, rebuke your disciples!"

"I tell you," he replied, "if they keep quiet, the stones will cry out."

Luke 19:37–40

As a young man I was privileged to study in Israel for a short course on geography to better understand the context of biblical stories. For several weeks, we traversed the country from Galilee to the Negev. Every day we remarked about rocks. Israel is really a rock pile. It is almost impossible to comprehend, unless you travel it, how littered the landscape is with stones.

Stones played a central role in constructing the temple, forming altars, and memorializing places of redemption, and were also used as weapons and a means of executing judgment. Jesus often made use of this ubiquitous daily presence to reverse his listeners' understanding of reality. According to the Gospel of John, he picked up a stone in the presence of a crowd about to kill a woman accused of adultery and said, "Let the one who has never sinned throw the first stone!" (8:7 NLT). He also reminded his religious accusers that the temple would one day be dismantled stone by stone, but in three days it would rise again.

As he entered Jerusalem, a few days before he would be humiliated and killed, he was accused of promoting a riot as the crowd shouted in frenzy. According to the Gospel of Luke he told those who wanted order and decorum: "'I tell you,' he replied, 'if they keep quiet, the stones will cry out'" (19:40). It was a prophetic hyperbole that was meant to reveal truth in a way that intrigues and disturbs. Earlier in Luke the prophet John told the religious leaders not to be too proud of being children of Abraham and Sarah, because in their place God could raise up a people from the stones if they failed to repent (see 3:8).

In both passages, Jesus and John are comparing the hearts of their listeners to stone and reminding those with hard hearts that they need to look around and see that God will raise up life from what is inert and dead. It is an indictment; it is also an invitation. There is a warning: these stones can expose and shatter you! And there is also a promise: from these stones God will raise up a people whose hearts are tender and alive.

Stones are also gathered into piles to mark places where remembrance is required. We are always prone to forget. We need icons, symbols, stones, paintings, Bible verses on the mirror, strings tied to our wrists, sacred places, favorite sweaters, and faces that call us to remember. We are not to live in the past but we are to be accompanied into the future by memory. We must create stone gardens to remind us of God's delight in raising the dead, remember the past, and anticipate the day of full restoration and justice. If we fail to become a witnessing people, God will raise up stones to cry out on his behalf. He will raise up his people in preparation for the moment called "the day of the Lord." It is the day when all things are put right and all suffering and injustice are banished in the new heaven and earth. It is a day we ask for each time we pray, as Jesus taught us, "Your kingdom come, your will be done, on earth as it is in heaven" (Matt. 6:10).

Like much of what Jesus says, these words have radical implications. Are we ever able to bring to this earth what will be fully true in heaven? No, we only have a taste, a small hors d'oeuvre of what one day will be the full banquet. But it is nonetheless real and true, even if small and limited. And what are we to bring to this earth? The best answer is the kingdom of God in all its glory.

The kingdom of God is a good story that reverses expectation and reveals the surprising complexity and goodness of the coming King. Jesus described his kingdom most often with stories so simple and elementary that those who heard him were confused by what he was saying (see Matt. 13). He would say, "The kingdom of God is like a man who sows seed." He told this story to a community of farmers who had been sowing seed for a long time. Another time he told a story that commended shrewd managers who took money from their masters to cover their tracks and provide for themselves when they lost their jobs (see Luke 16:1–15).

He might as well have said, "The kingdom of God is like a sexually abused man whose life was ravaged by hatred, who stumbled into an awareness of God's delight in his body—holy, broken, ripped into pieces by contempt, but blessed and honored with the royal robes of righteousness and a crown of thorns."

Jesus purposefully surprises, confuses, and disrupts in order to expose assumptions about God and life that serve as our false foundation to make life work. The kingdom is a legion of stories too simple, perplexing, bizarre, and complex for us to comprehend, let alone live. Yet God intends for those stories to form for us a picture of his person and his kingdom that is a lived reality now and will one day be fully revealed.

Prophet, Priest, and King

The King himself also comes to us as the Prophet. The King as Prophet testifies to the truth that a kernel of wheat must die to produce many seeds. The Prophet spins stories that reveal and expose and invite those who have ears to hear the knowledge of himself. The King also comes as the Priest who offers the sacrifice of himself to cover the sins of his people and restore them into relationship with himself.

When we bring our story to the story of the Prophet, Priest, and King of the kingdom of God, something happens. We become his ambassadors. We actually become kings/queens, prophets, and priests—just like him. We don't lose our story or unique life; instead, we live out the kingdom we are given. We have a story that needs to be told, a healing path that needs to be walked, a way of leading in which we limp yet stumble forward and kneel before our King.

Jesus told his disciples at the Last Supper that he was conferring to them a kingdom so that they would one day be able to dine with him in his kingdom (see Luke 22:29). We are given the right to serve his kingdom as kings/queens of the kingdom he has bestowed on us. It is crucial to consider what it means in light of the material of this book to be a prophet, a priest, and a king/queen in this kingdom he has given to us.[1] This requires careful consideration of how our story reveals the story of the King of kings.

Priestly Care: Clearing Space

> He brought me out into a spacious place;
>> he rescued me because he delighted in me. (2 Sam. 22:20)

> The LORD is my shepherd, I lack nothing.
>> He makes me lie down in green pastures,
> he leads me beside quiet waters,
>> he refreshes my soul. (Ps. 23:1–3)

A priest opens a spacious place for the heart to speak what is felt by allowing the story of how we got to this place to be told. A priest invites the lived stories to be sung in praise, lament, and thanksgiving. But most of the songs our heart needs to sing are ones of lament and complaint. These are the stories that are seldom told, sung, suffered, or engaged. We are reluctant to hear the wail in the other for fear of what it will provoke in us. A priest must be subjectively at home with both grief and joy—a characteristic formed in the paradox of death, tears, and resurrection laughter.

The image of Jesus as Priest is most powerfully seen during the Last Supper, especially as told in Luke 22. Jesus is the host who serves at the table like a servant, not like a king. He tells his friends that one who sits at that table will betray him. The scene demands that the disciples ask, "Who?" But no one asks; instead, the conversation immediately turns into a food fight of accusation and eventual boasting. It is beyond bizarre. After three and a half years of daily engagement with Jesus, his disciples still have no more maturity than drunken frat brothers.

Jesus allows the space for the dark matters of the heart to come pouring out without condemnation or indulgence. He engages the debris of their fear, shame, and pride and invites them to imagine the calling of living hospitably. A priest is a host or hostess who spreads an abundant table and invites stories.

I have been to many lovely homes and sat at countless meals that were graciously served. Lavish. Delicious. Elegant. These meals were polite and socially appropriate. The same is true for most of our church services. Truth is spoken but the raw reality of life is seldom exposed or engaged during our worship. I don't expect this to change, and likely it shouldn't. But every now and then I need to let my soul wail.

The last time I was in Ethiopia to address issues of sexual exploitation and human trafficking, our friends gathered to pray over us and send us off. They laid hands on us and began to pray in Amharic. Soon a woman I adore prayed partially in English to tell Jesus on our behalf of her sorrow in our departure. She began to wail. It was a staggering sound. It began so suddenly and out of context that my limbic system, my mirror neurons, set off a deep, piercing cry in my soul.

I didn't wail. I am an older American male. But tears flowed out of my eyes with such force that I couldn't see. I may not have had the courage to wail, but I did whimper. And in my tears, I felt the kindness and the delight of Jesus.

We desperately need space to feel, tell, and hear the broken heart tell the truth. Sadly, too little space exists in families, churches, schools, bars, movie theaters, art galleries, or coffee shops. We have few spaces to tell and feel the truth other than a therapist's office. But we all need a witness to the particularities of our story, someone who takes in and holds everything from banal trivialities to what is so horrendous it can barely be seen, let alone spoken. This need was voiced well in the movie *Shall We Dance*:

> We need a witness to our lives. There are a billion people on the planet, what does any one life really mean? But in a marriage, you're promising to care about everything. The good things, the bad things, the terrible things, the mundane things, all of it, all of the time, every day. You're saying "your life will not go unnoticed because I will notice it. Your life will not go unwitnessed because I will be your witness."[2]

Even truer, however, is that we are a proxy witness for the One who reminds us that our life is seen and held by a great cloud of witnesses. We are not alone. Our days have been accounted for and remembered by the One who has saved every tear that has fallen and every tear that refused to fall. To create a rock garden of holy remembrance we must take ownership of the ground we are given and begin the backbreaking work of clearing the space. This space is both internal (our heart) and external (our calling).

A friend told me that she was required in college to take a language course, and because she learns better by using her body, she chose to learn sign language. She enjoyed it and did well, but she seldom used it, except for occasional signing for her church. This apparently random experience from her college years was not a conscious choice to seek the kingdom of God. As the years went by she pursued a job, family, and life like most of us. Her story also included sexual abuse, but she viewed those events as irrelevant to her current life and gladly left in the past.

In her midthirties she met a deaf woman at her church and began signing for her during services. Her new friend eventually told her of her past sexual abuse, and for the first time she was compelled to address her own story. Their stories converged and she was introduced to a number of deaf women who had no access to therapists due to their hearing impairment. She was not a therapist and knew little about sexual abuse, but she attended therapy with one of her new friends to sign for her and translate for the therapist. The experience propelled her into her own story and to develop a ministry to hearing impaired women in her community.

The ground God gives us to witness to and clear for others as well as ourselves is not often what we choose. It is truer to say the ground calls to us. It tells us what we are chosen to do, and we need to respond and answer the call.

We must listen to the voice of the witness of our life and know that as the Spirit invites us to care for others, he intends as well for us to know redemption for ourselves. The Spirit calls us to see, feel, suffer, cry out against, and delight in, and to commit ourselves to the arduous process of healing. God has called us to be priests as well, priests who open space for stories to be entered with truth. Whatever space needs to be opened, it will require us to dig up tree trunks, move boulders, and hack away at dense, prickly foliage. But nothing is more worth living for than witnessing and opening terrain for the kingdom of God to thrive in.

Prophetic Creativity: Imagining Redemption

> If you do away with the yoke of oppression,
>> with the pointing finger and malicious talk,
> and if you spend yourselves in behalf of the hungry
>> and satisfy the needs of the oppressed,
> then your light will rise in the darkness,
>> and your night will become like the noonday.
> The LORD will guide you always;
>> he will satisfy your needs in a sun-scorched land
>> and will strengthen your frame.
> You will be like a well-watered garden,
>> like a spring whose waters never fail. (Isa. 58:9–11)

Priests have the locale of the temple and eventually the church. Kings and queens have the castle and throne. In both worlds, there is specified space, ritual, and hierarchy. Not so for the prophet. The prophet is a desert rat: a writer, poet, painter, therapist, blogger, musician. A prophet is a truth revealer who tells truths that arouse the heart to desire redemption and restoration.

I spoke to an African-American woman, a pastor in a Harlem church, who told me, "I just sing the blues in prose and coax the heart to kiss the dreams that cry out for justice and mercy." I know she does even more in the pulpit, but what she described is the work of a prophetic voice. She crafts beauty to awaken the heart to taste and see the goodness of God. She is a truth teller who uses her creativity to forge words, images, music, and art to capture the heart.

A prophet exposes the heart's proclivity to idolatry and intensifies the desire for what we are most meant to enjoy. A prophet's art creates beauty that makes it difficult to accept injustice as it is. The art form may be a rose garden, a chocolate cream pie, a poem, a song, a legal brief, a sand tray, or a sermon. A prophet uses beauty to name and to testify to our dark propensity to oppress, point the finger, and speak maliciously. It seems simple enough: whomever we oppress, use, and exploit we will eventually point at with contempt and undermine with words. We will dehumanize. Mock. Objectify. We stand above, aloof, and separate from, and we blame.

We were created to be in restored relationship even with those with whom we differ. And the movement toward restoration can only be entered through the doorway of disruptive beauty. A prophet's space is anti-Eden—the realm of the broken, the waterless world where the absence of the verdant sweetness of Eden creates a hunger and hope for restoration. The prophet comes to the throne and says to the ruler, "You favor the rich," and comes to the altar and says to the priest, "You say 'peace, peace' when there is no peace."

All over the world, beauty has disrupted the status quo of a cruel and heartless world. There has long been a movement to teach addicts, prisoners, and the homeless how to write poetry—to help them to regain their dignity through the creation of beauty. Beauty awakens, exposes, and disrupts the ugliness of the expected and instead re-creates a vision of what is meant to be.

Prophets are often stoned and hated. It is no wonder that being a prophet is rarely a career choice but rather an intrusive calling. Consider the cost for anyone who disturbs the comfortable status quo and invites the heart to yearn for what is not yet realized. At best, we are curious about these odd creatures, but mostly we prefer to buy their music or art and let them haunt the world we don't want to enter.

But we are called to be these creative, disruptive people ourselves. We are called to say to other victims of abuse, "Your thick skin doesn't hide your wounded heart." We are meant to say to our political leaders, "Sexual abuse is an expensive social evil," and to our religious leaders, "God cares about the orphan, the stranger, and the widow—who are all vulnerable—and it is the weak who are most often sexually abused." We are called to be prophets in our families, churches, and communities.

At the close of this book is an appendix written by my colleague and friend Linda Royster. She is an African-American woman and is on staff at the Allender Center for Trauma and Abuse. Her appendix speaks to the (often) unaddressed issues of sexual abuse in the African-American community. She tells truths that disrupt her African-American world. She tells truths that expose the long history of sexual abuse of people of color by whites. She exposes the cowardice of men and the complicity of women, and she calls for all men and women to dream the dream of redemption. The price for Linda is far higher than the realized gains because every pioneer must endure pushback from those reluctant to face the truth.

Like Linda, we are called to use our story to disrupt the reenactments of abuse and not settle for anything less than heaven on earth. Our voice is to be used creatively to tell the truth. This requires living into and becoming a paradox. Jesus often urged his followers to lose their lives so they could find their true lives. He told his disciples on their first missionary trip, "Be as wise as a serpent and as innocent as a dove" (see Matt. 10:16).

One client remarked, "I have spent my life striving to fit in and not cause disruption. You are telling me that I have to be like a prophet who wears weird clothing and eats locusts? I have succeeded in hiding how odd I am, and now I am supposed to use my strange imagination for the kingdom of God?" In fact, she is meant to bless her disruptive imagination, create beauty, tell the truth, and invite others to something well beyond the status quo.

My client had been gifted with creativity and a keen imagination, but she always wanted to stay off the radar screen. Thus for years she had been viewed as having little to offer in her church. She seldom volunteered, and when she did, she did only what was required. But as she worked through issues of her past sexual abuse, she began to step into the freedom she had been given as a broken and beautiful woman who was no longer defined by her past. In fact, she entered her world with panache.

When the church staff and leaders had a major gathering, she offered to make dessert for the fifteen who would be at the meeting. She discovered each person's favorite pie and crafted a miniature pie with homemade ice cream for each of them. After the meal they asked who had made the stupendous dessert, and many were surprised that she had such skill.

Weeks later a pastor asked her why she had hidden her exquisite baking abilities. She asked him, "Are you teasing or do you really want to know?" He was surprised at her candor and said, "No, I'd really like to know why you have been hiding." She replied, "Pastor, I have been hiding my whole life from people in power because of some terrible things that were done to me when I was a little girl. If you want to hear more, I'd be glad to tell you. I am not hiding anymore—not my baking or anything else."

This pastor followed up later and asked her to tell him her story. She did. Months later he called her and asked if she would meet and pray with a woman who had shared with him stories of past sexual abuse. No one can predict where a good dessert in the hands of a prophet might lead.

Given that redemption is always a turnaround, a turn upside down, it is inevitable that the prophet will sometimes be considered far worse than weird. Therefore, prophets are meant to fit in and be as normal as they can—that is, living in accord with the norms of family, friends, epoch, and culture. This is being a dove. Be pleasant, if not at times obsequious. Do what is right in the eyes of others. But remember you are also a snake, capable of blending in and striking at the right time. The strike is not about vengeance or retaliation. It is not a form of passive-aggressive spirituality. Instead, being a dove and a serpent means plowing up the field to prepare it for good seed, then seeding the soil with truth and waiting.

This is particularly the calling of prayer and perseverance. We will seldom see what we dream in our life or the lives of others if we fail to seed the heavens with our desire. Prayer is storming the heavens with hope. It inevitably demands that we live the prayer we pray and become the king we ask God to deliver. Just as a fiction writer is often challenged to tell the truth through the characters he or she has created, so are we called to become what we request of God to do. Our fiction becomes real. Our dreams become true. And realizing our dreams demands that we lead.

Kingly Initiative: Ruling with Strength and Wisdom

See, today I appoint you over nations and kingdoms to uproot and tear down, to destroy and overthrow, to build and to plant. (Jer. 1:10)

Then Jesus came to them and said, "All authority in heaven and on earth has been given to me. Therefore go and make disciples of all nations, baptizing them in the name of the Father and of the Son and of the Holy Spirit, and teaching them to obey everything I have commanded you. And surely I am with you always, to the very end of the age. (Matt. 28:18–20)

An ancient Near Eastern king was often referred to as a shepherd—one who protects and provides for his sheep. The kingly/queenly work of God is providing strength and wisdom to rule so that space, including natural resources, people, and goods, is not proportioned unfairly. A king must make space for the priest, who reminds us of how we came to be here. A queen must allow the time for stories to be told, processed, and pursued. She must also make room for the prophet, who exposes the failures of the present and invites us to dream of the future.

A king or queen is far more than a manager or decision-maker. He is the gardener-shepherd-leader who authorizes the uprooting and tearing down. She knows the past but refuses to be bound to systems or buildings that are no longer inhabitable. He authorizes the removal of debris and the building of temporary structures that will suffice until what is desired is constructed. And she authorizes resources to be spent to create what is not now but will one day come to be.

A woman we know discovered that her daughter was dancing in a strip club. She was beside herself with grief and confusion. What could she do? She knew her daughter had been sexually abused as a child, and at the time they had sought counseling. Her daughter went for a few sessions and then said she was fine. A decade later she was working in the club. Our friend felt powerless, but she knew she had to do something.

One night she felt compelled to stop in at the club. She sat in the audience and felt sickened and enraged. The bouncer was suspicious and gave her a hard time, but she held her ground and ended up talking with him about his life.

Our friend is a kind, thoughtful, and generous woman, but no one would mistake her for a fearless advocate or reckless risk taker. Still, she prayed with a few friends, and this small group of women decided to visit the strip club every Tuesday night. Her daughter was too ashamed to have her come on any day that she was dancing, and she guaranteed her mother that she would never dance on Tuesdays. Her mom and her friends got to know the bouncer, the owner, and the other girls. They never caused trouble, and they drank their diet colas and sparkling waters, tipping generously. After a few months, the husbands also got involved, dropping their wives off at the club and then driving a block away to meet and pray together.

The owner was happy because the girls felt cared for and honored. The bouncer loved the visits because the older women mothered him, baked him cookies, and entered the heartache of his story. The girls, including our friend's daughter, were never scolded or condemned; instead, they were offered caring and honest conversations about their lives. Over time her daughter heard from the other girls about the "church ladies" who hung out in the club and offered makeup and certificates for massages. Their kindness and care softened hearts to consider the gospel.

Our friend now leads this lovely ministry through her church. She has become more bold and free, and there are many young women who have been accompanied into the kingdom of God because of her queenly presence. After several years of dancing, her daughter was exhausted by the relentless exploitation and asked her mom for help to develop a career in nursing.

A kingdom led by good leaders will produce more goods than it needs. It is the responsibility of a king or queen to distribute the goods for the benefit of the kingdom, not themselves. This is where most kingdoms turn foul. The produce of the kingdom is a gift to those whom it serves. Its ruler must prioritize commitments, allot funds, and focus on the good of the many while also saving and providing safety and protection against the few who would impose their will on the many.

To say the least, to rule is to use power to serve and do the seemingly impossible. It requires immense courage, wisdom, and willingness to suffer for good. Tragically, kings and queens are often cowardly, foolish, and indulgent. When this happens, the kingdom turns dark and soon everyone suffers. In contrast, a king or queen who stands against evil and honors dreams will work for justice and peace. He or she will not pick a fight or feel the need to prove himself or herself, nor will he or she concede to injustice or to the mockery of a bully.

For an abused man or woman, this means taking back the authority given them by Jesus over his or her body and heart. There has to be a willingness to go to war against the dark accusations and vows formed in earlier periods of one's kingdom that mar the present and future. The claims and accusations of the kingdom of darkness need to be revoked and vows broken.

Using Your Kingdom Gifts

So take the bag of gold from him and give it to the one who has ten bags. For whoever has will be given more, and they will have an abundance. Whoever does not have, even what they have will be taken from them. (Matt. 25:28–29)

Then the righteous will answer him, "Lord, when did we see you hungry and feed you, or thirsty and give you something to drink? When did we see you a stranger and invite you in, or needing clothes and clothe you? When did we see you sick or in prison and go to visit you?"

The King will reply, "Truly I tell you, whatever you did for one of the least of these brothers and sisters of mine, you did for me." (vv. 37–40)

Once authority to live is restored and the kingdom is set in the direction of life, then it is imperative all gifts, talents, and assets be directed for the sake of the kingdom of God. Our story is not our own. Our past abuse, current struggles, and future redemption are not ours alone. All my stories and yours, in due season, are *ours*. Nothing, ultimately, is private or personal. Our lives are revelatory and belong to generations before and after. Our suffering and incomplete but full redemption are part of the story that seeds the kingdom to come.

Equally, our gifts of gold are not our own. As greater freedom grows in our life to live out the work of a prophet, priest, and king/queen, we will need to allocate our time and resources to fulfill our calling. Our calling is not a job, a career, or even a vocation. Our calling is to live out the character of God.

I am a therapist, teacher, writer, and fly fisherman. That is my current set of skills and passions, but my calling is primarily about exposing the shame and contempt of the kingdom of darkness as it relates to our broken sexuality. Even more I am called to live out and indwell the delight of God. My kingdom is focused primarily on exposing shame and elevating delight. It permeates all my writing, teaching, and activities. I have a job, but if I were to get fired or move on, my calling wouldn't end. It would only have a new realm in which to flourish. I am highly verbal, bright, entrepreneurial, quick-witted, unafraid of a fight, extremely hardworking, hyperfocused, and loyal. I also have my share of flaws. But all combine into a way of being that makes the possibility of retirement unlikely if not impossible. I am called to wage a war, and I see no way to step off the dais until I am incoherent and/or incontinent.

We all need to account for our gifts and the talents (gold) we are given by God for his use. God intends for our work in his kingdom to produce fruit. The parable of the talents given in order to create profit indicates that what God gives he intends for us to use and not hide (see Matt. 25:14–28). We serve Jesus and his kingdom by how we care for the broken: those who are hungry, thirsty, estranged, unclothed, sick, and imprisoned. This is both a concrete statement and a metaphor. Jesus tells us that we give him a drink of cold water when we give a thirsty child a drink. We give him a warm coat when we give a man who has no coat our covering (see vv. 31–46). Part of what it means to be a king or queen is to distribute our gifts and wealth to those who are broken and need our care. If we choose not to do so, what we have will be given away to someone else.

A dear friend, who is a world-class bamboo rod maker, told me the story of a fellow craftsman who was twenty years older and considered the best in the world. This man hoarded his knowledge and refused to give away his techniques and wisdom. His rods were inconceivably expensive, but when they aged or snapped no one else could fix them. The rod maker refused to help, and over time his rods came to be worth nothing since a broken rod or the prospect of one is valueless.

Hoard, and your produce will rot. Some of the unhappiest people I have ever worked with are staggeringly wealthy and terrified of loss. Some of the happiest people I have ever been privileged to know are staggeringly wealthy and committed to dying as near paupers. They keep the gift until it matures them in gratitude and then they give it away. Our gifts and talents are to be returned ultimately to the One who gave them to us. We do so not by some religious act but by caring for the hungry. Everyone is hungry; some don't have food.

We are to feed everyone what we ourselves are meant to partake. The issues of sexual abuse require that we address the harm of abuse with everyone, especially those who are uniquely vulnerable to the misuse of power and lust: the poor; orphans; people of color; immigrants; the blind, deaf, mentally ill, and developmentally challenged; prostituted boys, girls, women, and men; LGBTQ youth; child soldiers; people with disabilities; prisoners; the bullied and sexually harassed; victims of domestic violence; and anyone else who has been used as a dumping ground for sexual violence. It is never enough merely to care for oneself and one's household. We are an extended family, and everyone who has known sexual harm or has harmed another sexually is our brother and sister. Blood and tears bond us. Our bodies bear similar scars. We need to open the field of our heart and begin the hard labor of clearing the land. We need to dream redemption for ourselves and others.

Every dollar you give to any organization gives you the right to ask: How are you addressing sexual harm? How can we provide medical care or new wells or restore nutrient-deprived lands when the sons and daughters of those we serve may be sexually violated? Every hour you volunteer at church gives you the right to ask: How are we addressing sexual abuse in our community? What is our policy when abuse is suspected? What are the provisions for those who begin to face this harm? Who is trained to engage or be the conduit for a wise referral? Do we have a policy if we discover that someone who has abused a child is beginning to attend this church?

We have no right to ask those questions of any person or community that has not felt our desire to learn about and delight in their lives. And we can't offer our own stories unless we are far, far more committed to suffering their stories than telling our own. We have to be priests and kings before we will ever be endured as prophets. But at some point, we must speak. The issues of sexual harm can't remain a hidden, unspoken issue in our families, churches, and culture. It can't remain a private, unspoken issue in our own life. There is a time for healing—and a time for piling rocks into a configuration of beauty and meaning.

I have written this whole book in the presence of one rock. It is a small, pink stone with sixteen concentric circles in an egg-shaped loop. I found the rock as I sat on the bank of a Montana river that will one day receive my ashes. It is a holy space that has saved my life more often than it has nearly taken it. I sat praying one day as I watched a dear friend catch yet another trout. I looked down at my feet and saw the stone and I heard Jesus say, *For you. Take and eat.* I laughed. I may be addled, but I am not inclined to eat any small stones.

But that is when I began thinking again about the stones in Israel. They call me to build a garden of remembrance. To not cast judgment. To bless the temple—my body—made of flesh and not stone. To bear witness to the ferocious kindness of a God who will raise up a people from stone to address these issues if we fail to speak.

Look at your feet. Listen to the voice of God. Hear the impulse to act and enter the waters and see if the Jordan is stopped. If the waters hesitate, pick up a stone and mark the place so that when your children and your children's children one day ask, "Papa, what did you do in the war?" you will have an answer worthy of your one beautiful, scarred, precious life.

APPENDIX

The Implications
for African-American Women

by Linda Royster

W hat does the content of this book have to do with African-American women? Posing this question reveals its premise: there are notable differences in how assaults on faith, hope, and love are metabolized in black women, but this premise is valid only when one contextualizes African Americans' trauma within African-American history. That said, there is no uniform response to trauma that applies to African-American women in all places at all times. We are a sisterhood with as many disparate experiences as any other group. Therefore, as you read, hold in mind that what is written here is not applicable to every woman of color. The shaping of identity and the lenses we develop do not escape the influence of religion, gender, or ambiguous categories of race. Yet, as varied as our experiences are, every African-American woman who is not alien to herself or her experiences knows that she is affected by the stories of her ancestors.

Words hold the power to transform cultures, systems, and individuals. For example, grandmothers, historical and flawed cornerstones

253

within black culture, know the power of words to buoy up themselves and others through tumultuous seasons by their faith and testimonies. Likewise, words have the power to tear down and deface, disempowering and infuriating at will.

Abusers often use words to produce an array of emotions in their victims, known as a type of speech act. Their intention is to coerce and entangle their victims in a net of lies that bond victim to abuser. The act of abuse is both physical and verbal. An act can either unify or fragment. Acts of kindness can unify our body, our thinking, and our will, creating a capacity to love with the fullness of God's intent for each human being. Adversely, physical and speech acts of abuse can fragment our sense of self, leaving us to do the work of salvaging the wreckage.

The Field of Debris

A field of debris is the area of wreckage left behind as a result of the destruction of something that was once intact. Forensic investigators examine wreckage and by doing so create a story of how that wreckage probably happened. This is not unlike the experience of entering our stories of harm, where much is uncertain but the likelihood of certain events or sequences of events is highly probable.

Shame, distorted loyalty/idolatry, and fear are debris left from the wreckage of slavery. Black women across history who are victims of sexual abuse suffer similar rubble, especially since the bridge that connects generations is relatively short.

Shame

Shame is no small matter to acknowledge or relinquish. As African-American women, we have suffered shaming experiences regarding every aspect of our being. We are a people who through legal, psychological, social, and religious means were robbed of our right to our own bodies. The press for ownership, and therefore power, has been a founding principle of America that has vastly different outcomes depending on the clan to which one has been born. Historically, the world has gazed upon, analyzed, appraised, owned, abused, and ridiculed our body. Because of that degree of shaming and violence, our mind, emotions, and desires are rarely known and valued.

It is unwise and disingenuous to write about the impact of sexual abuse on African-American women without acknowledging that American history shapes the expression of black women's trauma. Neither should we ignore the dark work of evil in its convergence of familial failure, social ostracization, and systemic oppression. All make fertile ground for shame to take root.

At the place where desire for love and loss of love intersect, shame takes root and grows deep, choking out life in places that are meant to bring glory and joy. As an embodied experience, shame obscures reality, altering our perception of the world and our experiences, making it virtually impossible to orient ourselves to truth that has been captured in ancient teachings. Jesus's parable of the two foundations in Matthew 7:24–27 might seem completely disconnected from this description of shame, but it is a fitting framework. Jesus lays out the differences between a wise and foolish builder: one who built on rock and the other who built on sand. The foolish man built his construction on shifting sand, perhaps with the full expectation that his house would serve its purpose. But skilled and unskilled builders alike know that buildings need a firm and level foundation; otherwise, its rooms and all their contents will be crooked too.

The implications of "the crooked room" study from Melissa Harris-Perry's seminal work can be applied to shame. She references the work of H. A. Witkin et al., who conducted psychological studies that tested the cognitive phenomenon of field-dependence (reliant on surroundings) or field-independence (undistracted by surroundings).

Basically, participants were blindfolded and instructed to sit on a crooked chair in a crooked room of which they were initially unaware. The experiment was to determine if they could find a truly upright position or if their posture, or way of being, was field-dependent. Some found the true upright, but others, being out of kilter by as much as 35 degrees, assumed their positioning as normal.

Black women are daunted by the way shame from sexual abuse puts us in "crooked rooms." Often we have shame for disavowing our commitment to live out an intracultural stereotype that says we are always resilient, capable, and indestructible. Shame deceives us into becoming insular and steals our freedom to function with liberality.

Consider a young African-American woman who was sexually and physically abused throughout her childhood and teen years and date raped as a young adult. As expected, she struggled with her sexuality. In her youth she never spoke of her abuse because she read in her family dynamic that she could not report her victimization and receive any modicum of aftercare. Both awakened to and frustrated by her desire for intimacy, she rarely blessed either. She was often bewildered by what it meant to be a follower of Christ, unmarried and simultaneously alive to sexual desires. She loved her church communities, but each was profoundly anxious and avoidant about addressing sexuality for a single woman.

Having a history of abuse created caverns in her heart that predisposed her to longing for men who harm sexually, verbally, and emotionally, or harm by their absent heart. She found herself repeatedly falling in love with the same man—different face, different frame, but no less the same man—and felt compelled by her desire for him. Anything different made her bored, disinterested, or even angry. Apart from the enlightenment that only awareness brings, she proceeded into a deeper relationship with a new guy. Within months, they spiraled downward and she knew they would come to the end she expected.

After one particularly long workday, she anticipated his arrival. They both knew why he was there, but she, pretending happiness, convinced herself she was glad to see him, banishing her anger, fear, and disappointment. After having sex, which left her feeling used, she knelt on the floor feeling immense shame and anxiety while he excused himself to the bathroom. He returned, stood over her, and said he thought it would be best if they were just friends. Still kneeling on the floor, eyes filled with tears and heart ripping open, she begged him not to leave. He turned and walked out, leaving her devastated but not surprised. The crooked room of sexual abuse had stolen this woman's joy in trusting her goodness and her desire for kindness, killed her imagination to craft a future different from her past, and destroyed the freedom to liberally give and receive pleasure in the here and now.

By divine design of being African American, we are born in a crooked room. When sexual abuse and misuse are added, the room tilts further. For us, as with all abuse survivors, whether we acknowledge it or not, finding the true upright requires the active presence of the Spirit.

Writing about abuse within black communities is the equivalent of galloping on horseback with a sword through an old but active battleground. Exposing violence that black people perpetrate against each other feels much like using weapons meant to war against evil to strike behind our own defenses and wound each other in our most vital places. This imagery may seem violent and unnecessarily provocative. However, when considering all that has been and is still being stolen from African Americans through internal and external thievery, strategic engagement is necessary to reclaim what is ours and to oust occupying forces. More specifically, reclaiming our body from the power and presence of our abusers must become part of the process of liberation. Our body does not belong to our abusers. This point is not to be missed.

The girl who suffered significant trauma through each stage of development into her adult life learned to believe the lie that she did not own her body or her voice. Having a heart that was hungry for love and attention made the soft caresses of her abuser a taste of heaven. Her abuser's touch was far kinder than the abrasive and utilitarian touch of her mother and the lack of touch from her father. Her fear, ambivalence, and suspicion that she was a dirty little girl were not enough to make her run from the gentle touches of her abuser. To whom could she have run? Certainly not to her mother, whom she suspected despised her.

However, as nurturing as that moment was for the abused young girl desperate for her parents' affection, it is no less true that ancient lies are communicated when abusers go untrammeled as they wound through the violence of sexual and emotional abuse. As a result, girls who have been starved of love and affection grow into women who congeal their identities around lies that say they are not worthy of fidelity, protection, advocacy, or support, and they conclude that their being is not innately good or desirable. Interpersonally, they develop styles of relating that, no matter where they land on the continuum, prevent their heart from being accessed and enjoyed. Shame often becomes the end result of having built a house on shifting sand.

Distorted Loyalty/Idolatry

There is immense tension in addressing abuse within black communities. Certainly, shame silences, but a distortion of our loyalty perpetuates harm. In one direction, there is a commitment to protect black men and women from suffering harm at the hands of those unsympathetic to their plight. In the opposite direction is a desire to live free of the horror of intracultural abuse, which requires exposing abusers and heightening cultural shame. Protecting and exposing abusers cannot co-occur; this creates a double bind.

Effectively, loyalty that has been distorted is no more than an illusion of belonging and safety. Every culture has extremist factions that hold to a rigid set of beliefs and have disdain for anyone who disagrees. Political parties, some church communities, and racist ethnic groups are reminiscent of gangs that demonstrate how loyalty can become idolatrous.

Consider an example of how a black community set up an adolescent to be victimized and then protected the abuser. An African-American girl entered her adolescence bold and courageous, but left it cursing her voice and her heart for advocacy. She was not the most brazen in her circle of friends, but neither was she the wallflower. Like most teenage girls, she had a growing awareness and curiosity about her sexuality and her changing body, and she was unsure of how to navigate the terrain between girlhood and womanhood, especially since none of the women in her life dared to have conversations about what it meant to mature.

Observant and sensual, she knew that she drew attention. People noticed her; men decades older undressed her young body with their eyes; eager and awkward teenage boys stole touches of her bottom and breasts. What remained of her sensual joy and youthful playfulness was incinerated when a man who ideally should have been protector and advocate violated her trust. Previously, he had indeed shown himself within his family as abusive and scandalous, but somehow he was allowed access to her. His sexual assault was violent and left wounds on her body and heart.

With the courage of a thousand Zulu warriors who fought against invasion, she pressed charges against her assailant knowing that her private hell would have to become public. His family and hers soon took matters into their own hands and fought both physically and verbally. Each side defended their own. As far as she knew, no one in his family ever held him accountable for his actions. They vehemently protected him. However, no one talked to her to see how she was faring. She lived with PTSD and ensuing terror for many years, hypervigilant and secretly blaming herself for causing disruption in her community because she dared to speak out against her abuser.

As some communities cover or excuse abuse, they make themselves look more like gang participants in that they engage in activity that undermines the goodness they desire. They believe that concealing harm and protecting abusers will save them and their community. It will not. Since African Americans have been victims of historical and localized terrorism, of course we want to protect our own; it is written into our cultural DNA. While honorable, this has its limitations. Unexamined loyalty to any person, system, group, or set of beliefs is at best foolish and at worst idolatrous. Distorted loyalty is an attempt to escape the heartache of loss of hope.

At the place where abuse and economic insecurity intersect, the devastation of distorted loyalty is multiplied and makes black women and children even more vulnerable. There are some black mothers, as well as some mothers from every race and every socioeconomic class, who have joined in their child's abuse through betrayal, choosing not to believe or to blame their daughter or son when the child makes the immensely courageous decision to report her or his abuse. Undoubtedly, a parent's failure to believe and protect has everything to do with his or her own story, which is likely one of harm, and has little to do with the child. These families sacrifice children to keep abusers safe by not addressing their shame or the broader shame found within black culture. Thus, these families retain a false hope of having stability, economic security, physical safety, and romantic love in an environment that is violent and precarious.

An African-American family caught in the throes of poverty and dysfunction captures this reality. The young, gentle, caring, and beautiful girl in that family had become the scapegoat long before her fifth birthday, and this was her enduring role in their family. Her stepfather soon learned that she was the scapegoat and treated her with disdain, eventually physically and verbally abusing her. With gusto that she had managed to retain in the face of constant humiliation, she sought help and safety from her biological father, who advocated in small measure on his daughter's behalf, albeit with woeful inadequacy. He communicated his anger over her abuse and invited her to live with him and his family, but she remained in her primary home, where she continued to suffer hatred and violence. Already on the brink of sinking further into poverty, her deeply wicked mother blamed her for inciting her husband to violence. She assured her daughter that if her husband, who provided their only source of income, left them it would be solely her daughter's fault.

African-American women and girls, like all survivors of abuse, pay a high cost for their own victimization. We carry not only the physical effects of abuse but also its social effects. Many survivors feel the pain of having been abused but are also fearful of what may happen to one more black person who enters the legal system. Well aware of the imbalance of our justice system, survivors often are more loyal to protecting black culture than to doing the heartrending work of genuine healing. This loyalty bind creates an idolatrous turn to protect the family and culture instead of pursuing truth. The duality of surviving and protecting represents a multiplicity of existence. The conflict of some African-American women who have survived abuse is similar to W. E. B. Du Bois's notion of "double-consciousness"—a two-ness of being: one that is innate and the other that is birthed within social systems.

Fear of Vulnerability

Racial and sexual trauma, which are essentially identical, influence us physiologically and psychosocially. Many black women have persistently heightened levels of fight/flight/freeze responses. While some have found bastions of hope within church communities that provide true comfort to survivors of abuse, infuriatingly there are some who fail to provide succor. They evade speaking of sexual abuse from the pulpit as if trauma were not central to the Passion of Jesus. Ironically, we are a people accustomed to storytelling and trauma, but we too often tell familiar and safe stories. Traditional black churches have kept their tradition of "testifying," wherein congregants tell of God's goodness and how they made it over or through or endured some difficult fate. However, we mostly fail to tell the truth of our lives. We fail to tell the shame-filled stories that wreak the most havoc. I understand this silence. It is risky and disruptive to name our harm, and we cannot engage sexual trauma narratives in our communities without disrupting the entire system.

Some African Americans experience the invitation to enter more deeply into their stories with a sense of suspicion and question why anyone might want to know about their most painful experiences. It goes against what many African Americans have been trained to believe: we are strong; do not show weakness because doing so makes you a target of contempt; real women and real men can and should pull themselves up and through any difficult circumstance. These are beliefs that are strongly held, and they also reveal places of idolatry where we worship at the altars of strength, suprahumanity, and false beliefs of womanhood and manhood.

Such is the case of one black mother's stance toward her daughter who only hours earlier had suffered a sexual assault. This mother's words to her daughter, who sat in the living room in tears and in the early stages of PTSD, were, "You need to stop crying and go to bed because he didn't actually rape you." If you are not chilled by those words, then I invite you to consider what has calloused your heart. Her words were icy and they captured her attitude: *What happened wasn't that bad; pull yourself together because there is no time, space, or energy designated to heal. If you receive healing, it will be happenstance, not because of any intentionality. Your harm belongs in your past; look forward.*

However, it should not be ignored that Jesus says, "Let the little children come to me, and do not hinder them" (Matt. 19:14). I am certain he speaks of literal little children but, by using my holy imagination, I suggest that he refers to our inner young selves as well—those parts of us that were deeply trusting and deeply betrayed.

African-American pastors, churches, and families, with all diligence, must not contradict their calling by willfully turning their faces away from abuse survivors and unwittingly colluding with evil.

Fear of bringing more harm to sexual abuse survivors through willful ignorance or deliberate silencing has a legitimate place; either is dangerous. However, fear of vulnerability within black communities is understandable but illegitimate. Such fear is an expression of a loss of faith, forgetting that God is trustworthy and good. I am not equating vulnerability with weakness but rather I am describing it as the opening up of oneself to the reciprocal process of being known and knowing others with the added risk of being hurt. An African-American woman who has suffered sexual abuse might tremble internally at the invitation and call to live in vulnerability. Pressured expectations to keep the façade of *We are strong and capable of enduring immense harm without significant effect* must be deconstructed.

Deconstructing fear of vulnerability does not have a formulaic solution. However, it is a process that requires intentionality to counter what has been constructed over centuries through injustices wedded to evil. If we have not been kind to ourselves and, certainly, if we have not been shown kindness, then vulnerability is transformed into an enemy. Living with a stance of vulnerability is developed through praxis, a process of becoming, as African Americans well know.

As black women, our fluctuating life, in all its facets and settings, demands that we suit up in the attire each milieu requires. However, what we usually put on is made of something equivalent to emotional and psychological Teflon. Some black communities recognize a central theme for black women as caretakers and fixers who hold together systems and families. Black women's bodies have been used to maintain the agendas of those who lord their power over them. Many black women, regardless of the type or magnitude of difficulties, find a path forward, even if they must create paths for themselves. Yet black women are not impervious to harm.

Some women have not allowed themselves the right to grieve. Ambivalent and frightened, we ask, "Why cry? Who will attend to our pain? What good does it do to revisit our dark places?" Some of us reason that if we cannot hold life together then we have failed at being a black woman, because black women are not weak. If we are, then something must be wrong with us. Many fear that feeling the depth of harm they've suffered will be like opening up the dam that has held back centuries of tears yet to be shed. The tears we need to cry for ourselves, for our ancestors, and for our daughters are of oceanic proportions.

Commonly, people both within and outside black communities call us strong, as a favorable description. It is an act of naming our goodness; a blessing. Many consider our perseverance, in spite of immense harm, as equivalent to strength; they are interconnected. However, the implication of their naming us as strong is invisibility. If our defining descriptor is strength, then that signals to others that we need less care and attunement. It signals that we can be left alone to mend ourselves because we are resilient enough to pull ourselves up and gritty enough to move ourselves forward.

Ignoring our stories of sexual abuse will not undo the harm we have suffered. The debris of our abuse will surface eventually. It affects our memories, aspirations, and relationships.

The interplay of our fear of vulnerability and perceptions of us as strong and unbreakable suggests that some unwittingly bless our defense mechanism. Some black women even become contemptuous toward themselves or other women if they show any indication of what they misconstrue as weakness. This approach tends to obscure or transform what once served as a gift into an issue used by evil to keep the cycle of harm in place.

Defensive structures are developed for one or more reasons. They serve a purpose, often one of keeping us sane and stable when we are incapable of changing threatening circumstances. Many black women are tender beneath a sometimes impenetrable external shroud, but there is no rest there. To be constantly on guard against being hurt is a defeatist approach to gaining what we really want: a capacity to play out our role in the kingdom of God. Playing is imagining without limits, giving ourselves over to the thrill of creating with others or alone. It is regenerative and shapes our reality.

Now, as always, we can name ourselves in our context, redefining what *strong* and *tough* mean. As I am learning, advocating for the attunement to the young girl in us who was deeply violated is crucial in ushering us more deeply into our rich and awe-filled stories.

Notes

Introduction

1. If there is good news regarding sexual abuse over the last twenty-five years, it is that we have seen a decrease in the number of children molested. One estimate is that there has been a drop of up to 49 percent. There are other studies that indicate a smaller change, but this decrease has been noted in more than forty-one states. These figures are subject to debate and are neither final nor conclusive, but they do indicate that the fight against sexual abuse is going in the right direction. (See David Finkelhor and Lisa Jones, "Why Have Child Maltreatment and Child Victimization Declined?" *Journal of Social Issues* 62, no. 4 [2006]: 685–716.)

Researchers have taken into account many issues that might cause a drop in the number of cases of reported childhood sexual molestation, not all of which indicate a true decrease in sexual abuse. Those factors can't be ignored; nevertheless, it is with reasonable optimism that we can say changes for the good have occurred. (See Lisa M. Jones, David Finkelhor, and Stephanie Halter, "Child Maltreatment Trends in the 1990s: Why Does Neglect Differ from Sexual and Physical Abuse?" *Child Mistreatment* 11, no. 2 [2006]: 107–20.)

Still, vast numbers of children are being abused. It is highly probable that in the past, as in the present, the majority of abuse never gets reported or factored into the statistics. One research study found that among younger women (ages 18–24) sexual abuse had slightly decreased in early years but had increased in the years of early to mid-adolescence. The perpetrators in these cases were peers and older adolescents. (See Eric Casey and Paula Nurius, "Trends in the Prevalence and Characteristics of Sexual Violence: A Cohort Analysis," *Violence and Victims* 21, no. 5 [2006]: 629–44.)

Chapter 1 The New Face of Sexual Abuse

1. American Psychological Association, "Report of the APA Task Force on the Sexualization of Girls" (2007), http://www.apa.org/pi/wpo/sexualization.html.

2. Donna Freitas, *Sex and the Soul: Juggling Sexuality, Spirituality, Romance, and Religion on America's College Campuses* (Oxford: Oxford University Press, 2008), 148.

3. Todd Melby, "Teens, Porn, and the Digital Age," *Contemporary Sexuality* 44, no. 9 (2010): 1–5.

4. Julie Albright, "Sex in America Online: An Exploration of Sex, Marital Status, and Sexual Identity in Internet Sex Seeking and Its Impacts," *Journal of Sex Research* 45, no. 2 (2008): 175–86.

5. Jodi Lipson, ed., "Hostile Hallways: Bullying, Teasing, and Sexual Harassment in School," AAUW (Washington, DC: American Association of University Women Educational Foundation, 2001), http://history.aauw.org/files/2013/01/hostilehallways.pdf.

6. US Department of Education, Office for Civil Rights, "Revised Sexual Harassment Guidance: Harassment of Students by School Employees, Other Students, or Third Parties," Office of Assistant Secretary of Civil Rights (January 19, 2001), http://www2.ed.gov/about/offices/list/ocr/docs/shguide.html.

7. Linda Charmaraman, Ashleigh E. Jones, Nan Stein, and Dorothy L. Espelage, "Is It Bullying or Sexual Harrassment?: Knowledge, Attitudes, and Professional Development Experiences of Middle School Staff," *Journal of School Health* 83, no. 6 (2013): 438–44.

8. Donna Freitas, *The End of Sex: How Hookup Culture Is Leaving a Generation Unhappy, Sexually Unfulfilled, and Confused about Intimacy* (New York: Basic Books, 2013), 40.

9. William F. Flack Jr., Kimberley Daubman, and Marcia Caron, "Risk Factors and Consequences of Unwanted Sex among University Students: Hooking Up, Alcohol, and Stress Response," *Journal of Interpersonal Violence* 22, no. 2 (2007): 139–57.

10. Freitas, *End of Sex*, 49.

11. This section has borrowed heavily from these works: Donna Freitas, *Sex and the Soul: Juggling Sexuality, Spirituality, Romance, and Religion on America's College Campuses* (Oxford: Oxford University Press, 2008); Lauren Winner, *Real Sex: The Naked Truth about Chastity* (Grand Rapids: Brazos, 2005); and Mark D. Regenerus, *Forbidden Fruit: Sex and Religion in the Lives of American Teenagers* (Oxford: Oxford University Press, 2007).

Chapter 2 The Role of Evil

1. In a state of hyperarousal, part of the brain called the insula sends signals to the amygdala to secrete adrenaline, norepinephrine, and cortisol, which prepare the body for fight, flight, or freeze. This process radically decreases the activity in the left frontal lobe and especially Brocca's area, the portion of our brain that controls speech. This process is so rapid that it precedes our capacity to "think" and shuts down the mind in a state we call *dissociation*. Dissociation is not a choice; it is a God-given physio-psychological process similar to what we call *shock*.

2. G. K. Chesterton, *Orthodoxy: The Romance of Faith* (New Kensington, PA: Whitaker House, 2013), 66.

Chapter 3 The Body's Response to Abuse

1. Scan a sample of these books and articles and see if any prompt some openness or some curiosity to contemplate the ways in which your body has held mental and

emotional pain: Bessel van der Kolk, MD, *The Body Keeps the Score: Brain, Mind, and Body in the Healing of Trauma* (New York: Penguin, 2014); J. Douglas Bremner, MD, *Does Stress Damage the Brain?: Understanding Trauma-Related Disorders from a Mind-Body Perspective* (New York: W. W. Norton, 2002); Sonia J. Lupien et al., "Effects of Stress throughout the Lifespan on the Brain, Behavior, and Cognition," *Nature Reviews* 10 (2009): 434–45; Michael D. De Bellis and Abigail Zisk, "The Biological Effects of Childhood Trauma," *Child Adolescent Psychiatric Clinics North America* 23 (2014): 185–222; and Sandra Odebrecht Vargas Nunes et al., "The Impact of Childhood Sexual Abuse on Activation of Immunological and Neuroendocrine Response," *Aggression and Violent Behavior* 15 (2010): 440–45.

2. Bremner, *Does Stress Damage the Brain?*, 274.

3. For example, neuroendocrinology. Bruce McEwen is one leading researcher and voice in this area. "Stress is a state of the mind, involving both brain and body as well as their interactions; it differs among individuals and reflects not only major life events but also the conflicts and pressures of daily life that alter physiological systems to produce a chronic stress burden that, in turn, is a factor in the expression of disease." This is the opening sentence of the abstract in his recent review article in which he describes the historical context of this field, the physiological adaptations our bodies make to handle stress, the consequences of chronic stress, and what we can do about them. See Bruce McEwen, "Brain on Stress: How the Social Environment Gets under the Skin," *PNAS* 109 (2012): 17180–85.

4. Oxytocin is released by the hypothalamus, directly linked to the pituitary. It has been linked to pair-bonding (including parent-child); attachment; mothering activities such as milk letdown; contractions post-labor; buffering against stress, anxiety, and depression; and more. See Kayt Sukel, *This Is Your Brain on Sex: The Science behind the Search for Love* (New York: Free Press, 2013) for a discussion of oxytocin in pair-bonding and sexuality. See Daniel A. Hughes and Jonathan Baylin, *Brain-Based Parenting: The Neuroscience of Caregiving for Healthy Attachment* (New York: W. W. Norton, 2012) for a discussion of oxytocin with regard to parent-child relationships.

5. Nurturing touch is so important that when rhesus monkey babies were separated from their mothers and forced to choose between a wire "mother" that provided milk or a cloth "mother" that provided softness and warmth but no sustenance, the monkeys consistently chose the cloth mother. This is a classic psychology finding by Harry Harlow with rhesus monkeys in the 1950s and '60s, reviewed by Robert M. Sapolsky, *Why Zebras Don't Get Ulcers: The Acclaimed Guide to Stress, Stress-Related Diseases, and Coping* (New York: St. Martin's Griffin, 2004), 117–19.

6. See Hughes and Baylin, *Brain-Based Parenting*, and Sukel, *This Is Your Brain on Sex*, for more discussion of brain areas and biochemicals (such as oxytocin, vasopressin, dopamine, serotonin, and prolactin) that interact to promote feelings of love and connection, as well as how they are shaped by early experiences and influence future caregiving behavior.

7. Italian researchers accidentally discovered mirror neurons in 1994 while running experiments with monkeys using single electrodes to determine specific motor neurons activated when grasping objects. For historical review, see van der Kolk, *Body Keeps the Score*, 58–59.

8. Mirror neurons enable us to read others well, be in sync, imitate, and feel empathy for others. They also enable others to read us well, an important aspect of attunement. Abuse almost always disrupts this process. For review, see van der Kolk, *Body Keeps the Score*, 58–59, 111–12; and Hughes and Baylin, *Brain-Based Parenting*, 39–41.

9. Early development of secure attachment to the mother or other caregiver is foundational to healthy emotional and relational processing throughout the lifespan. There is much research in this area. "It is not an exaggeration to say, based on research across mammalian species, that good parenting sculpts the child's brain for emotional resilience and social competence while developing the child's capacity to trust other people and to sustain positive, caring relationships" (Hughes and Baylin, *Brain-Based Parenting*, 6). For a review of how to help children develop secure attachment through emotionally healthy parenting, see Hughes and Baylin, *Brain-Based Parenting*. For research on the development and disruption of healthy attachment, see Pat Ogden, Kekuni Minton, and Clare Pain, *Trauma and the Body: A Sensorimotor Approach to Psychotherapy* (New York: W. W. Norton, 2006).

10. Serotonin is linked to feelings of happiness and well-being, and is considered our body's natural stress buffer. It is also important in many other physiological processes throughout the body. For a review of the vital role of serotonin in mental and physical health, as well as strategies to improve your health, see David Edelberg with Heidi Hough, *The Triple Whammy Cure: The Breakthrough Women's Health Program for Feeling Good Again in Three Weeks* (New York: Free Press, 2006).

11. Our sexual desire, feelings, and behavior are shaped by three systems in the brain: desire (lust), attraction (romance), and attachment. Lust is the desire for pleasure. Attraction is the prompting for someone who not only arouses desire but also offers intimacy. The third area of the brain is related to attachment. The same portion of the brain that fires when a mother securely attaches to her child is energized when we are sexual. Consequently, sexuality is bound to arousal (dopamine), intimacy and attachment (oxytocin), and many more biochemicals. See Daniel G. Amen, *Sex on the Brain* (New York: Random House, 2007); and Kayt Sukel, *Dirty Minds: How Our Minds Influence Love, Sex, and Relationships* (New York: Free Press, 2012).

12. See Dan B. Allender and Tremper Longman III, *God Loves Sex: An Honest Conversation about Sexual Desire and Holiness* (Grand Rapids: Baker, 2014).

13. van der Kolk, *Body Keeps the Score*, 55–65.

14. Ibid., 60.

15. Ibid.

16. The sympathetic nervous system gears the body up, and the parasympathetic nervous system slows the body down ("the brakes"). Both systems can be stimulated through inhaling and exhaling, respectively, which is why meditation and breath work can be so effective in bringing our body back into balance, peace, and homeostasis. For an overview of these systems, including how they prepare the body to respond to stress, see van der Kolk, *Body Keeps the Score*, 76–77; Hughes and Baylin, *Brain-Based Parenting*, 14; and Sapolsky, *Why Zebras Don't Get Ulcers*, 20–23.

17. A major player in our body's stress response system is the hypothalamic-pituitary-adrenal (HPA) axis. When a stressor is detected (by the amygdala), this system sets in motion a cascade of events aimed at quickly preparing the body to handle the

stress. The hypothalamus is immediately signaled to release corticotrophin releasing hormone (CRH) and vasopressin (AVP), which then stimulate the pituitary gland to release adrenocorticotrophic hormone (ACTH), which in turn stimulates the release of glucocorticoids, such as cortisol, from the adrenal glands to gear the body for responding to the acute stressor.

Each day our body produces and regulates cortisol in a diurnal rhythm, with a healthy cortisol curve rising in the morning, preparing the body to wake and equipping it to respond to any upcoming stress, peaking around 6:00–8:00 a.m., then falling (variably, responsive to food, time, and stressors) throughout the day, reaching its lowest levels during nighttime sleep, around 2:00–4:00 a.m., and then climbing back up to reset for the next day.

For an accessible overview of the anatomy and physiology of the stress-response system, see James L. Wilson, *Adrenal Fatigue: The 21st Century Stress Syndrome* (Petaluma, CA: Smart Publications, 2001), 255–301; also Shawn Talbott, *The Cortisol Connection: Why Stress Makes You Fat and Ruins Your Health—and What You Can Do about It* (Alameda, CA: Hunter House, 2007), 14–50.

Much research has been done on the HPA axis, cortisol in particular, and the multitude of biological, psychological, and social factors that affect its healthy functioning or dysregulation. See reviews throughout Sapolsky, *Why Zebras Don't Get Ulcers*; Wilson, *Adrenal Fatigue*; and Eamon McCrory, Stephanie A. De Brito, and Essi Viding, "The Impact of Childhood Maltreatment: A Review of Neurobiological and Genetic Factors," *Frontiers in Psychiatry* 2 (2011): 1–14. Also, for an interesting discussion on how cortisol response to stress changes over multiple timescales (from minutes to days, weeks, months, years, across developmental stages, and even across generations), see Emma K. Adam, "Emotion-Cortisol Transactions Occur over Multiple Time Scales in Development: Implications for Research on Emotion and the Development of Emotional Disorders," *Monographs of the Society for Research in Child Development* 77, no. 2 (2012): 17–27.

18. Messages are sent from the thalamus simultaneously to the amygdala along the "low road" (automatic, bottom-up processing) and the prefrontal cortex along the "high road" (conscious, effortful, top-down processing). The amygdala receives messages just milliseconds quicker than the prefrontal cortex, almost determining whether or not there is a threat to our system, and will then signal the hypothalamus to activate the stress response throughout the autonomic nervous system if so, even before the prefrontal cortex brings conscious awareness to the situation. These two pathways are reviewed by van der Kolk, *Body Keeps the Score*, 60; see more comprehensive discussion by the neuroscientist who named these pathways, Joseph LeDoux, in *The Emotional Brain: The Mysterious Underpinnings of Emotional Life* (New York: Simon & Schuster, 1996).

19. van der Kolk, *Body Keeps the Score*, 62–64.

20. Freezing: in this case the parasympathetic system activates and the sympathetic system is suppressed (a reverse pattern of activation from the fleeing or fighting response). For review, see van der Kolk, *Body Keeps the Score*, 71–73, 82–83.

21. For a more detailed overview of the stress response in the brain and body, see Bremner, *Does Stress Damage the Brain?*, 38–70; Sapolsky, *Why Zebras Don't Get Ulcers*, 20–36; and van der Kolk, *Body Keeps the Score*, 55–65.

22. van der Kolk, *Body Keeps the Score*, 39–44.

23. Ibid., 43–44.

24. Ibid., 42–47.

25. Ibid., 71–73. In terms of treatment, depersonalization is particularly resistant to talk therapy and instead requires mindful engagement with the body.

26. Allostasis refers to our body's ability to maintain internal balance or homeostasis by perceiving and adapting to our environment and therefore setting new "normal" ranges for physiological functioning (such as increased stress hormone secretions). Homeostasis, on the other hand, has historically referred to our body's unchanging normal levels of physiological function, without regard to the body's adaptation to the environment—in other words, not taking into account our body setting a "new normal." See Robert Paul Juster, Bruce S. McEwen, and Sonia J. Lupien, "Allostatic Load Biomarkers of Chronic Stress and Impact on Health and Cognition," *Neuroscience and Biobehavioral Reviews* 35, no. 1 (2010): 2–16.

27. For an in-depth discussion of these concepts, including the many individual factors that comprise allostasis and allostatic load, see Juster, McEwen, and Lupien, "Allostatic Load Biomarkers."

28. For review, see McEwen, "Brain on Stress," and Juster, McEwen, and Lupien, "Allostatic Load Biomarkers."

29. See van der Kolk, *Body Keeps the Score*; this is both the book's title and the reoccurring theme of the book.

30. The shrinking of these areas can take various forms, such as decreased growth and branching of dendrites, less neurogenesis, and so forth. For overview, see McEwen, "Brain on Stress"; Sapolsky, *Why Zebras Don't Get Ulcers*, 210–25; Bremner, *Does Stress Damage the Brain?*, 108–120; A. F. T. Arnsten, "Stress Signalling Pathways That Impair Prefrontal Cortex Structure and Function," *Nature Reviews Neuroscience* 10, no. 6 (2009): 410–22; and Nunes et al., "Impact of Childhood Sexual Abuse." Also see review highlighting the impact of duration and developmental timing of stress on the brain: Sonia J. Lupien, Bruce S. McEwen, Megan R. Gunnar, and Christine Heim, "Effects of Stress throughout the Lifespan on the Brain, Behaviour and Cognition," *Nature Reviews Neuroscience* 10, no. 6 (2009): 434–45.

31. For review on the multiple ways estrogen (and other hormones) affects the brain, including the ways in which it benefits neurogenesis, see Bruce S. McEwen and Teresa A. Milner, "Hippocampal Formation: Shedding Light on the Influence of Sex and Stress on the Brain," *Brain Research Reviews* 55, no. 2 (2007): 343–55; also Bruce S. McEwen et al., "Estrogen Effects on the Brain: Actions beyond the Hypothalamus via Novel Mechanisms," *Behavioral Neuroscience* 126, no. 1 (2012): 4–16.

32. For review, see McEwen, "Brain on Stress."

33. Abused children show atypical development of the HPA axis (human and animal studies corroborate these findings), making them more vulnerable to psychopathology later in life. For review, see McCrory, De Brito, and Viding, "Impact of Childhood Maltreatment"; and Nunes et al., "Impact of Childhood Sexual Abuse." Also see Lupien, McEwen, Gunnar, and Heim, "Effects of Stress," for a review of stress-related changes in the HPA axis and brain structure and function in relation to timing and duration of stress across developmental stages over the lifespan.

34. For review, see De Bellis and Zisk, "Biological Effects of Childhood Trauma." For example, adults with childhood trauma, compared to those with adulthood trauma, show flatter diurnal cortisol rhythm, culminating in higher overall daily output of cortisol (meta-analysis). Sexually abused girls vs. nonsexually abused girls showed initial higher levels of cortisol in childhood and then attenuated levels beginning in adolescence and continuing into young adulthood (the only longitudinal psychobiological study to date). For more discussion on how HPA axis activity and cortisol output change across multiple timescales in relation to chronic stress, see Adam, "Emotion-Cortisol Transactions Occur over Multiple Time Scales in Development."

35. For overview, see Bremner, *Does Stress Damage the Brain?*, 265–76. Additionally, Sapolsky, *Why Zebras Don't Get Ulcers*, devotes many chapters to a comprehensive yet accessible review of the effects of stress on specific body systems.

36. Respiratory system: for example, asthma is aggravated by stress; see interesting line of studies in Richard. J. Davidson and Sharon Begley, *The Emotional Life of Your Brain* (New York: Hudson Street Press, 2012), 127–32; also Michael L. M. Murphy, George M. Slavich, Edith Chen, and Gregory E. Miller, "Targeted Rejection Predicts Decreased Anti-Inflammatory Gene Expression and Increased Symptom Severity in Youth with Asthma," *Psychological Science* 26 (2015): 111–21; and Stacy L. Rosenberg, Gregory E. Miller, John M. Brehm, and Juan C. Celedón, "Stress and Asthma: Novel Insights on Genetic, Epigenetic, and Immunologic Mechanisms," *Journal of Allergy and Clinical Immunology* 134 (2014): 1009–15.

37. Digestive system: for review, see Sapolsky, *Why Zebras Don't Get Ulcers*, 71–91.

38. Metabolic system: for review, see ibid., 60–70.

39. Endocrine system: for example, given the adrenal glands' central function in pumping out the steroids our body uses to gear up in stressful situations, such as cortisol, a common consequence of chronic stress is literally stressed adrenal glands, a condition known as adrenal insufficiency or fatigue. For a helpful, accessible resource for identifying and correcting this condition, see Wilson, *Adrenal Fatigue*. For a brief review of the relationship between positive emotion and daily cortisol patterns, see Andrew Steptoe, Samantha Dockray, and Jane Wardle, "Positive Affect and Psychobiological Processes," *Neuroscience & Biobehavioral Reviews* 35, no. 1 (2010): 69–75.

40. Cardiovascular issues are linked to chronic stress; for example: hypertension, plaque formation, increases in CRP (C-reactive protein, a marker of inflammation now commonly tested), atherosclerosis, damage to inner lining of blood vessels, platelet clumping, decreased heart rate variability (especially during depression), and more. For review, see Bremner, *Does Stress Damage the Brain?*, 270–72; Sapolsky, *Why Zebras Don't Get Ulcers*, 41–54; and Davidson and Begley, *Emotional Life of Your Brain*, 117–36. For a brief review of the relationship between positive emotion and cardiovascular function, see Steptoe, Dockray, and Wardle, "Positive Affect and Psychobiological Processes."

41. The immune system gains a boost during acute stress but is weakened by chronic stress. For a detailed overview, see Sapolsky, *Why Zebras Don't Get Ulcers*, 144–85; for a brief review, see van der Kolk, *Body Keeps the Score*, 126–27, 240; and Daniel G. Amen, *Change Your Brain Change Your Body: Use Your Brain to Get and Keep the Body You Have Always Wanted* (New York: Three Rivers Press, 2010), 217–18. For a review of many immunologic components (such as proinflammatory cytokines, antinuclear

antibody titers, and activation of T cells) that show dysregulation in relationship to childhood trauma, see De Bellis and Zisk, "Biological Effects of Childhood Trauma"; also Nunes et al., "Impact of Childhood Sexual Abuse." For a review of the relationship between positive emotions and immune function, see Davidson and Begley, *Emotional Life of Your Brain*, 117–33; also Steptoe, Dockray, and Wardle, "Positive Affect and Psychobiological Processes."

42. Reproductive system: for review, see Sapolsky, *Why Zebras Don't Get Ulcers*, 120–43.

43. For example, even our skin holds the effects of chronic stress. In one research study, plastic surgeons examined photos of 186 identical twins and tried to determine the age of each individual based on his or her facial features. The results indicated that the twin who had experienced more stress (such as divorce) was rated as looking older than their twin counterpart; see Bahman Guyuron et al., "Factors Contributing to the Facial Aging of Identical Twins," *Plastic and Reconstructive Surgery* 123, no. 4 (2009): 1321–31 (reviewed by Amen, *Change Your Brain Change Your Body*, 216–17). Even our hair holds our cortisol levels and can be used to determine our past stress levels; see Brittany Sauvé et al., "Measurement of Cortisol in Human Hair as a Biomarker of Systemic Exposure," *Clinical and Investigative Medicine* 30, no. 5 (2007): E183–91.

44. Stress and autoimmune disorders are linked. See Sapolsky, *Why Zebras Don't Get Ulcers*, 154–60, for physiologic explanation; and van der Kolk, *Body Keeps the Score*, 126–27, 291. Also, for an interesting study linking previous periods of chronic stress to current periods of amplified inflammatory response, see Gregory E. Miller and Steve W. Cole, "Clustering of Depression and Inflammation in Adolescents Previously Exposed to Childhood Adversity," *Biological Psychiatry* 72 (2012): 34–40.

45. Telomeres are the protective ends on each strand of DNA within our chromosomes (composed of repeated DNA sequences and specialized proteins), often compared to the plastic tips on the ends of shoelaces. When cells divide, telomeres shorten, which is associated with aging (for an interesting tutorial on telomeres, see http://learn.genetics.utah.edu/content/chromosomes/telomeres/). Telomeres also shorten as a result of chronic stress, starting in infancy (and perhaps even in utero) and continuing throughout the lifespan. For example, children who have experienced trauma typically have shorter telomeres than children who have not experienced trauma. Stress-related shortening of telomeres (and reduced telomere maintenance, via the enzyme telomerase) is a sign of premature aging and a potential mechanism for abnormalities in brain development, mental health, and physical health. The good news is that more current research is beginning to suggest that telomere shortening can be slowed, or even reversed, through healthy lifestyle adaptations such as stress reduction, exercise, and dietary improvements. For an interesting review and commentary on this research by two of the field's pioneers, see Elizabeth H. Blackburn and Elissa S. Eppel, "Telomeres and Adversity: Too Toxic to Ignore," *Nature* 490 (2012): 169–71; also review by De Bellis and Zisk, "Biological Effects of Childhood Trauma," 197; and Amen, *Change Your Brain Change Your Body*, 216–17.

46. Powerlessness during harm is an intensely stressful, traumatic state—resulting in persistent and destructive psychological and physiological consequences such as learned helplessness and chronically increased levels of stress hormones, among others;

for review, see van der Kolk, *Body Keeps the Score*, 29–31; Sapolsky, *Why Zebras Don't Get Ulcers*, 260–63, 267–69, 300–304, 403–6; and Sally S. Dickerson and Margaret E. Kemeny, "Acute Stressors and Cortisol Responses: A Theoretical Integration and Synthesis of Laboratory Research," *Psychological Bulletin* 130 (2004): 355–91.

Shame is also associated with increases in stress hormones such as cortisol, as well as increases in the secretion of proinflammatory cytokines (which "initiate and maintain the inflammatory response") from the immune system. See Sally S. Dickerson, Tara L. Gruenewald, and Margaret E. Kemeny, "When the Social Self Is Threatened: Shame, Physiology, and Health," *Journal of Personality* 72, no. 6 (2004): 1191–216; and Dickerson and Kemeny, "Acute Stressors and Cortisol Responses."

47. The combined experience of powerlessness and shame is intensely stressful. In research studies that asked participants to give a public speech or do a math task, for example, in which social evaluative threat (being judged by others) was paired with uncontrollability, "in which participants could not succeed despite their best efforts," (powerlessness, in the form of exposed failure)—eliciting shame—participants reliably showed the largest cortisol response in a meta-analysis of 208 acute laboratory stressor studies (very large effect size, d = .92, nearly three times greater than stressors with only one of those two components); also cortisol was slower to recover to baseline in these conditions. See Dickerson and Kemeny, "Acute Stressors and Cortisol Responses."

48. Trauma often leads to addictions such as eating disorders, substance abuse, and more. For discussion, see Sapolsky, *Why Zebras Don't Get Ulcers*, 343–52; and van der Kolk, *Body Keeps the Score*, 70, 98–99, 120, 146–47, 266, 286–89.

49. The connections between past abuse and current physiological functioning can be powerfully illuminated within a trusted community. As one woman said after being in a Wounded Heart group, "When it's in yourself, you can't connect the dots as much, but when you hear it in someone else, all of a sudden you can't let it go. It's like a war has started, and you can't just shove it under the rug anymore. It starts the wrestling in the soul, and it ends up being about the soul more than the physical body."

50. For a brief review of the role of the medial prefrontal cortex, self-awareness, and interoception (now often called mindfulness), see van der Kolk, *Body Keeps the Score*, 95–96, 206; also Ogden, Minton, and Pain, *Trauma and the Body*, 218–21, for a more clinical discussion on fostering interoception.

51. Bremner, *Does Stress Damage the Brain?*, 275.

52. Serotonin is our body's "factory-installed buffer against stress." Dr. Edelberg thoroughly discusses the vital role of serotonin as the body's natural stress buffer, as well as the importance of reducing stress and balancing hormones (the three components of his "triple whammy"). See Edelberg and Hough, *Triple Whammy Cure*.

53. See a recent review article for exciting new advances in this area of neuroscience research on neural plasticity, or the way the brain changes in response to environment and experience, and how these changes include neurogenesis, or the growth of new neurons: Richard Davidson and Bruce McEwen, "Social Influences on Neuroplasticity: Stress and Interventions to Promote Well-Being," *Nature Neuroscience* 15, no. 5 (2012): 689–95.

54. So many great resources are available to help us understand how our emotions, particularly stress, affect the brain and body and how to care well for both. Here are a few:

Daniel G. Amen, *Change Your Brain Change Your Body: Use Your Brain to Get and Keep the Body You Have Always Wanted* (New York: Three Rivers Press, 2010).

J. Douglas Bremner, *Does Stress Damage the Brain?: Understanding Trauma-Related Disorders from a Mind-Body Perspective* (New York: W. W. Norton, 2002).

David Edelberg with Heidi Hough, *The Triple Whammy Cure: The Breakthrough Women's Health Program for Feeling Good Again in Three Weeks* (New York: Free Press, 2006).

Pat Ogden, Kekuni Minton, and Clare Pain, *Trauma and the Body: A Sensorimotor Approach to Psychotherapy* (New York: W. W. Norton, 2006).

Robert M. Sapolsky, *Why Zebras Don't Get Ulcers: The Acclaimed Guide to Stress, Stress-Related Diseases, and Coping* (New York: St. Martin's Griffin, 2004).

Shawn Talbott, *The Cortisol Connection: Why Stress Makes You Fat and Ruins Your Health—and What You Can Do about It* (Alameda, CA: Hunter House, 2007).

James L. Wilson, *Adrenal Fatigue: The 21st Century Stress Syndrome* (Petaluma, CA: Smart Publications, 2001).

Bessel van der Kolk, *The Body Keeps the Score: Brain, Mind, and Body in the Healing of Trauma* (New York: Penguin, 2014). This book is a treasury of up-to-date scientific research on how trauma affects the brain and body, and specifically highlights much research on the effects of sexual abuse, as well as explaining many potential avenues toward recovery.

55. Be encouraged that even deciding to start somewhere can make a significant improvement; see the "80/20 rule" for stress management in Sapolsky, *Why Zebras Don't Get Ulcers*, 414–15.

56. Sleep: Amen, *Change Your Brain Change Your Body*, 195–212; Wilson, *Adrenal Fatigue*, 124–27; Edelberg and Hough, *Triple Whammy Cure*, 170–76; Sapolsky, *Why Zebras Don't Get Ulcers*, 226–38; and Talbott, *Cortisol Connection*, 141–44.

57. Eating well: Edelberg and Hough, *Triple Whammy Cure*, 245–73; Talbott, *Cortisol Connection*, 147–54; Amen, *Change Your Brain Change Your Body*, 81–108; and Wilson, *Adrenal Fatigue*, 133–91, including detecting food sensitivities and allergies that could be causing inflammation and taxing the body. Also, Dr. Andrew Weil is renown for developing a repertoire of anti-inflammatory foods and diet—see his website (http://www.drweil.com) for his work and available resources, including a cookbook, *True Food: Seasonal, Sustainable, Simple, Pure* (New York: Little, Brown and Co., 2012). See also many other available cookbooks for practical ideas on how to eat "clean," reduce inflammation, promote healing, and optimize health through quality nutrition; for example, Alejandro Junger, *Clean Eats: Over 200 Delicious Recipes to Reset Your Body's Natural Balance and Discover What It Means to Be Truly Healthy* (New York: HarperCollins, 2014).

Eating well is not about dieting or attempting to lose weight. Diets are destructive and ineffective. An approach to eating is not possible to develop in this book, but to consider a radically different approach to food, please consider: Evelyn Tribole and Elyse Resch, *Intuitive Eating: A Revolutionary Program That Works*, 3rd ed. (New York: St. Martin's Griffin, 2012); Linda Bacon, *Health at Every Size: The Surprising Truth about Your Weight*, 2nd ed. (Dallas: BenBella Books, 2010); Anita Johnston, *Eating in the Light of the Moon: How Women Can Transform Their Relationship with Food through Myths, Metaphors, and Story Telling* (Carlsbad, CA: Gurze Books, 2000); and Linda Bacon and Lucy Aphramor, "Weight Science: Evaluating the Evidence for a Paradigm Shift," *Nutrition Journal* 10 (2011): 9, http://www.nutritionj.com/content/10/1/9.

58. Exercise has consistently proven to have many health benefits. Even short bouts of exercise can help the body come back into balance and promote healing. For example, Dr. Edelberg encourages a twenty-minute walk each day (in sunshine), which raises phenylethylamine and triggers the release of endorphins, including GABA, norepinephrine, dopamine, and serotonin. For review, see Edelberg and Hough, *Triple Whammy Cure*, 47–48, 216–20; Amen, *Change Your Brain Change Your Body*, 109–26; Talbott, *Cortisol Connection*, 144–47, 249–60; and Frank J. Penedo and Jason R. Dahn, "Exercise and Well-Being: A Review of Mental and Physical Health Benefits Associated with Physical Activity," *Current Opinion in Psychiatry* 18 (2005): 189–93. For motivation, Ken Adams has written an enlightening and inspiring book about living more fully each day, which among other things includes daily doses of fun, movement, play, and exercise: *Fully Alive: A Journey That Will Change Your Life* (Nashville: Thomas Nelson, 2012).

59. Sunlight: walking briskly in the sunlight twenty minutes a day (without sunglasses, unless needed for an eye condition) will boost serotonin. See Edelberg and Hough, *Triple Whammy Cure*, 47–49.

60. Prayer: research on the potential cognitive, emotional, and physiological benefits of prayer has increased dramatically in the last fifteen years and is also becoming an increasingly popular topic in neuroscience research, as researchers aim to see how prayer changes brain activity. Prayer research is challenging, however, as it is a deeply personal process and highly variable, not to mention supernatural! Findings to date are mixed, and this field is continuing to refine its methodology and grow. See Andrew Newberg and Mark Robert Waldman, *How God Changes Your Brain: Breakthrough Findings from a Leading Neuroscientist* (New York: Ballantine Books, 2009); see also a recent review article, Kevin L. Ladd and Bernard Spilka, "Prayer: A Review of the Empirical Literature," in *APA Handbook of Psychology, Religion, and Spirituality: Context, Theory, and Research*, vol. 1, ed. K. I. Pargament, J. J. Exline, and J. W. Jones (Washington, DC: American Psychological Association, 2013), 293–310.

61. Gratitude: Amen, *Change Your Brain Change Your Body*, 227–29, 257; for a theological discussion of gratitude and how to grow in gratitude, see Ann Voskamp, *One Thousand Gifts* (Grand Rapids: Zondervan, 2010).

62. Kindness and/or service to others raises serotonin (see Edelberg and Hough, *Triple Whammy Cure*); for a compilation of research on the multiple benefits of altruism, see Stephen G. Post, ed., *Altruism and Health: Perspectives from Empirical Research* (New York: Oxford University Press, 2007).

63. Laughter: see an inspiring story about Norman Cousins on the healing power of laughter reviewed by Wilson, *Adrenal Fatigue*, 128–29; see also Amen, *Change Your Brain Change Your Body*, 174, 234; and Edelberg and Hough, *Triple Whammy Cure*, 18–19, 203.

64. Music: for a diverse compilation of research on the multiple benefits of music (of various modalities, such as listening to, singing, playing an instrument) on the brain and body, see Raymond MacDonald, Gunter Kreutz, and Laura Mitchell, eds., *Music, Health, and Wellbeing* (New York: Oxford University Press, 2012). For numerous

real-life stories highlighting the power of music on the brain, see national bestseller written by Dr. Oliver Sacks, *Musicophilia: Tales of Music and the Brain* (New York: Vintage Books, 2008); also van der Kolk, *Body Keeps the Score*, 242–43, 330–46, for a discussion of the therapeutic benefits of expressive therapies such as music, art, dance, and theater. For an insightful Bible study on the power of song as a tool of expression for the soul, see Beth Moore, *Stepping Up: A Journey through the Psalms of Ascent* (Nashville: LifeWay, 2007). For the best theological work on the power of music and worship, see Reggie Kidd, *With One Voice: Discovering Christ's Song in Our Worship* (Grand Rapids: Baker, 2005).

65. Social support: van der Kolk, *Body Keeps the Score*, 79, 210–15, 230–47; and Sapolsky, *Why Zebras Don't Get Ulcers*, 164–66, 256–58, 406–7.

66. Mind-body connection: many techniques are available to help the mind become increasingly aware and open to what the body is holding and telling, powerful tools toward recovery. For example: mindfulness, meditation, yoga, Tai Chi, Qi Gong, and so forth. For overview, see van der Kolk, *Body Keeps the Score*, 203–29; and Hughes and Baylin, *Brain-Based Parenting*, 200–204. For in-depth discussion, theory, and practice of sensorimotor therapy, see Ogden, Minton, and Pain, *Trauma and the Body*; for a recent meta-analysis on the effect of mind-body therapies on the immune system and lowering inflammation, see Nani Morgan, Michael R. Irwin, Mei Chung, and Chenchen Wang, "The Effects of Mind-Body Therapies on the Immune System: Meta-Analysis," *PLoS ONE* 9, no. 7 (2014): e100903, doi:10.1371/journal.pone.0100903 (freely available online).

67. Yoga: for discussion on how yoga helps restore balance in the nervous system, foster connection between the body and mind, cultivate self-awareness, and promote healing from trauma, see van der Kolk, *Body Keeps the Score*, 263–76; for practical tips on getting started, see Edelberg and Hough, *Triple Whammy Cure*, 230–32. Also see an enlightening review article for a comparison of the health benefits of yoga and exercise, highlighting the overlapping and unique benefits of each, such as decreasing stress reactivity of the HPA axis and sympathetic nervous system, alleviating symptoms of disease, and improving normal physiological function: Alyson Ross and Sue Thomas, "The Health Benefits of Yoga and Exercise: A Review of Comparison Studies," *Journal of Alternative and Complementary Medicine* 16, no. 1 (2010): 3–12.

68. Meditation has received increasing attention from various fields of research for its benefits to the brain and body. For an interesting historical overview of contemplative neuroscience (studying how the brain responds to meditation) as well as a review of scientific findings, see a recent book written by a leading researcher and pioneer of the field: Richard J. Davidson and Sharon Begley, *The Emotional Life of Your Brain* (New York: Hudson Street Press, 2012), especially pages 177–224. For brief research reviews and practical tips to get started, see also Amen, *Change Your Brain Change Your Body*, 223–26; van der Kolk, *Body Keeps the Score*, 208–10; and Edelberg and Hough, *Triple Whammy Cure*, 215–16.

69. EMDR: for an inspiring overview, see van der Kolk, *Body Keeps the Score*, 248–62.

70. Bodywork: many practices are available to bring healing to the mind and body through working with the body through movement, touch, rhythm, breathing, observation, and so forth; for example: yoga, music/dance, sensory integration, sensorimotor

psychotherapy, somatic experiencing, therapeutic massage, Feldenkrais, craniosacral therapy, and mindful touch. For overview, see van der Kolk, *Body Keeps the Score*, 203–29, more specifically, 213–17; and Edelberg and Hough, *Triple Whammy Cure*, 236–44. For in-depth discussion, theory, and practice of sensorimotor therapy, see Ogden, Minton, and Pain, *Trauma and the Body*.

71. Aromatherapy: for example, lavender has been found to reduce stress and cortisol levels; see Amen, *Change Your Brain Change Your Body*, 231–32; and Edelberg and Hough, *Triple Whammy Cure*, 210–12.

72. Supplements: see advice throughout Edelberg and Hough, *Triple Whammy Cure*; Talbott, *Cortisol Connection*, 154–240; Amen, *Change Your Brain Change Your Body*, 320–49; and Wilson, *Adrenal Fatigue*, 193–221.

73. Medication: see discussions about the pros and cons of medications (and supplements), how they affect the brain and body, and so forth: van der Kolk, *Body Keeps the Score*, 223–27; Wilson, *Adrenal Fatigue*, 209–21; and throughout Talbott, *Cortisol Connection*; Edelberg and Hough, *Triple Whammy Cure*; and Amen, *Change Your Brain Change Your Body*.

74. Integrative medicine (previously called *holistic*) and functional medicine are branches of medicine that aim to look at the mind and body as an integrated unit, considering both in prevention, diagnosis, and treatment of illness. One concern about these approaches is the cost. Some of these doctors are covered by insurance at the same level as more conventional doctors; however, this is not always the case. It is crucial to check ahead of time about fees and insurance coverage, as well as to get feedback about the physician from reliable sources and test the effectiveness of the treatment with precise record keeping and scrutiny. One way integrative medicine doctors can be located is through professional organizations such as American College for Advancement in Medicine (http://acam.site-ym.com) and American Board of Integrative Holistic Medicine (http://www.abihm.org).

In his book, Dr. Bremner advocates for modern medicine to embrace a comprehensive, integrative approach; for discussion, see Bremner, *Does Stress Damage the Brain?*, especially pages 272–76.

75. For example, keeping a spreadsheet or tracking document of your lab results can illuminate patterns and connections. Looking at your data will allow you to more clearly see patterns, reflect on changes in your results, and also help doctors see your health profile at a glance. Bremner urges patients to become their own body scientist by making observations (mental, emotional, and physical—and the connections between them), keeping careful objective notes, and being ready to communicate them to their clinicians (*Does Stress Damage the Brain?*, 275).

76. Stress journal: Edelberg and Hough, *Triple Whammy Cure*, 46–47, 197–200.

77. Sex: Amen, *Change Your Brain Change Your Body*, 272–86; and Allender and Longman, *God Loves Sex*.

Chapter 5 The Damage of Covert Abuse

1. Diana E. H. Russell, *The Secret Trauma: Incest in the Lives of Girls and Women* (New York: Basic Books, 1987).

2. Murray Bowen, *Family Therapy in Clinical Practice* (New York: Aronson, 1989), 379.

3. See Ogden, Minton, and Pain, *Trauma and the Body*, 41–64; Allan N. Schore, *Affect Regulation and the Origin of the Self: The Neurobiology of Emotional Development* (Hillsdale, NJ: Erlbaum, 1994); and Daniel J. Siegel, *The Developing Mind* (New York: Guilford Press, 1999).

4. The primary parent for establishing attachment is the mother. Research is less clear on the role of the father, but it has progressed over the years. A good review is found in Robert Karen, *Becoming Attached: First Relationships and How They Shape Our Capacity to Love* (Oxford: Oxford University Press, 1994), 198–201.

5. See Michael John Cusick, *Surfing for God: Discovering the Divine Desire Beneath Sexual Struggle* (Nashville: Thomas Nelson, 2012); Mark Laaser, *Healing the Wounds of Sexual Addiction* (Grand Rapids: Zondervan, 2004); and Patrick Carnes, *Out of the Shadows* (Minneapolis: Hazelden, 2001).

Chapter 6 Men at War

1. Matthew Parynik Mendel, *The Male Survivor: The Impact of Sexual Abuse* (Thousand Oaks, CA: Sage Publishers, 1995).

2. David Finkelhor, *Child Sexual Abuse: New Theory and Research* (New York: Free Press, 1984); Paul N. Gerber, "Victims Becoming Offenders: A Study of Ambiguities," in *The Sexually Abused Male: Prevalence, Impact, and Treatment*, vol. 1, ed. Mic Hunter (Lexington, MA: Lexington, 1990), 153–76; and Mike Lew, *Victims No Longer: Men Recovering from Incest and Other Sexual Child Abuse*, 2nd ed. (New York: Harper & Row, 1990).

3. Natacha Godbout, Yvan Lussier, and Stephane Sabourin, "Early Abuse Experiences and Subsequent Gender Differences in Couple Adjustment," *Violence and Victims* 21, no. 6 (2006): 744–60.

4. Finkelhor, *Child Sexual Abuse*; Lew, *Victims No Longer*; and Jim Struve, "Dancing with the Patriarchy: The Politics of Sexual Abuse," in *Sexually Abused Male*, 3–46.

5. Mendel, *Male Survivor*, 21–35.

6. John Briere and K. Smiljanich, "Childhood Sexual Abuse and Subsequent Sexual Aggression against Adult Women" (paper presented at the 101st annual convention of the American Psychological Association, Toronto, Ontario, August 1993).

7. The debate rages about the role of sexual abuse in the lives of gay men and women. This is not a realm where research can be conducted or passed through university ethics committees that must approve research design for doctoral students or professors. It is simply too politically complex to assume that homosexuality has any social causative influences, including past abuse, attachment structure, or relationship with the same-sex parent. The dictum is simple: one is born gay or heterosexual. My opinion is that sexual orientation is not a choice, and though sexual abuse has an impact on everyone's sexuality, it is not a simple structure of causation: if you were abused by a male, you will struggle with homosexuality. There are simply too many heterosexual men and women who have been abused by both men and women who do not have a same-sex attraction. On the other hand, there is a strong distaste in the gay community for addressing

sexual abuse due to the assumption that if one were to address the harm, one's sexual orientation ought to change. As difficult as these issues are politically and in the church, as a therapist I have seen men and women who struggle with homosexuality address sexual abuse and find heterosexual desire less bound in shame and disgust. In many of these cases, there is a growing awareness of both same-sex desire and a competing opposite-sex desire. Is this merely discovering the person was neither gay nor straight but in fact bisexual? Perhaps. Perhaps our categories are so politically striated that we can't really explore the complexity and brokenness of all sexuality, including LGBTQ and H. I have also worked with gay men and women who have addressed sexual abuse and remained gay. Perhaps in a less politically/ecclesiastically intense day, the question of sexual desire and orientation can be approached with more kind, lucid, open, and dialogical interaction.

Chapter 7 The Drama of Reenactment

1. See Proverbs 26:11–12.

2. Louis Cozolino, *The Neuroscience of Psychotherapy: Healing the Social Brain*, 2nd ed. (New York: W. W. Norton, 2010), 279.

Chapter 10 Caring for Another's Story

1. Shelly Rambo, *Spirit and Trauma: A Theology of Remaining* (Louisville: Westminster John Knox, 2010), 6.

2. Ibid.

3. Presence in telling a story of abuse requires being aware of how one's body is experiencing the telling; theallendercenter.org has instructional videos to help you assess a person's capacity to be present in the telling and how to invite the storyteller to return to be "in" his or her body.

4. M. Main and R. Goldwyn, "Adult Attachment Scoring and Classification System" (unpublished manuscript, University of California at Berkeley, 1998), as quoted in Cozolino, *Neuroscience of Psychotherapy*, 201–6.

5. Ibid., 203.

6. For additional understanding of memory issues related to sexual abuse, including what has been termed "False Memory Syndrome," see Dan Allender, *The Wounded Heart*, 2nd ed. (Colorado Springs: NavPress, 1995), 23–39.

7. Memory is the integration of our felt body sense of being in the world (right brain) and our capacity to understand and encode our experience in language (left brain). Two parts of our limbic system that are in both hemispheres of the brain are the amygdala and the hippocampus. The amygdala is the constantly on siren that warns us of actual or perceived danger. It is unbound by time and doesn't "learn" by multiple experiences as to what is and isn't dangerous. It is moderated by the hippocampus. The hippocampus learns through experience and helps form memory as a progression in time and space. It is the foundation for enabling us to be a "storyteller." The greater the trauma, the more likely there is division between our discursive memory—a story with a beginning, middle, and end—and our affective memory (the state of felt body experience). Some victims remember the event of abuse with intricate detail but with

little or no emotion. Other memories may not be encoded as a story but are only felt in the body with no context or details. This is a profound division, or split, in the brain.

8. Linda M. Williams, "Recall of Childhood Trauma: A Prospective Study of Women's Memories of Child Sexual Abuse," *Journal of Consulting and Clinical Psychology* 62 (1994): 1167–76.

9. Like everything with the brain, the process is more complicated than can be easily described. In fact, all bonding "increases the secretion of oxytocin, prolactin, endorphins, and dopamine" (Cozolino, *Neuroscience of Psychotherapy*, 184). Further, the secretion of endogenous endorphins increases even when we are looked at with warmth and kindness.

10. Cozolino, *Neuroscience of Psychotherapy*, 84.

Chapter 11 Restoring the Marriage Relationship

1. Susan M. Johnson and Lyn Williams-Keeler, "Creating Healing Relationships for Couples Dealing with Trauma: The Use of Emotionally Focused Marital Therapy," *Journal of Marital and Family Therapy* 24, no. 1 (1998): 25–40; Heather B. MacIntosh and Susan M. Johnson, "Emotionally Focused Therapy for Couples and Childhood Sexual Abuse Survivors," *Journal of Marital Therapy* 34, no. 3 (2008): 298–315; and Carolynn Maltas and Joseph Shay, "Trauma Contagion in Partners of Survivors of Childhood Sexual Abuse," *American Journal of Orthhopsychiatry* 65, no. 4 (1995): 529–39.

2. Dan Allender, *To Be Told: God Invites You to Coauthor Your Future* (Colorado Springs: Waterbrook, 2006).

Chapter 13 Thy Kingdom Come

1. It should be readily apparent I follow the theological premise that the priesthood of all believers equally includes men and women. Utilizing the offices of Christ as a heuristic to speak of our calling to fulfill his work as prophet, priest, and king is meant equally for women as for men.

2. *Shall We Dance?*, directed by Peter Chelsom (Santa Monica, CA: Miramax, 2004), DVD.

Dan B. Allender (MS, Barry College; MDiv, Westminster Theological Seminary; PhD, Michigan State University) is a professor of counseling psychology and former president of the Seattle School of Theology and Psychology in Seattle, Washington. He travels and speaks extensively on sexual abuse recovery, love and forgiveness, worship, and other related topics. Allender is the author of fifteen books, including *The Wounded Heart*, and is coauthor of *God Loves Sex*.

ALSO BY DAN ALLENDER
Healing *the* Wounded Heart Workbook

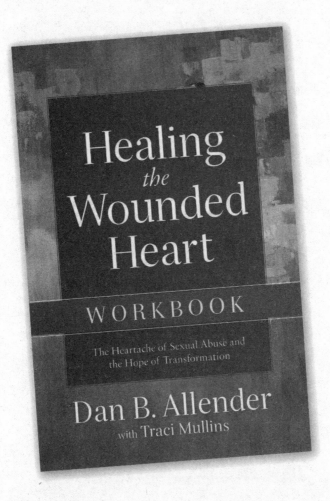

Counselors, pastors, and friends of those who have suffered sexual harm will find in this companion guide to *Healing the Wounded Heart* a helpful tool to effectively minister to the sexually broken around them. Victims themselves will find an invaluable resource to walk alongside them on the road to healing.

The Allender Center
at The Seattle School

Everyone has a story that needs to be told—whether it is a story of faith, hope, and love or a story of betrayal, powerlessness, and harm. We all have core stories from our past that deeply shape us and unwittingly impact our present and future. These are the stories that work as barriers to our truest calling—to love God, ourselves, and one another. The Allender Center joins people in the sacred work of identifying and telling these core stories, creating space for people to turn toward these stories and to begin to listen to what they have to say. And in this process, something transformative happens: people find the hope of redemption.

"Our own life is the thing that most influences and shapes our outlook, our tendencies, our choices, and our decisions. It is the force that orients us toward the future, and yet we don't give it a second thought, much less a careful examination. It's time to listen to our stories."

– Dr. Dan B. Allender

We believe that by courageously stepping into stories of pain and harm, restoration occurs. The Allender Center is committed to boldly engaging the core narratives of relationship, sexuality, trauma, sexual abuse, and sabbath through innovative conferences, in-depth workshops, and facilitated groups. We shape and embolden leaders through an integration of dynamic instruction, praxis-oriented group work, and rigorous personal work in their own narrative.

theallendercenter.org